THE NEXT BIG STORY

THE NEXT BIG STORY

MY JOURNEY THROUGH THE LAND OF POSSIBILITIES

SOLEDAD O'BRIEN

with

ROSE MARIE ARCE

A CELEBRA BOOK

CELEBRA
Published by New American Library,
a division of Penguin Group (USA) Inc.,
375 Hudson Street, New York, New York 10014, USA
Penguin Group (Canada), 90 Eglinton Avenue East, Suite 700, Toronto,
Ontario M4P 2Y3, Canada (a division of Pearson Penguin Canada Inc.)
Penguin Books Ltd., 80 Strand, London WC2R 0RL, England
Penguin Ireland, 25 St. Stephen's Green, Dublin 2,
Ireland (a division of Penguin Books Ltd.)
Penguin Group (Australia), 250 Camberwell Road, Camberwell,
Victoria 3124, Australia (a division of Pearson Australia Group Pty. Ltd.)
Penguin Books India Pvt. Ltd., 11 Community Centre,
Panchsheel Park, New Delhi - 110 017, India
Penguin Group (NZ), 67 Apollo Drive, Rosedale, North Shore 0632,
New Zealand (a division of Pearson New Zealand Ltd.)
Penguin Books (South Africa) (Pty.) Ltd., 24 Sturdee Avenue,
Rosebank, Johannesburg 2196, South Africa

Penguin Books Ltd., Registered Offices:
80 Strand, London WC2R 0RL, England

First published by Celebra,
a division of Penguin Group (USA) Inc.

First Printing, November 2010
1   3   5   7   9   10   8   6   4   2

CELEBRA and logo are trademarks of Penguin Group (USA) Inc.

LIBRARY OF CONGRESS CATALOGING-IN-PUBLICATION DATA:

O'Brien, Soledad, 1966–
The next big story: my journey through the land of possibilities/Soledad O'Brien
with Rose Marie Arce.
p.   cm.
ISBN 978-0-451-23137-6
1. O'Brien, Soledad, 1966– 2. Television journalists—United States—Biography. 3. African-
American television journalists—Biography. 4. Women television journalists—Biography.
I. Arce, Rose Marie. II. Title.
PN4874.O355A3 2010
070'.92—dc22   2010029396

Set in Fairfield LH
Designed by Elke Sigal

Printed in the United States of America

To my mom and dad and Brad,
whose appreciation and support have never wavered,
even when I didn't necessarily deserve it

CONTENTS

THE NEXT BIG STORY

· INTRODUCTION ·

I am crammed in an uncomfortable little stick-shift car climbing over the edge of the Patagonia region of Argentina into Chile. It is the middle of the night and these huge bare trees with peeling white bark stand out against the sky like creepy phantoms. We swing left and right, zigging and zagging, up, up, up, past a forest of ghosts.

I've been diverted by CNN from reporting in Haiti to cover an earthquake in Chile. I have flown through Miami, Panama, Lima, São Paulo, Buenos Aires and Bariloche in twenty-four hours to end up on this mountain road. The plan is to enter the disaster zone by land because the Chilean airports are closed. We finally hang a hard left turn and climb over the top of the last big mountain. A huge white ball rises above the landscape and lights up the night. I have never seen a moon so large, so round and so close, floating in vast black space like a beacon for travelers.

My journey as a journalist takes me to places of great beauty and deep sorrow. I never know what or who will emerge past the next turn. I just know that being a reporter has given me a unique opportunity to bear witness to the humanity of another moment, to follow the magnetic pull of a bright moon into uncharted territory. In a few hours, I will walk the streets of Concepción, Chile, and see looters thrown down by water cannons. I will sleep stranded by a roadside as the earth rocks from aftershocks. I will tell the world via satellite that help needs to be on the way. I will once again see people rescued from disaster, not by nations or organizations, but by the kindness of a stranger who decides to reach out beyond themselves. I will record the latest opportunity in life to do right by each other during the worst of times. I have told this story in places as far-flung as Thailand, New Orleans, and Port-au-Prince. Bad things happen until good people get in the way. I learned this life lesson growing up in Smithtown, Long Island, and I see it almost everywhere I go in pursuit of the next big story of the moment. People have an incredible potential to do good and make good and seize good from bad if they will only make the choice to do it.

I have had that same chance many times over and I am so thankful for the opportunity. I began life as the child of a mixed-race marriage growing up in a white suburb, treated sometimes as a creature of bad circumstance. My immigrant parents made sure I had the potential to capture my American dream anyway. I was handed a life of possibilities. That experience left me with the urge to chart how those around us get their chance at life and whether they go on to share their good fortune with others when the time comes.

So often I am disappointed one minute only to be elated the next. In Concepción, I see adults whose homes and lives were spared by an earthquake trolling a shopping mall to steal cell phones. Then, a block away, a line of volunteers work all night to clear the way for rescuers to pull total strangers from the rubble of a building. You can be a looter or you can be a lifeline. The choice is yours. That is often what I report.

I am lucky. I get to leave Chile in its crisis. I return home by barreling through the chilly skies above the Andes on a Peruvian police transport plane. I ache from the bitter cold and loud buzz that shakes my senses. But the pretty moon shines slices of light through the windows. There is always good with bad. It's all in how your mind wraps around the moment. I think of the people lifting those heavy blocks of rock to help out no one in particular. I look to the part of the journey that reveals the best in us. I always try to remember the beautiful moon and how it draws me back home and then out again on the next assignment.

CHAPTER ONE

My Life of Perpetual Motion

I'm eleven. My sister Estela is fourteen. We're at a photographer's studio to get a picture taken to give to our parents. The studio is on the main street in Smithtown, Long Island, not that far from where we live. The photographer says, "Forgive me if I'm offending you, but are you black?" For a moment, I'm speechless. I turn the comment over in my head. I can't figure out what he means. My sister is light-years ahead of me. She starts to shred the guy. "Offend us? Offend us? By asking if we are black?" He is maybe thirty but he seems old to us. He has dark brown hair and he's tall. He's white and we're two mixed-race girls trying to get our picture taken as an anniversary present for our parents. It's 1977. I'm this cheery, optimistic kid who suddenly feels quite sunk.

I just stand there in my big sister's shadow. I'm trying to figure out why the nice-sounding words make me feel small and embarrassed. The photographer is being exceedingly polite but he's crushing my girlish self-confidence. "Forgive me if I'm offending you . . ." What is that supposed to mean? Why would it be offensive if he were to call me black? I am black. I am also Latina, and half white through my Australian father. That isn't typical in Smithtown, but there is nothing wrong with me. My name is sort of long. I'm Maria de la Soledad Teresa O'Brien. I am fast becoming "Solie" to my friends. I'm a kid so I draw a little heart over the "i" when I write it. My hair's combed back in a bun and my clothes are what an eleven-year-old would wear. His tone makes it sound like something about me is off, especially the part about not offending me by assuming I'm black. I just don't understand how it could possibly be offensive to be black.

This is the first time I remember feeling like I might be disliked for who I am. My mind does leaps on this theme. But Estela is totally on it. I am very impressed that she can articulate her anger so well at fourteen. She is already able to take apart a grown man. She's so much more on top of it than me. "Forgive me if I'm offending you . . ." We don't have to take this crap. And from a photographer? Estela gives me the universal body language for "we're taking a walk" and off we go.

I think this was the day it began, my life of perpetual motion. There was a time when I was always walking away from comments or stares. There was the store where someone explained that I couldn't be black because black people were thieves and killers. Um, gonna put down this jacket and leave now. I didn't feel rejected; I felt annoyed and confused. I was proud of my identity. I thought I fit in comfortably in my suburban town. It was off-putting when someone came out with something nasty, something that signaled that not everyone saw me the way I saw myself. I always expected the best from folks so it came as a surprise. It would take me a moment to figure out if that's what they *really* meant to say. Then I would refuse to let it get to me. I was a middle-class girl in a middle-class Long Island suburb, but my young life became like those games of dodgeball we played in the school yard. When you move, you can't get hit. You survive to play again. By doing that you come out the winner.

There was the day I was walking down the hall to sixth-period science class. An older kid, eighth grade, came right up to me. "If you're a nigger why don't you have big lips?" he asked. It killed me that not only could I hear him: I actually could feel myself trying to formulate an answer, as if the question necessitated a response. There was no hostility in his voice. It was just this question he hurled at me in the rush to change class. He wasn't much bigger than me; he wasn't even scary. Just a guy with long sandy brown bangs swinging past his eyes like windshield wipers. I rushed past him, recording for some reason the colors on his short-sleeve shirt. I could pick him out of a lineup today, almost thirty-three years later. That day, I just pursed my mouth and kept moving, walking away. I wouldn't dignify him. I had to get to class.

I've been a journalist now for more than twenty years. I go sprinting from story to story. My life moves fast. I am a big version of the little girl in Smithtown except now I'm walking toward something rather than away from it. I force people to consider every word they've said in interviews. I dig in to the awkward question. I revel in making people rethink their words. Nothing stops me. I am not the type to dwell on bad things. I have no patience for people who do. I am the glass half full, the one who insists there must be a way to fix things. It's not that I'm propelled by unfounded optimism. I just can't suffer the small stuff or the bad stuff or the meanness we encounter in the world. I think better of life, that it harbors the possibility we can get past things and come out better on the other end. I see life as a series of victories, of wins. I live to capture that feeling when your chest cracks the ribbon at the finish line and tiny triangular flags flutter high above the track.

I graduated with honors from the school where being half black and half white meant I was the brunt of bad jokes. I went on to Harvard, just like my sister Estela, like all six of us, in fact. I am by all accounts a successful journalist. I produce award-winning documentaries about challenging subjects like race. I went on to write books, give speeches, marry a great guy, have four healthy kids, and anchor a network TV show. That eighth-grader in the hallway didn't hinder my forward motion one bit. Whatever became of him and his life, he was wrong about me. Whatever assumptions he made about me, I proved him wrong by succeeding.

I won not just because I charged on. I won because experiences like that changed me for the better, not for the worse. I learned that I didn't need to stop and confront every injustice thrown my way. That I could win just by moving along. That feeling angry was healthy, if I used it as a motivation and didn't let it fester. That anger could teach me. That my experiences would help my work as a journalist because I could identify with people with whom I had little in common. I refused to let anger find an ugly place to grow deep inside my gut. I refused to let it lie fallow inside of me, waiting for some new idiot to make it grow like a desert weed in a flash flood. I knew that if I let anger take hold of me, every person who rubbed me the wrong way would be paying for the guy back at the photo store in 1977. "Forgive me if I'm offending you . . ."

So I've figured out a strategy of pushing forward. And I think it's a good choice to make. One thing that's certain in this country is that not far around the corner from every ugly thing there's something really beautiful. And if you stop at every bitter comment you will never reach your destination.

My mom and dad initiated this life strategy long before I arrived. They lived their lives in flight. My father, Edward Ephram O'Brien, or "Ted," took off from a rural town called Toowoomba in Queensland, Australia. His family had a mill and wanted him to work there as a chemical engineer. He disliked the strictures of working for the family business, so he took off for the United States instead. He studied at Purdue in Indiana, then at Johns Hopkins near Baltimore.

My mother, Estela Lucrecia Marquetti y Mendieta, began her journey at the age of fourteen. Her family was poor and black and living in Cuba. She wanted to study and escape the sweltering heat, racism, and isolation of pre-Castro Cuba. She connected with the Oblate Sisters, a Roman Catholic order of women of African descent. She went to study with their counterparts in Baltimore, who raised her to adulthood. She was working in a science lab at Johns Hopkins University when she met Dad.

My dad had the build of a rugby player, which he was, and which he still has at seventy-seven. He had a firm, almost mischievous smile and ivory skin. There are old photos of my dad with his rugby T-shirt. Although he's one face among seventy, I can always pick him out by his smile. I think I look like him. His hair thinned young but he was always handsome.

Mom's skin was the color of a coconut shell. Her eyes were wide and bright. Her black hair was shiny and combed back. In those days a press and curl was in vogue and she was very fashionable. She had these full cheeks as a young woman, smiling cheeks. My mother was a natural beauty. My parents looked and spoke like immigrants making their way to a different life. Their accents faded with time but they were always present. The two of them were making their way separately to mass when Dad offered Mom a ride. She said no. My mother is the kind of woman who goes to mass every day. Yet she turns down a ride if it's offered by a man she doesn't know. That pretty much describes her. But my dad just kept asking, and I can imagine him tossing his funny little jokes through the car window, working his charming Australian accent and his easy smile. One day she finally said yes.

Dating for them was something like my experience in school, a game of avoiding issues with race. They traveled from place to place looking for someone willing to serve a young white man on a date with a black woman. It was Baltimore in 1958, so there were many places where eyes would follow them as they came to sit, places where folks would get up and leave or come over and say something offensive. But most places just wouldn't have them at all. It didn't faze them. My mother cooks great Cuban food. She had to bring my dad home when no one would serve them on their first date. She always advised us to learn to cook.

When they decided to get married their church said no. It wasn't legal in Maryland in 1959 for someone black to marry someone white. A lawyer asked them if they were willing to become a test case to challenge the ban on interracial marriage. They declined. They didn't want to be part of a legal case that would stop their forward motion. They drove to Washington, D.C., where it was legal for them to get married, got hitched, and came back to Baltimore.

My mother and father took no small risk when they decided to live outside D.C. back in Maryland. Just a year earlier, Mildred

Jeter, a black Virginia woman, and Richard Loving, her white husband, had traveled to Washington, D.C., to get married, just like my parents. They went back to Virginia to live until police stormed into their bedroom one night and arrested them. They became the test case. The U.S. Supreme Court overturned the ban against interracial marriage in the 1967 case *Loving vs. Virginia*. By then, my parents had been married for nearly ten years, had moved to Smithtown, Long Island, and were raising six kids.

My mom doesn't like to talk much about that period of her life. "You have to keep going in life, live every day and then the next day and then the next," she likes to say. So she did and we went with her. She got pregnant with my sister Maria within a year of getting married and then had a second daughter, my sister Cecilia, before leaving Baltimore. My oldest brother, Tony, then Estela, and then I were born in Long Island. My youngest brother, Orestes, was born when we went to visit my dad's family in Australia during a sabbatical. "With life, everything has to look forward," Mom says.

Forward to them was Smithtown, one of Long Island's classic suburbs, well-off and white, sitting along the North Shore, part of storybook America. On the surface, Smithtown is the living, breathing embodiment of why immigrants come to this country, the kind of place much of America aspires to become. The schools are good. The town is rich with history. One of the great things about this country is that we get to have a cumulative past. It doesn't matter when or how you come here; the past of this country and its principles belong to you, good and bad. It's what makes America special. It doesn't matter how you look or speak; you get to be an American because you're here. And I'm as much of an American as the eighth-grader or the photo store guy or anyone like them. I adopt their history and there's nothing they can do about it.

There is a large blue-green statue of a bull at a key intersection in Smithtown celebrating the town's founding. I've driven past it a thousand times and more, but I only recently found out he's named Whisper. Legend goes that Whisper belonged to an early settler named Richard Smith, who won land from the Native Americans by betting he could ride on the back of a bull across a piece of land big enough to build a whole town. He did it and today there is a town named for him, and a statue of his bull charges mightily at its center.

The schools are named for those Native American tribes like Nesaquake, my junior high, where I was asked about having thick lips. The Nesaquake were among the tribes who scoured the waters off Long Island looking for clams to eat and to bead together to make wampum. Then Smith and the Dutch came along and the natives all but vanished. But the names of their ancestors have been emblazoned on towns from Montauk to Manhattan. And, of course, they lived on in our public schools, where we learn to memorialize our collective roots. It didn't matter that the O'Briens were late arrivals to this history. My parents chose Smithtown as their outpost in this land of possibilities and opportunities. Smith and the Dutch and the natives that plied the Sound, even Whisper the muscular bull, now belonged to us, too.

I grew up unaware that there was anything significant about my parents' flight to Smithtown. It was just our home. If you had told me they were political I would have laughed out loud—we were very typically suburban, caught up in figuring out the latest ways to make the most of our suburban town. I had no idea what they'd gone through to create our tribe, and as a teenager I didn't much care. I knew they had joined a group of black families that pushed for integration and better housing. My mother thought it was a good way of meeting the other black families because there were so few. I remember it fondly. We would gather at a small park in Smithtown. Today it has a colorful jungle gym that wasn't there back then, but it had space to have a picnic, and well-manicured lawns and tables.

There weren't really enough black families to form any kind of critical mass. But we met the ones there were. There was my best friend in school, Shevoy Onley, one of the only black kids who wasn't related to me. She was also in constant motion. I met her in kindergarten, and our parents encouraged our friendship. She was considered different, just like me. That was part of what connected us, even though we didn't talk about it much. Shevoy had it better in one small way. She was from Bermuda, which seemed more exotic than Cuba, where my mother was from. Plus, she could go back and visit her relatives and see the place where everyone looked like her. I was stuck here with just my five siblings in Smithtown.

I was frustrated that I had thick bushy hair that was completely unmanageable. My mom would braid it, and I would take out the braids and pull them into a ponytail. Shevoy had hers pulled so tightly back, it seemed to be tugging at her eyebrows. That wasn't as much about us having black hair as it was about looking like everyone else. But we were also aware of our race. Shevoy's uncle once insisted on filling out a race question on a form by writing "Human Race." She tried that a few times but it didn't get her far. Shevoy and I didn't get noticed as much as we got looked at. Even through high school, when our class schedules separated us for most of the day, we would catch each other's eye and smile. No one really saw us. They just looked.

Smithtown was a wonderful place to be a kid, but like many

American towns, it sometimes had a split personality. When my sister Cecilia was a teenager, she got an internship at a civil rights organization. It was a big deal, very grown-up. She was doing research about women in untraditional roles. She remembers stumbling upon some files on allegations of police brutality, cases in which black people talked about how the police treated people who looked like us. We never even spoke to the police.

We all had great friends. I would go all the way across town to ride horses at the homes of girls who were white, have dinner and while away an afternoon playing in the yard. Then one day at a friend's house, I sit next to her little sister to eat dinner. "Why do I have to sit next to the black girl?" she asks, and suddenly I see another side of my hometown.

My siblings felt it, too. A guy comes up to Cecilia at school and says, "I saw your father and your brother on the highway changing a tire." He'd seen some black folks and figured they must have been us. That was how limited their knowledge was of black people. They must all be related! When my parents first moved to Smithtown, white people wouldn't sell their homes to black people. My parents had to buy land from a rich, liberal philanthropist. They saved every dime and built a small ranch house on it. Smithtown was close to Dad's work at the state university and an easy commute. That was how we bought into this town with its dual personality.

But I did know that my parents on occasion marched through Smithtown's narrow streets with some of the black families to fight for housing integration, singing and chanting and banding together. My mother says now she doesn't think they accomplished much. My parents were involved enough that the group tried to recruit my dad to be a leader. My dad remembers thinking there were guys that would make better leaders than he. The lack of leadership meant there were squabbles, and my mom and dad eventually withdrew. They were raising six kids in Smithtown and they were busy. Maybe raising us was enough of a statement. We walked those streets. Sometimes people looked at us as if we had two heads and were completely out of place. We always ignored them.

The ugliness of what was quietly happening around us in Smithtown way back then has only been revealed more recently. The town began participating in a federally funded housing program in 1985. The program is called Section 8 and it allows low-income people to apply for housing vouchers that pay up to two-thirds of their rent. The program helps out poor people and also works to desegregate a town. But Smithtown required that you already be a resident to apply. The town was already more than 90 percent non-Hispanic white, so the residency requirement would mean almost no one of color would ever be given assistance to move in. In 1997, the U.S. Department of Housing and Urban Development told the town that the policy had a "racially exclusionary effect." Smithtown did nothing.

By 2007, a group of civil rights lawyers felt they had a case and filed a class-action suit against Smithtown. The suit was filed on behalf of a group of people like Corinne Vargas, a Latina mother of two. Corinne had grown up in nearby Oakdale, a working-class town. She was the only child of Puerto Rican parents. Her father, George, worked in Smithtown for Animal Control. She remembers how her father's coworkers would always steer him to certain parts of town. "Give that territory to George. He can deal with those kinds of people," she remembers them saying. But he wouldn't take that to heart. He would cruise around

Smithtown and see a great place to raise kids. Her parents had grown up in Spanish Harlem in Manhattan, and moving to Long Island was for them a big step up. Once they got to Oakdale, they looked at Smithtown as the next rung on the American ladder, the place Corinne dreamed she would one day make a home. Her father figured working there was one pace closer to that dream.

Corinne's childhood in Oakdale sounds a lot like my own, which is ironic since she assumed that Smithtown would be better. Her parents were Americans, like all Puerto Ricans, although their home was culturally Latino. "Why are you so dark?" they'd ask her in the hallways. "Goya O-boya! Spic and Span." There were comments about her "big bubble lips" and people would constantly assume Corinne was from Mexico. "We kind of co-existed," Corinne remembers. "It was all so weird and shocking. I have cousins who have blond hair and blues eyes. I felt like I was just like everyone else until someone came up and put me in some new category."

Corinne left Oakdale and made a great life for herself, until she gave birth to her first child, Jasmine. She was born with cerebral palsy and spina bifida. She is a quadriplegic confined to a wheelchair. Corrine's marriage fell apart and she moved to Florida to live with her parents, but the available health care wasn't great for her daughter. She returned to Long Island with a well-paying job when suddenly her daughter began to have severe seizures and she ended up sitting by her hospital bedside for weeks. Corinne lost her job and her health insurance and became homeless in December of 2005. That's when she put herself on the Section 8 list.

Section 8 was a way out of a very tough spot. Corinne couldn't raise a sick child in a homeless shelter. She was unaccustomed to poverty and all the bureaucracy it comes with, the paperwork of social services and the humiliation of constantly asking for help. She was worn down by her situation and calculated that if she could get a Section 8 housing voucher, she could raise her daughter on child support and Social Security payments. She was told there were available vouchers in Smithtown and to get on the waiting list. A dream was about to come true.

By the following summer she was told she should come into the Smithtown offices because her number was up. She remembers the day. "I was so excited," she said. She recalls walking into the town offices in Smithtown fully expecting to walk out with her housing voucher. She said she had every piece of paperwork completely filled out. She wasn't in the office for more than a few minutes when a woman behind the desk took a thick black Sharpie and wrote "INELIGIBLE" across the top of Corinne's form and circled it. She withheld the desire to lose her cool and asked a lawyer to join her. Robin Nunn, who was doing pro bono work for the firm of Sullivan and Cromwell, was working on a potential lawsuit and was accompanying people to their appointments. Robin explained to the Smithtown officials that residency could not be a requirement. But the town took a position that they held on to—that they could require applicants to already live in the town. They were sent on their way.

"I didn't know what to do," Corinne said. "I live for my kid. She is my life. She is my everything. I was living in a motel with a sick kid. And this place was denying me my one shot at life." Corinne joined the lawsuit. The others in the suit included Keisha Trent, another homeless mother of two who is black, and Anne Smith, a disabled black woman who lives with her adult child. These are the people Smithtown was trying to keep out.

According to the suit, Smithtown had issued 102 vouchers. Seven had gone to black families and two had gone to Latinos.

Together they made up half the waiting list. When the waiting lists got shorter, Smithtown would simply go out and recruit more people with Smithtown addresses, who were usually white, to fill the top slots. That suit revealed the housing issues my parents were marching about way back when. It chronicled the history of race friction in my hometown. In 1971, the local NAACP had asked the town to develop low-income housing, but Smithtown's council had rejected the idea because low-income housing lacked "pride of ownership." A board member named Robert Brady said publicly that the problems in Smithtown "had been caused by the new people that moved here. The only way to solve our problems is if [they] get back on [their bicycles] and move back to Jamaica." Corinne was trying to make a jump from Oakdale, a town close by.

The complaint talks of cross burnings and home arsons in the 1980s. A real estate agent is threatened with death in 1995 for selling to a black person. The Trinity AME church had "Go Home Nigger" scrawled on its side. In 2004 a minority family got menacing phone calls and had a brick thrown through the window. The next year a black family moved because of racial epithets and threats stuck in their mailbox. This sour legal document painted an ugly picture of my hometown. Only last summer did a federal judge approve a ten-year consent degree placing Corinne and the others back on the waiting list and a $925,000 compensation fund was set up. After years of homelessness, they were back waiting for a crack at a life in Smithtown, Long Island. I knew none of this until recently.

This is one of the reasons my town was split in two, a landing place for the American dream had slammed the door shut on anyone new. That is not what being American is about. Our communities thrive because they renew themselves with people who bring in new ideas and refresh our culture. Smithtown could have only gotten better by welcoming people aspiring to make good. The duality of my town didn't have to exist. They had the choice to embrace new people and encourage change or reject newcomers and limit growth. My parents had so much to contribute to Smithtown, including six children who appreciated the obvious benefits of where they lived and went on to succeed. We are proof that a choice to welcome newcomers can help a community thrive. My parents still own the house where we grew up. They go there summers. I go visit and I bring my kids. The joy I feel there, as the joy I felt way back when, conjures up the promises of my hometown.

I remember a totally different Smithtown from the one denied to Corinne Vargas. My family embraced Smithtown's typically suburban lifestyle and became a part of its DNA. My father taught mechanical engineering at the local state college. My mother taught Spanish at one of the local high schools, Smithtown West, and then at East, where I also studied. My parents were focused on education. They wanted us to study whatever they were teaching us and bring back good grades. They were religious and strict and kept us kids tightly controlled. I couldn't watch TV during the week or stay out late with friends. My mother's child-rearing prescription was this simple: "Studying is what children do, study hard, and the parents provide them with three meals a day and very little TV, like three or four hours only on weekends. That's all there is to it." It was never hard to figure out what was expected of me. "Do your work," my mother said so many times.

In so many ways, we seemed to fit right in. My mom dressed very simply and kept her hair cut into a short Afro. My dad dressed like you'd expect a college professor to dress and kept himself neatly groomed. We all saw ourselves as unremarkable and un-complicated. It only became apparent we were different when we stepped outside our home. Not everyone ate rice with every meal, sometimes with guava jelly and fried plantains. There is a photo of the six of us that spells out who we were. We are wear-ing 1970s shirts with stripes and flared pants with stripes going the other way. We all have giant Afros and big smiles, and we are leaning against our VW bus. There was no way we could avoid looking a little different when we stepped out onto the streets of Smithtown. I sometimes wonder if that's part of the reason my parents encouraged us to be a tight gang of six. We needed one another. We became one another's closest friends.

I have great memories of our life in Smithtown. I remember the evenings when we piled up the dinner dishes and retreated to a double-wide hallway that we had converted into our place to play. We were never allowed to go out after dinner. I remember our dance parties, our funny gyrations, how we would collapse into giggles to the sound of a 45. I can still hear the monotonous lyrics of "Billy, Don't Be a Hero" as we shook our heads and shoulders to the sound. We created a Television Constitution for the weekends, when we were allowed to watch. We got to vote on *Star Trek* or *The Waltons*, though I was too little to stay up for *The Waltons* for the longest time. Every now and then, one of us would just get our night to pick to avoid a tyranny of the majority.

The vast lawn outside our door and the labyrinth of trees that lined our property was our refuge, a place of endless games of softball and tag and hide-and-seek, of tree climbing. These are the things that Smithtown means to me. Holding on to those memories and the psychic peace they forged in my soul is part of what makes me press on. That's the home my family created in this promising little part of the globe, because they got the opportunity.

When I was little, my oldest siblings were like this gang of four. They were born one right after the other. The oldest is Maria. She is crazy smart and somewhat bossy. She vacuums without being asked. She kisses up to the teachers at school. We are all in awe of her. She is short, energetic, and driven. Her strategy is to be better, kinder, faster than anyone. The teachers love her and respect her intelligence. They call on her when they want the right answer. Maria opens a door of opportunity for all of us by getting into Harvard. The next three siblings go to Harvard, too, as if they are walking right in behind her. As one is going off to college, the next one is working on his application.

Cecilia is next in line. She is more argumentative than Maria. She loves to argue and uses words to get what she wants. She acts like a lawyer even as a teenager. Tony is the oldest boy and likes to be in charge. I look like a female version of him. He is the most athletic of us, though none of us are exactly jocks. Estela is grumpy in the mornings but she has this gentle side when she deals with me and she deals with me a lot. She sleeps in the bunk bed above me. She makes up stories to tell me—murder mysteries and tales about Sinbad the Sailor. She is a Renaissance kid. She paints and sews and is good at science and math at the same time. She is the smartest person I know.

The four of them set a fast pace at Smithtown High. My mom tells them to stick together, watch out for each other. It's easy for the four of them because they are close in age and naturally together. Some girl in Estela's second-grade class tortures her. Maria walks in and asks the teacher if she can talk to the kid. In a whisper she basically tells the kid she'll kick her ass if she messes with Estela. Problem solved. A goofy neighbor boy says something racist on the bus. The four of them hang out the windows heckling him: "You flunked first grade, you idiot."

There are something like twenty-seven hundred kids surrounding the O'Briens and the four of them represent more than half the black population. But they have each other. Mom teaches them comebacks. They practice on each other. The only place they are lonely is in class. A teacher says something nonsensical about Africa and no one is there to dispute it. Another teacher stages a debate about apartheid and wants one of us to take the "pro" side. Then class would end and there is another O'Brien—there is Maria or Cecilia or Tony and Estela in the hall or all four of them on the bus.

They all descend on our great front lawn, where the raspberries grow among the wildflowers. They explode through the front door of our eighteen-hundred-square-foot house, disappearing into one of the five tiny bedrooms carved from this box. Forests and horse farms and beach surround us. We make forts in the brambles and I ride a horse named Strawberry who lives across the street. Dad gathers up kids from the neighborhood for a game of baseball. He always takes the weaker side, so Orestes and I often get to play with him because we're the youngest.

Our little neighborhood is perfect for us. There is a Quaker Meeting House down the road where I sometimes babysit the kids. There are a few rentals around us, something rare in this upper-class part of town. There is wealth around us even though we are solidly middle class. Vast parcels of land surround us like a moat. There are enough tall blue spruce that the neighbors can't tell my mom is raising pigs and geese. We use a barbecue fashioned from a pile of loose bricks. The ivy hides the fading paint color. But life is good. We walk just a quarter mile to the beach and learn to swim and boat and not harass the horseshoe crabs. Once a year a fox scrambles for its life and a string of hunters on horseback follows aggressively behind. Because of my mother's insistence that we do everything as a family, the four big ones drag Orestes and me along to everything. There is enough laughter in our tiny world to lift a sunrise.

Then suddenly, in what seems like an instant but was really a few years, they are gone. The four of them go off to college, one by one. Out of the house. Away from Smithtown and all its constraining homogeneity. There we are, Orestes and me, with our oddball names, all by ourselves. Hard to threaten somebody or cough up a comeback when you're all alone. No cavalry for us. Orestes and I barely see each other, even in the halls. He is a little quiet. If some kid grabs his lunch bag, I'd grab it back. That is the extent of our opportunity to express solidarity, but we are very close at home.

Shevoy is still there. She has these glass blue eyes but they are hidden behind some proper glasses. Her cousins used to throw her in the ocean back in Bermuda to teach her to swim, so she knows survival. Shevoy gets her feelings hurt just like I do. She doesn't know why, either. We have our pain in common. Kids walk up to her and say, "Hi, Soledad." She says "Hi" back because she figures she's talking for the three of us, me, her, and Orestes. Shevoy is an advocate of not picking fights. Shevoy figures no one is going to defend us. I like that strategy so I sign up for it. We know that no family invites us over unless they have a conversation about it first. We figure it out when younger siblings sometimes let it slip that we're the black guest.

But it's not like that when Shevoy and I go see each other. I sleep over at her house sometimes. She is an only child and I feel special when I'm with her. She has this tiny front living room and her parents let us camp out on the couch. We look out the window and giggle at the neighbors. Her mother makes these terrific crab sandwiches on white bread. I've never had crab and I eat two and three sandwiches at a time. Shevoy's mother says not to worry about other people because we all have each other. We do what our parents tell us to do. We worry about the person we're becoming inside. And we giggle through the night, together.

School gets challenging. The four older kids had set these expectations of Orestes and me. They had been tracked for college. They were considered bright as a group. That was their good legacy. Then there was the other expectation, that we'd stick our noses in a book and keep to ourselves. My sisters had warned me about what was coming. "A guy would be crazy to date a black girl in that school," Cecilia remembers. Maria and Cecilia didn't date. They didn't go to prom and it was never expected that they would.

I vaguely remember some conversations about whether Tony should ask out the one black girl. Mom had warned us, "A guy may like you but he may not be comfortable dating you." We are actually pretty fair-skinned in the broader spectrum, though we don't think of ourselves that way. We are black in our heads, and Latino, but it's nothing we talk about or work to define. We look black, or at least we don't look white. I find it odd later when some black folks would suggest we weren't black enough. Black enough for what? We grew up in Smithtown in the 1970s. We were black.

It wasn't until I was a teenager that I realized that school would just always be difficult. Because I am not white I accept the expectation that I can't ever have a boyfriend. Plus, I have these strict parents. And I am this nerd who can't stop moving, taking AP classes in biology and physics. It dawns on me that my race isn't a good thing, or even neutral. I try to push past that thought. I tell myself my mother will kill me if I go on a date anyway. I am smarter than the boys, so who cares? They aren't going to find me cute because in this town I am not ever going to be considered cute. No one rejects me. It is so far out of the realm of possibility that rejection would have required an inkling of hope.

My mom keeps telling me I'll date in college. Another reason I have to study, as far as she is concerned. I dive headlong into books, rush off to after-school activities—student government, track and field—rip through my assignments and bypass any temptation to stop and socialize. Things happen around me, dances and sports events; chatting and laughing erupts in the hallways. I have friends and I charge ahead. Kids can be mean to anyone.

There is a girl named Angela Cinqmani. With a name like that I figure she must be a Latina. She is short and curvy and by third grade she has an enormous chest. Boys practically fall over a railing trying to get a look. She says a teacher tells her to dress more conservatively and that makes her mad, so she flaunts what she's got and she taunts people. But she struggles. She is constantly absent and spends a lot of time in detention. She works jobs at a local factory just to get away, she tells me later. The guy she asks to the prom goes instead with her best friend. She hates Smithtown, but never moves away. I figure a lot of people have it bad for lots of reasons.

As I get older I begin to move toward things instead of away from them. I am student government president in the eighth grade. I run the quarter mile and the high hurdles for the track team and I'm good. I win medals. I am AP Physics, AP English, AP Biology, and AP History. I join the do-gooder arm of the Rotary Club, called Interact. I play the flute and piccolo. I wear a red and white military-style band uniform and I love the feeling of being part of the marching band. Other than the fact that the uniform is wool and it's hot, I feel great when I'm performing before a crowd. After struggling some, I am an excellent student just like my siblings. I find ways to fill every space, book every moment of time. I find a weird comfort in racing from one thing to the next, conquering, achieving, dominating, commanding. It makes it easier to ignore unpleasant remarks, to be too busy to realize you don't belong. No time for the chance encounter in the hallway. No time to date should anyone ask. No time to think about why, just moving fast.

In the back of my mind there is this question mark that travels with me—Is it race? Or is that person just a jerk?—and it annoys me that the question takes up any space in my head. But all I can do is keep going. I will not let any teenager's stupidity or ignorant mouth spoil it for me. I refuse to allow anyone to rob me of the promises of my wonderful middle-class existence—the well-kept lawns and suburban box houses of Smithtown. I have too much to lose. So when nonsense gets in the way, I learn to push it aside. Very little stops me, and I've been blessed with a terrible memory. Even when people insult me, I opt to forget it. And I do forget it. But my mom remembers everything and proactively dismisses the bad stuff. She likes to say: "We all live with so many people and work with so many people that if we fight with them every day we won't get anywhere." I have places to go. I can't let myself get stopped.

America is a wonderful land of opportunities—if you're in a position to take them. I don't think that requires as much luck as it does strategy. My parents found ways to get what they wanted for themselves—a family, education, and a way of life. They picked a place to live where their kids could as well. What they couldn't have themselves as children, they tried to give to theirs. Smithtown was their storied American dream: Immigrant parents get an education, work hard, plant a flag in a suburban wonderland, then have a pile of kids, whose achievements sparkle like sunspots on an asphalt driveway.

My parents positioned us well to enjoy all of life's possibilities. I learn to seize them. I get a plan, then work hard and sidestep adversaries. I hope for the best. Life can derail your highest ambitions. I try not to make things harder by holding myself back. I keep a fast pace. I fight distractions and fading hope. Achievements happen in forward motion. I don't encounter anything that truly sets me back. But mostly, I am never in a position for something truly bad to happen to me. I live a wonderful middle-class American life, and my parents never let me be at risk. My last days in Smithtown are filled with sunny afternoons and lazy evenings, of my siblings' raucous laughter and my mother's black beans, of my dad's constant smile and his get-up-and-go. I pack to leave a house with warmth in the air and positive energy, a place where the tallest blue spruce outside our front door is our annual Christmas tree. It is a place where a family thrived. I feel like this home life is within reach to just about anyone if they just work hard and try. At least, that is the promise of America.

But before I leave Smithtown to venture off into adulthood, I learn one last lesson about where I stand in the world. I borrow my mother's car. I'm eighteen, young enough that borrowing the car still comes at a price. I have to pick her up at school. She is the language teacher. She walks around in this gigantic purple hat with little skunk stripes. She is very comfortable with her race and everyone has become accustomed to her Cuban accent. This is one very proud black lady. I am very proud to be her kid. She has this torturously slow walk, but on this day I don't mind.

We walk around the halls saying "Hi" to everyone, until something happens that brings us both to a stop. A teenage black boy is running madly through the halls of this nearly all-white school. He comes to a halt when he comes upon the school administrators, who just happen to be in the hall. Their faces are clear. This kid does not belong. My instinct is to keep walking. The kid just stands there with this startled look. My mom stops, which means I stop. "I imagine he was probably scared with so many adults around him," my mom would say later. "So I did what had to be done." And that was to stay and watch. But I suddenly feel in a rush. This is not our business. One of the administrators is my former principal and my mother's boss. The broad shiny halls close in around us. "It's okay, Mrs. O'Brien," he tells her. "We have it under control." He obviously wants her to move on.

"That's okay," she says. "I'm just going to stay here for a while." She is five feet two. She clutches her macramé handbag and just stands there. The power of her immobility is awesome. I am entranced. The men are growing very uncomfortable. The boy's eyes shift from the men to my mom and back. I can almost feel his sense of relief. She isn't leaving him. This important black lady is fulfilling her unspoken obligation to watch after this trapped black boy. The principal reaches over and gives him a pat on the back. "Don't run in the halls," he says.

I am intrigued by my mom's subtle power play. She is teaching me a lesson without saying a word. Sometimes you have to make things your business, as uncomfortable as that may feel. My mother transforms the moment. Her presence says, "Yes, I'm the black employee so this is my business." She gives me the same body language my sister Estela had given me years ago at the photo shop. Then we turn on a heel and walk. I am in motion once again.

· CHAPTER TWO ·

GETTING STARTED

I start my freshman year at Harvard just before my September birthday. I'm eighteen. I'm stunned by the wealth of many of my new classmates. People drive Saabs and vacation in Switzerland. Mom and Dad mail me a Seiko watch. I live in Straus, a dorm like all the others on the Ivy Yard. It's brick, like everything else. It has tall windows with tiny little squares and white lintels. Three alumni who are heirs to a department store fortune built it. Their parents sank with the *Titanic* so they named a dorm after them. There are fireplaces in the suites. I've never lived away from home before. I've never lived in a big city. I am so small-town that my first night at school I'm afraid to cross the street to Harvard Square. I do it anyway. I am the fifth O'Brien to walk these yards. I decide I'm going to study medicine like my sister Estela. I am supposed to be here. But I don't totally feel like I belong.

I get a job. My family is middle class so I have to work to pay for everything. I sell clothes. The clothing store is Rogers of Harvard Square. It's only women's clothes, stuff a professor's wife might wear. They sell cashmere sweaters and velvet wraps. I love it there. I love the feel of a job. I like rushing in and checking off a list of things to do. I love the feeling of work. I love working hard. I do catering on the side. I get to see the inside of people's houses. I also edit stacks of scientific abstracts. I don't understand a word but you don't have to—you just have to understand grammar. I love the writing. I babysit. I'm premed so I become a certified nurse's aid for the summer. I make just over $6 an hour. That's great money. Everyone else is earning just over $3. I work at a pharmacy. I feel on my way to being a doctor.

I begin to make a place for myself. I develop the social life I'd never had. I try out for the lacrosse team. I join the running club at my house. I play rugby until I tear my ACL, ending my career in competitive sports. I volunteer to work with kids at a school across the street. I get to feel comfortable with myself in college. Being multiracial is suddenly cool. A new world opens up for me. The place seems big but I make it feel small. There are kids from everywhere. My rooming group includes an Asian girl from Michigan, a wealthy Tex-Mex girl from Laredo, a lawyer's daughter from Scarsdale, New York, and a girl from Berkeley. I go to parties for the Black Students Union and get rushed by the black sorority. College allows for diversity. I can be half black here and still be considered one of the family. The fact that I'm different is just okay. Difference is suddenly a plus. It was clear that no one in high school found me attractive. In college, I'm suddenly exotic and cute! I date for the first time—white guys, Asian guys, Puerto Rican and black guys. I start to slow down.

I learn to choose good friends. I assign high value to nice folks, low value to the pretentious. The place is full of people who will later put their college on their business cards. People live large. Some of them think being here makes them better,

better than other people, on their own way to better. I don't feel better than anyone. It's not how I was raised. I am a middle-class kid from a Long Island suburb. My parents are immigrants. Paying all these college tuitions is tough. I don't relate when folks say we're special for being here. Not me. I know I am not. I am here because I had strong grades. They like strong grades. I was a woman and they needed women, a person of color and they wanted more people of color. Three other O'Briens have blown through here, one is still here, and there is another on the way. I am not here because I am special. I am not special at all. I am just here.

Estela is the one still at Harvard when I get there. She is also premed. I take lots of science classes, studying at all hours. I become a candy striper, the old-fashioned way to get a taste of medicine. Then I take organic chemistry with Estela. I can get through. But she really gets it. She can figure out how to deduce formulas. I have to stuff this crap in my brain. I have to memorize everything. It's not fun. It's frustrating. I realize I can't apply to medical schools and condemn myself to a life of this. I just don't have a passion for practicing medicine.

Suddenly I am totally lost. I'm not inheriting a job or a secret fortune at the end of four years. I'm lugging around a history of family expectations. My parents are already on the road to having two lawyers, a doctor, and a businessman in the family. I lack a sense of purpose that I should have by now. They are worried that I have no idea what I am going to do with the rest of my life. By then, I'm living in Cabot House. It has a shield with three fishes swimming upstream. It makes me think of the *Titanic* again. Not hopeful. I charge on with premed. I have to major in something.

I run to be house president so I can be in charge of social events. I troll for votes at the dorms, where I'm friendly with everyone. There is this one room of handsome guys. Everyone promises to vote for me, including one lacrosse player named Brad Raymond. His hair is sandy brown. He is friendly enough that day we meet. We are both dating other people. There's nothing flirty between us. He's just like, "Sure." He doesn't get up off the couch. I like him anyway. He has this intensity. We are both always on our way to something. But he is strategic about it. He is practical. He becomes a friend very quickly. It's not until we were expecting our first child that he admits he didn't vote for me.

My junior year I get an internship at WBZ-TV, a Boston television station. This is one place where going to Harvard is of no help, which makes me like it immediately. Gritty newsroom managers aren't big on snooty kids from Ivy League schools. They need someone to fetch coffee and rip copy. I know some Spanish so I get in through their weekly Spanish-language show, *Centro*. I step into a newsroom for the very first time. What a place. The electricity in the room is overpowering. Everyone is rushing around putting together this complicated puzzle of a newscast. It's like one of those memorable scenes on *Star Trek* when the Klingons have entered the zone. An eclectic group of people zooms through space on a mission to someplace. People my age race down the hall cramming three-quarter-inch videotapes into players to cue them up. It is all tape-to-tape editing. Slide it in, spin these big rubber wheels, slam the button, flash red to edit.

When I'm in the studio I know there's no way I am going back to my life as a student at Harvard. *This* is important. Things are happening. There is nothing like the feeling of telling someone else's story, of saying something that needs to be said. In an instant, the shows go live. The anchors begin to talk from behind a little box to the entire city of Boston. It's downright intoxicating.

I use my premed background to land an interview with the medical unit. The medical reporter is Jeanne Blake. She needs a production assistant. She is a force at WBZ, which means I'll be in the newsroom if I work for her. Jeanne walks around with the sense of purpose of an athlete, like every day is an emergency. She has blow-dried feathered-back hair. Her eyebrows are manicured and intense and every bone in her face has shape. She is all business. I walk into her office wearing a carefully chosen red suit with a gorgeous Italian handbag. I ooze self-confidence even if I don't feel it. To this day she remembers how I looked. She asks me what the most important medical story is at this moment. I say, "I think it's the AIDS epidemic," and her eyes light up.

I face a series of decisions. Mostly, I need a new direction in life. I really want this job. I tell her I need a decision. Jeanne remembers me saying something like, "I have to know by tonight or I'm going to medical school." I think I said I had to decide in a week. But I definitely conveyed a sense that this production assistant job was a make-or-break deal. She marches down the hall to the office of the assistant news director and declares they can't let me get away. They hire me.

I tell Harvard I'm not coming back. I'm a few classes short of graduation but I have a new goal in life. I want to be Jeanne Blake. Some people at the station are a little intimidated by her. The girl is wound tight. I adore her. She looks into the camera like she has something important to say. She is very, very smart, intuitive, cunning, street smart. She is obsessed with getting it right. She doesn't just move; she charges around like hurricane wind. She flies through life, reeling past obstacles like a superhero in flight. She sets the agenda. A story comes along that no one wants to do and she just does it. She hardly even has to ask people above her for permission to do it. She gets onto something and flies out the door on a mission. I am awed by her sense of purpose.

She is one of the first reporters covering AIDS. She sees a fascinating human story unfolding. She sees this rainbow of humanity afflicted by a mystery virus, a medical whodunit unraveling the lives of people in their prime. No one else is covering it. She gets carte blanche from the bosses. She embarks on this reportorial journey through the ravages of the disease. She follows the destruction of whole communities. She predicts the political inferno over the identity of the afflicted. She exposes the latest snake oil being peddled as the cure. I am mesmerized. Of the five hundred stories she reports on HIV and AIDS, I have a role in about half. I am the girl at the desk making the phone calls, pulling the tapes, organizing this chaotic work life Jeanne keeps so she can go out and shoot stories. I learn so much so quickly. She is in constant motion and I am right behind her.

I tell my interns these days to not be afraid to pick up a little dry cleaning or fetch an occasional café au lait. It's the little crap that gets you in the door with people. I write notes and tack them to Jeanne's desk. This person called, this report is coming out, attend this event, and don't forget this list of appointments. I am so hyper about the notes that one day I leave one that says "Carolyn died." It doesn't occur to me that this might just be someone she cares about. Jeanne had reported a story about Carolyn, who had AIDS. She looks at me, appalled by my detachment, and stunned that I put efficiency before compassion. Carolyn is not just a story. She is a person. This is something I never forget. In time, she begins to trust my work and trust my judgment. I become her shadow. She takes me everywhere.

We drive twenty minutes to the local hospital most afternoons. She eats lunch there. We walk in, stand in line, order the same tuna sandwich every time, and then sit to eat and say hello to all the doctors. I sit there poking at the miserable food waiting for her to work a source. IVs dangle from a few arms. Hospital gowns split in the back to reveal the occasional backside. I figure it's the price you pay to get access to doctors. The food is limp. The smell is medicinal. I'm always hungry because I can't bear to eat there. I don't want to piss Jeanne off. One day we get into her car and I snap. I tell her we need to skip the hospital lunch. I can't do it anymore. I will never eat there again. I demand she not take me there anymore. I worry because I really want to keep this job. She laughs out loud. She's not there to develop sources. She's just this oddball who likes their tuna sandwiches.

The most important thing I learn from Jeanne is to never look at individuals as a group. It wasn't a hard concept to embrace. I had been a victim of that as a kid, reduced to my skin color and the stupid stereotypes created around it. She didn't give me didactic lectures about how the media shouldn't paint people with a broad brush. She just doesn't do it.

While I am at WBZ, a story unfolds that underscores everything she has taught me about not making assumptions about people. Charles "Chuck" Stuart, the manager of a high-end fur store, and his pregnant wife, Carol, a lawyer, are on their way home from a childbirth class. A few hours later she is dead and he is lying in the hospital with a gunshot wound. Their son, delivered two months early by cesarean section, later dies.

Stuart tells police that a black man carjacked them at a red light and made them drive to Mission Hill. Then the "black man" shoots Stuart in the stomach and Carol in the head. Somehow Stuart manages to drive away. There is a frantic 911 tape where a badly wounded Stuart struggles to lead dispatchers to his dying wife. A CBS crew doing an early reality show has a dramatic tape of the response. A frenzy of reporting erupts in the newsroom. It's all hands on deck. This is big.

The story has all the elements—race, class, and a murder mystery. I am working in the newsroom so I soak it all up. This is the biggest story to hit Boston in ages. The police fan out across Roxbury, questioning people in search of the "black guy." The police announce they've got their man. Our newsroom comes alive to cover the moment. There are doubters. I only know four black people in the newsroom. I don't think there were many more at the station. They don't think Stuart's story adds up. The "black guy" supposedly thought Stuart was a cop because he had a mobile phone. But he's a cop driving around Boston with his pregnant wife in the front seat? The doubts don't seem to resonate in the coverage. The story is a horse race. But it is real life. The rush to get information is intoxicating. Everyone wants to figure it out.

Then the story begins to unravel. Stuart's brother, Matthew, confesses that he'd helped his brother set the whole thing up because Stuart didn't want to be a father and feared losing his wife's salary. A black man's life is almost destroyed because of his lie. The black community is in a rage. Stuart leaps off a bridge to his death a day after his lie is revealed.

Jeanne takes me out on another story with her. We pull up outside a homeless shelter. It's across from Boston's city hospital, located over the morgue. The story is simple. There are a lot of people with HIV losing their homes. They are sick and their immune systems are faltering. They are living in shelters alongside people with TB and other infectious diseases. Our guy sleeps on this super-thin mattress with a dark green army blanket.

We meet Jim. Jeanne has found him through the AIDS Action Committee. He doesn't look sick. He is pale, though, and sweaty. He has gray bushy hair and a professor's mustache. He's white. He wears a hat, thick glasses, a rumpled sweater, and an overcoat. With his shabby briefcase, he looks like a Harvard professor making his way to class. The shelters are only for sleeping. They kick out the men in the morning. Jim is standing on the street. We say "Hi" and he smiles.

Jeanne believes you can take a big giant story and reduce it to one person. She doesn't need a load of drama or breathless writing, just one good personal story that viewers can connect to. Jim is homeless, sick, and a former intravenous drug user. Jeanne likes him instantly. So do I. He is sweet. He appears to be this friendly, very regular guy, neither frail nor homeless. He worries about his health. He has delicate lungs. He doesn't want to be around sick people. He is plaintive. Jeanne remarks that he looks like someone you might know already. She wants to tell the larger story through him.

Jim spends his day wandering the streets looking for a place to go to the bathroom. He has a raging infection. "I've got the sweats from medication or whatever and diarrhea and you're fighting to just not embarrass yourself. There's just no place that you can really go and rest," he says.

We walk around with Jim. He collects his bimonthly $46 welfare check. He buys a burrito, two tacos, and a Pepsi at Taco Bell. He saves the rest for shampoo, toothpaste, and bus fare back to the homeless shelter. Jim was fired from his job as a checkout clerk at a department store for taking so many sick days. His story haunts Jeanne. She stays up half the night thinking about him. I do, too. He has no place to go to the bathroom. He has diarrhea. "How do you do that?" Jeanne asks. "How do you handle being that sick and not have a place to even go to the bathroom?" The shelters are filling up with guys like Jim. She is obsessive about getting his story right. Her empathy is so obvious it consumes her. It leaks out into her writing. The viewers trust and like Jeanne. She cares about this guy. So they care, too. I just stand there and watch.

The piece airs on TV. I watch. A lot of people watch. The public outcry over who is getting AIDS is drowning out all reason. A lot of folks are lost in the debate over who has the disease and who can catch it. Jeanne just tells a story about a man wandering the streets looking for a place to go to the bathroom. She makes it impossible to walk past this guy. I do a lot of work on that story. I watch when it flashes onto the TV screen. I think about Jim, walking around looking for a bathroom in gray, chilly Boston. Jeanne is so right about this guy. He could be anybody. That's why people can relate.

Jeanne is writing a book, *Risky Times: How to Be AIDS-Smart and Stay Healthy*. I do some research. The AIDS crisis is the result of random events. A gambit of biology conspires against vulnerable people. There is the guy who grew up Catholic. He is sick from denial and HIV. He keeps having sex. There is the gay man whose family kicks him out when they find out he is ill. He weeps while we interview him. People keep getting sick. There needs to be a way to dodge this. There has to be something a parent can do to safeguard their child. Jeanne taps into that need in the book. She includes the stories of six Cambridge high school students, including Ben Affleck, who is just fifteen. "I want to be given the chance to become someone. I want to see how the story ends. I don't want to die," he says. He is nobody famous at the time. The message is this could happen to you. "Can you get AIDS from a mosquito bite? from a sneeze? from a kiss?" Jeanne's book asks.

Alison Gertz is also in the book. She grew up on Park Avenue in New York, the granddaughter of the Gertz Department Store founder. She contracts HIV from her first boyfriend and she goes public. Parents are in a panic. That could be my kid. Alison warns other kids about what happened to her. She gives practical advice. I am in the acknowledgments with all the doctors and researchers.

The book lands Jeanne on *Oprah*. Alison Gertz goes on with her. We ride together in a limo. I try to be perky. She has thrush in her mouth. She is an Upper East Side girl all the way, proud, defiant. She tells her story. Jeanne tells the audience she has written a nonjudgmental book about how to be careful. The audience is captivated. The WBZ news director gives me permission to go as long as I keep it a secret. He says to lie low because I'm just a lowly production assistant and he's given me the day off with pay to go sit in a talk show audience. I sit in the audience and end up in all the cutaway shots, so, not only does everyone find out I went, I'm even on TV. I am in awe of Jeanne. I know what I want to do in life.

· CHAPTER THREE ·

A Place at the Table

I am supposed to be a recent college grad, class of 1988, making my way to medical school for years of study and application followed by a respectable career. Instead, I'm at WBZ-TV in Boston making $6 an hour, where I live in the world of what's possible. I rush from one opportunity to the next, grasping at that American promise that hard work and high risk might reap sudden rewards. I am in fast motion once again. I see the newsroom like a mythical starship. I race around its serpentine cubicles. Dusty overhead lights beam down on the reporters as they're about to spring to life. I dream of putting words in their mouths. I dream of being one of them. I am living my life like a voice-over—direct and declarative, life in the active voice. The place is humming with information, fast decisions, chaos, disorder, and stress. I love every minute I am there.

I apply for a job as a "minority writer trainee." Jeanne cries. It means we won't be working together anymore. But she helps me. She has that high-test energy that women need to make it in TV.

She sees it in me. The industry isn't quite ready for her. Maybe it's ready for me? She teaches me to be strong, "tough" in the eyes of the people around us, but strong is what it really is. The trainee program will teach me to write for TV and it's the station's way of increasing the ranks of "minorities." It is my way in.

The door to the media world—and many other worlds—is opening a small crack wider. Women are rushing through it and blacks and Latinos want in, too. Like a lot of industries, journalism needs to diversify and look more at talent and perspective when they hire and less at connections and traditions. It's not just about equal opportunity. Journalism needs diverse people to cover a diverse world. But it's clear that this is neither happening overnight nor easily. The vibe I feel is similar to the one an interracial couple—like my mom and dad—might feel taking a hand-in-hand walk down an American street. Everyone is watching. They tighten their grip. At the same time, they're dying to just let go.

I am starting at the very bottom of the ladder of journalism and have my eyes on the top. I write in short TV sentences, the kind of writing you need to be able to read aloud. I am to the point, full of facts. My official title is "minority writer trainee" so I am in no doubt as to where I stand. Once you've been tagged a minority, this strange process begins. At times I feel like I have a question mark hovering over my head. Why are you here? Is it your race? Do you have any skills, anyway? I approach each day like a job interview. Nothing comes out of my mouth until I've given my thoughts the once-over. The bosses set the bar low. I move it higher. If I hit, I point it out. It's an act of subtle self-promotion, meaning I won one. But when I'm wrong, I suffer. I demand to know what I need to know to get to the next level. Making long lists of goals, I set and reset expectations.

I wasn't even born in 1961 when President John F. Kennedy issues Executive Order 10925. He calls on government contractors to take "affirmative action" to ensure people are given jobs without regard to race and treated fairly once they are hired. The Civil Rights Act in 1964 desegregates public facilities, like schools, and enforces voting rights. A year later, Executive Order 11246 enforces affirmative action. I am born in 1966, black, Latina, a child of immigrants, and a girl. These executive orders are about people like me. President Lyndon Johnson talked of centuries of "scars" that could not easily be wiped away. He pledged to create "not just equality as a right and a theory, but also equality as a fact and as a result."

There are days in the TV station that feel like America is a broad canoe that capsized and I am part of a rescue party thrown in the water to go set it right. I walk around the newsroom with this smart-as-a-whip attitude and this label on my chest. I'm a pioneer and I know it. I know I can't just do this job well and get moved up. I need to prove myself worthy of this opportunity for which I am immensely grateful. This is a country of chances but not of endless chances.

The American Society of Newspaper Editors counts minorities each year with a goal of achieving some level of parity. In 1978, minorities are 3.8 percent of the newspaper workforce and 20 percent of the general population. In 2010, we are at 13.2 percent. That gain would be remarkable if it wasn't that in those twenty-two years we have become 34 percent of the U.S. population. Broadcast journalism does a bit better, but the gains are smaller. The Radio-Television News Directors Association says minorities were 17.8 percent of their workforce in 1990. That number was 23.6 percent in 2008. Progress in this country can be wicked slow, as they say in Boston. As I start out my career in

1988, I know there is a world of opportunity available to me. I also know I need to be extraordinary to make it.

My young career rolls out in fits and starts. One moment I impress everyone. Then suddenly I feel very small and irrelevant. I am the so-called minority trainee and one day I confuse Martin Luther King Jr.'s birthday with the anniversary of his death. The news director finally calls me into his office and tells me not to be so hard on myself. A year flies by. I am promoted to "Writer/Associate Producer." I am assigned to the morning show, the first of several opportunities in my career that require turning my sleeping clock upside down. I am foggy with exhaustion. The show airs from 5:00 to 7:00 a.m. It is a warm-up to when NBC takes over our air with *Today*. I work from 2:00 a.m. to 2:00 p.m. and I am chronically tired. I eat donuts and gulp coffee to stay awake. My eyes don't as much open as they get unstuck each morning. I never feel completely bathed. I stare off into the distance at times, falling in and out of focus. If there is news, everyone snaps to attention.

But there rarely is news at that hour—there are single-alarm fires and car accidents. I'm so tired I rest my head on my keyboard to snatch a catnap. The only thing that rolls in is another torturously slow sunrise. I watch the anchors with their perpetual smiles pull questions from the air without scripting. The Soviet Union falls and there is a sudden burst of news. The anchor fills the time asking the most general questions. I watch and run copy and think to myself, "I could do that." But for now, I rarely even have a social life, much less a shot at being a TV anchor. My life blurs by. Every now and then, Brad invites me to a party. I step into this other world through him. There are young people, mostly Harvard graduates, investment bankers and law school students. They are my age, but they feel like younger people.

They have this glint in their eyes. They laugh and drink and date. I don't do those things. My mind has a day job. I have a plan.

Jeanne tells me not to blow it. Journalism isn't a job. It's not fame. You work lousy hours, she tells me. It's not always exciting. It's often pretty awful, emotionally taxing, unfulfilling. Your life is constantly interrupted by the joys and tragedies of others. So much of what you do seems repetitive. The schools open so you do a story. The kids don't learn so you do another kind of story. Then they do learn so you do that story. School ends and you are at it again. A guy kills his wife. A mom kills her kids. A house burns down. A plane crashes. Congress can't agree on anything. You become a player in the political or criminal or social drama of the moment. You don't want to be one, but you are.

I try to tell the story of the moment differently. That's not hard. There is a template most people work from. You hear the tease and you know what the story is about already. "When we come back . . . tragedy strikes in Anytown where a family loses everything to an early morning fire." The piece will open with video of flames leaping from a window, followed by a sound bite from a firefighter, then a neighbor, then video of the house charred, the mystery of how the fire began, a sound bite from a family member about the loss and back to the anchor in the studio.

The more stories I do, the more I realize it doesn't have to be that way. We've grown so accustomed to hearing the same voices, the same stories. We forget that every story is different. Every tragedy and triumph is personal. Our country is full of people whose perspectives are never heard, people who have something to say. The trick lies in listening to them. I'm dying for a chance to do stories of my own.

Jeanne hooks me up with Bob Bazell, the NBC network's science correspondent. Occasionally I shoot video for him for *NBC*

Nightly News, scramble around gathering material. Jeanne helps me rent an apartment for 600 bucks. It's a basement studio on Marlboro Street, the leafiest, prettiest street in Boston. I feel like I am on the cusp of success even though I can barely pay my rent. Like Jeanne, Bob is also covering the AIDS epidemic, but he is much more fascinated with the science of this fast-evolving virus. There is an international dispute over who discovered HIV that prompts high drama. The debate over how this killer disease can be transmitted is in full tilt. There is a period when it feels as if mutating viruses are spreading through the population like a common cold. It's a terrifying and challenging time to be covering medicine. Jeanne keeps pushing me to focus on the people. This is not just about a fast-changing illness eating away at human strength; this is a story of lives destroyed, of public services failing the vulnerable. This is about people like Jim, whom she and I met together. Jeanne becomes one of my best friends even as she is my mentor.

My work is energizing and convincing enough for Bob to hire me as a researcher and field producer. I move to New York, the epicenter of media. Brad is living in New York, so I get to see him occasionally, and slowly, in spite of my crazy travel schedule and Brad's hundred-hour workweeks, we become close friends. He's like my guidepost. I bounce my frustration off of him. I try out my strategies. But dating is barely on my radar. I live alone in a crappy one-bedroom in SoHo on Thompson between Prince and Spring Streets. I paint it yellow. My rent is $1,050 a month. There are cockroaches everywhere that scramble when the lights turn on. I pour Borax everywhere. My room is shaped so weirdly that my bed is in the middle of everything. But I feel like I belong in the city.

People are from everywhere. Everyone acts like they have

someplace to go. I seem very serious in the midst of the artists and hipsters around me. I wear smart suits and low heels into the office, often passing nobody on the street during my morning commute. Eight thirty in the morning is much too early for the people in the community I am living with. I work at Rockefeller Center, which towers above the plaza like a national monument. Flags from many nations flutter beside the ice rink and the golden statue of Prometheus. The whole place feels like an enormous finish line, like the big tent at the circus. So many people originally from Long Island are scrambling to get out here. For me, Manhattan is the city on the hill. The place where dreams are made.

My first day at NBC I ride up in the elevators with Jane Pauley, and I am so excited I can't breathe. I race around the hallways of NBC working on stories that air on a network everyone is watching. I get to see important anchors with big jobs. I know I want to be on TV reporting the news. I know I can do it. I want to be Jeanne. I'm meeting the people that can get me there. Bob sends me all over the country as his field producer. I keep coming back with the same thing, a story with a person as its center.

I fly to Phoenix to do a story about a man with strep B. His family talks about watching him dying because bacteria are eating him alive. He has two small kids. He survives and now he takes walks on his prosthetic legs because his legs have been eaten away. He also has a prosthetic hand. He can't toss a ball with his kid, but he is alive. Bob is very focused on the science, the "why" of medicine. I am consumed by the humanity. I learn a lot from Bob—it's like going to college, but sometimes I wish I can do it differently.

TV is a team sport. You get a piece on air with no less than a half dozen people working together—cameraman, audio technicians, editors, producers. But the TV reporter is at the top of that team. If I can get that job, I can frame the story the way I want to. I bump into Elena Nachmanoff one day on the elevator. She is in charge of what they call "Talent Development," which means she is the gatekeeper for anyone who wants to be on TV. She has a serious look and she dresses in that stylish New York corporate way that portrays how powerful she is. In our two-minute ride she asks what I want to do next. I don't hesitate: I tell her I want to be an on-air reporter, a concept I find exhilarating but that also makes me feel a bit ill. She says she thinks that can happen and walks off the elevator with the polish of the high-ranking executive she is. That's all we say. I'm stunned.

Brad moves to California in 1992. The moment he's gone, I start to miss him. He has been in and out of my life forever. We have gone out a few times but really we are just friends. I suddenly feel his absence, which is weird because we're just friends. I can call him and he encourages me to do things. I am lonely even though my family lives all of an hour away. I have five siblings, loads of coworkers. But I feel disconnected. I fly out to San Francisco to do a piece for Bob. Brad picks me up afterward. We go to the Tiki Lounge at the Fairmont Hotel. There is a pool in the middle of the bar and the band floats on top of it. It's really tacky. I suddenly feel that this is a date. We're not just catching up from some other time. I'm so comfortable it's like I'm visiting my family. I have so much to tell him. He is so eager to listen.

We go to dinner in the North End. We stay out as late as possible. We both have so much to say to each other. I realize I have a crazy crush on him and I always have. I just haven't let it go anyplace. There were too many things in the way. I was too confused over what to do with my life. Then I was focused about making it in TV. He works all the time. He is calculating his next big move in his career in finance. I am dating other people and so is he. While the guys I date are sweet and generous, they bore me. Brad is focused and self-sufficient. He believes in strategy; he has a plan. He is philosophical. He thinks about what I'm saying and gives me a thoughtful answer. He is the living definition of what character means. It matters to him to get it right and be honest and compassionate and to work hard. His eyes are mischievous and make him look like he's smiling even when he's not. He's handsome and fair, with all-American looks. He carries not an ounce of arrogance. He is unimpressed by wealth or good looks. He could care less how I look or what I do. I am considered pretty but not like the girls I run into at parties. He is happy to have me and create our own category. Brad is a minimalist, no frills. Nothing is a big deal to him. He is happy to live in a place that makes him comfortable, no matter the address. He likes an edgier neighborhood. He drives an old Honda. He doesn't brag he went to Harvard or that he was a star athlete. Years later I will show up to black-tie dinners underdressed because it will skip his mind to tell me I need to wear a gown!

There are many reasons people fall in love. I was born to a family made of concrete. We were a team—solid. I learned from my parents to look for that in people. If you're going to make a lifetime commitment to someone, base it on something that's real. Often people seem to look for someone who looks like them—same race, same class, same school, and same ambitions. None of that mattered to my parents. My dad was a good man. He was present, loving, no drama, a good friend, and a good father. That he is white and Australian are just facts about him. My mother is driven, purposeful, devoted, detailed. My dad fell in love with that. He loves that she loves family, that she loves God, that she has that immigrant spirit. The fact that she is black and Cuban and from a poor background are just details. That is one of the wonderful challenges of living in a country of immigrants. You have to look past people's facade. Every face you meet tells the story of far-off places and snap decisions. The ruddiness and freckles and red hair of the Irish in a man can tell the story of a grandfather's sudden quest to the Americas for another life. You can jump to a million assumptions about a guy. But looks cannot tell you what's inside the grandson who grew up surrounded by other histories, other dreams. You have to look at the person within.

It was easy to figure out why I want Brad to be my husband. He lives in forward motion just like me. He makes up his mind to do something and just does it. At the end of our date, he suggests I move to California. I have no job, no car, and no money, but somehow it totally makes sense. Life in the United States affords you unending opportunities to do one better. There is always something flashier than the flashy thing you've got. So sometimes it pays to just choose the thing you want. I want Brad, the man that urges me on like a fan at the racetrack, who talks about me like I have limitless ability and potential. I am in New York building a job as a network producer. But I want to be with this guy.

At NBC, I treat every day as if it's my first day on the job. I make sure everyone knows what I want to do next. I want to be a reporter. I practice. And I make sure everyone sees me practice. Other people begin to root for me. I call Jeanne constantly. I send Jeanne tapes of my efforts. She tells me to lower my voice and not punch the words so hard. I ask Bob for advice. He doesn't say much, though he blurts out at one point that I need to focus on marrying Brad because he's too good a guy to lose. I begin to figure Brad into my plans. There is someone out there—a destination to go with my strategy. If you tell people what you're after, they help you get there. I check in with Elena Nachmanoff all the time, a serious customer. She looks my resume up and down. I work at my writing. I look at myself in the mirror, work on my voice, and watch the anchors.

Jeanne had a model of the reporter she wanted to be, a tenacious, unyielding woman who won't accept a "no," a woman who sees someone that needs help and sends out a cry. Jeanne tells me that she once had dreams of going to work for a network, but made a decision to not pursue them. "I'd end up sleeping in hotel rooms using those little bars of soap," she says. She wanted to stay in Boston and get married. She believed I could make it to the top. Back in the late 1970s, lots of women wanted to be Jessica Savitch. Jessica had practically created the role for women by sitting on the NBC desk with her reporter's intensity, messy personal life, and anchor hair. Going network meant you had made it. Jeanne had given up her anchor chair to be a medical reporter. No one ever does that, but Jeanne was a pure reporter. That's how much she lived and breathed her job. Jeanne looked at me and saw herself. She gives me advice every day. Sometimes it's warming, sometime it's harsh: "Try it this way," she says. "Do it again and again until you get it right." That is her way of putting me, and by extension her, one step closer to becoming the next network anchor.

Years later, I'm giving my daughter Cecilia a bath. Jeanne is there. Cecilia, who is four, asks Jeanne why she didn't have kids. I jump in: "She does. She's my TV mom!" I see Jeanne's eyes get teary. It stuns me.

Increasingly, women were being hired by networks. I knew it hadn't always been so. I thought that was really awful, stinging. Not fair. Not right. Intolerable. It's all those things. Now I also know it's typical. There's an asterisk in the promise of America—a clause in the social contract that so many of us forgot to read. Women brought a special sensibility into the workplace. Journalism was no different. We gave life to what were thought of as women's stories: education, the elderly, welfare, and children all became areas of serious news coverage. A certain sense of humanity entered reporting. The distance between the subject and the viewer became smaller. What women got in return was a place at the table—just one place.

This pattern repeats itself in every profession I've encountered. The United States has always been a land of opportunities. A place that advertises itself as somewhere anything is possible for anybody. It is in one sense, but it's not in many others. There is always one breakthrough person. The first this. The first that. The person who leaps over their stereotype and creates a new reality. But most folks spend their whole lives trying to come in behind them and they only get part of the way there. They get the opportunity to try. They get a shot. They get further than the last person. Then they end up making way for the next person to get a shot. That can make you bitter. That can make you angry. Or it can make you Jeanne, giving a hard push to make way for the next woman in line.

One day, I break through glass. I am offered a job at KRON, an NBC station in San Francisco. I pack six giant duffel bags and move across the country. I move into a studio with an alcove that faces Bush Street. I can hear the traffic heading for the bridge that unites San Francisco and Oakland and it wakes me up early. I pay $600 a month for this tiny apartment, but I am making less money and working four days a week. But back in New York I was a field producer who wanted to be a reporter. Now I live three thousand miles away with less space and I have less money, and early-morning traffic noise. But I am going to be on air!

In the newsroom, I see some familiar and friendly faces. Stan Hopkins, who had been the news director at WBZ, is there. The meteorologist is Janice Huff, who is black, and she is nice to me. I feel comfortable asking her where to get my hair done. There are several reporters who are members of racial or ethnic minorities—Belva Davis, Ysabel Duron, and Vic Lee. They go out of their way to support me. They are also very talented, so their warmth gives me some comfort.

But often it feels like people don't much like me. Nobody would quite say it but they don't see me as qualified. Their eyes seem to challenge why I'm here. They act as if I am stealing something. I am definitely in over my head as an on-air reporter. But I have come from producing at an NBC network. I know I can write a great story. I just don't know how to tell that story talking into the camera.

Pam Moore, who had been a reporter when I was back at WBZ, is KRON's evening anchor. Pam makes it clear that she thinks I am in way over my head on camera so early. She's right. There has just been a layoff of some staff after a strike by the writers and I am the first new hire, making a third of what the other reporters make. I am young and an ethnic and racial minority. People read something into that. I try to focus on working hard. I volunteer to cover fires in the middle of the night. I might not be good, but I'm willing. I have a lot to learn about being on air.

Ysabel Duron is the weekend anchor. She went to school with Geraldo Rivera on a Ford Foundation grant aimed at increasing the number of minorities in TV news. She seized the opportunity given her. She won an Emmy in 1974 for covering the Patty Hearst kidnapping. She is from an era when women didn't get to cover that stuff and she did it anyway. She also covered the Harvey Milk murder and Ronald Reagan. She was a female first more than once, a Latina first. At KRON, she does a series on the son she gave up for adoption. The reporting is forceful, rich with emotion. There are not many women. Not many minorities. It makes such a difference to see someone make it who looks like you. I look toward Ysabel, and dream.

I try very hard but I need to be better. After two weeks, I am sent out on my first live shoot. I completely flub it. The San Francisco Giants are in the playoffs. I go live from a bar where everyone is drunk, and just as I begin my report someone grabs my ass. I freeze. I stare into the camera like an idiot. They go to my tape of happy people talking about the Giants. They come back to me to close out my story. I mumble. It's over quickly, though it feels like a lifetime. Back at the station the boss calls me into his office. I am so ashamed as I walk through the newsroom. He suggests I quit. I should try Santa Barbara; go make my mistakes in a smaller market. I call Bob Bazell from a pay phone, where no one can hear. He makes me take a deep breath. He says, "Don't quit. No matter what, stick it out. Those jobs are hard to get." He's right so I stick it out.

I review every tape I shoot to see how I look on camera. Every thirty minutes I do live shots before *Today* comes on. Five times a day I do short news updates. I live on the air. I can tell I'm improving. I'm young and paid a pittance. That is the moment of opportunity in any business. I am not naturally talented and I know it, but I am willing to work harder than everyone else. Someone suggests I pretend that Brad is the camera. I find that so ridiculous I laugh, even though I am so stressed. My friend Sara James from NBC tells me to pretend the live shot is a call to my own mother. "Remember, she is not stupid but she can't see what you are seeing. Explain with clarity and detail." As if I'm not stressed out enough, I'm thinking about my mother. But I try it.

I learn to stop trying to say too much. Just focus on the three lines I'm trying to deliver. I wear black too much and I don't like being on camera. I feel awkward doing a stand-up—the break where the reporter addresses the audience. Why am I talking into the camera in the middle of a story about someone else? I listen to my own voice and I hate it. It doesn't sound like me. I stick to the three lines. I pick someone to talk to. I just say what is happening. I keep it simple. One day, mercifully, I stop hearing myself and I just talk.

I have always hated the way I look on camera. I don't feel authentic. I feel like an insert, an extra, one of those annoying people who step into the camera and wave when they're not supposed to. I long wanted to be a television reporter, but one who didn't have to be on TV. That's crazy, of course. But it's true.

I am reporting a story about the dangerous high winds on the Bay Bridge and I urge people to stay away. Later at the grocery store an elderly woman tells me she is praying for me and says she hopes I get a job "inside." I go to the ninetieth anniversary celebration of the City of Richmond in California. I attend as the event's emcee, wearing a dress with a green velvet top and a black skirt. When I arrive they don't recognize me and won't let me in. I'm the main speaker and they can't find my name on the guest list.

Years later I'll walk the red carpet at the Costume Ball at the Met in New York as a network reporter. There will be over two hundred photographers shouting my name and taking flash photos and pushing Brad out of the way. I push forward a toe and flash that smile created for the glow of paparazzi. People recognize me but I still feel like the girl in the green velvet top—a little bit over my head. Next to the willowy models I don't think I am particularly pretty, but I focus on looking appropriate. The runway photos look like an ego moment, but they are not. They never appear anywhere. I'm not fashionable enough or controversial enough ever in my career to be the instant photo pick. If I sit next to Uma Thurman, I get lucky if they don't cut me out. Looks are something that can help you out or get in the way. Good looks betray you.

There is an aspect of TV that is an extension of the beauty industry. Because we are journalists everyone avoids talking about it. I feel confident I was picked to go on air because of my abilities, but looks always play a part when it comes to TV. That means I have to make sure my looks work for me, not against me. I have to walk around life looking like I believe I am smart and confident, that I am beautiful but that my looks are not my main focus. I need my attitude about my looks to get out of the way so people listen to what I am saying.

The good news is that in this country, anyone can qualify for good-looking because there is really no American look. There is something unique about American beauty in that it allows for beauty by circumstance. The blue-eyed blondes from the toothpaste commercials may declare themselves on top. But there is room for Barbra Streisand and Lena Horne. They sing beautifully so they are beautiful. There is room for Nancy Kerrigan and Michelle Obama and Jessica Tandy—or at least their career-high moments make for the sudden recognition of their beauty.

In America, success is beautiful, as is notoriety, power, exposure, attitude, accomplishment, and smarts. Beauty in America is not just blue eyes and a mane of blond hair. I walked through high school as this nerd living in a place where race was the third rail of dating. I was sunk when it came to good looks. But once I left my hometown my looks became exotic. The difference wasn't me. It was about the audience, the timing, the moment of my big unveiling. The look of a mix of races and ethnicities combining spoke of the promises of racial peace and social harmony. I had, just by circumstance, the face America wanted to reflect its soul. This was a moment for people who looked like me to stand out.

In 1993 I'm doing live shots for KRON and feel like ducking when the camera goes live. By 2000, I am a weekend anchor at NBC and I'm named one of *People* magazine's "Most Beautiful." It feels a bit like it is just my turn. They declare me the portrait of America's multiracial future. By then I'm pregnant and I have gut-wrenching morning sickness the day of the photo shoot, which seems comical given that I'm being photographed for my beauty. They offer me grapefruit juice and red jellybeans and make me feel much more lovely than I am feeling that day. I wear leather pants with alluring zippers and curl my long hair. I'm cute enough, not crazy beautiful. I'm certainly attractive enough to report the news.

But in my early days at KRON, it's attitude that counts. I walk into KRON each day like a ray of sunshine. I never appear to be unhappy. I complain about nothing. I say yes to everyone. I love reporting so I focus on that. The camera crews like me. I work hard and I am willing to carry the gear. That's key in TV—an experienced photographer can teach you everything you need to know about reporting. I keep at it with the punishing live shots at dawn. Not many people are watching, but I really invest. I try and try to get better. I begin walking around like I actually belong there.

Then one day I am walking down the hallway and see a huddle of people. There is another young reporter who is also working four days a week, like me. She's kind of my competition in the new arrival category. Everyone is making a joke about the affirmative action hire. I smile and walk by. They are having fun. But suddenly they look embarrassed. It's me. I'm the hire they're talking about! I am so incensed. I want to remind them of my resume. I had been a network producer. I've worked so hard and achieved so much and now I'm mad. I'm embarrassed. It didn't even feel racial; it was just nasty.

I sink into myself. At twenty-six, I am always in fast-forward. I get lost in the story or at least the little piece of it I can grab for myself. Polly Klaas is kidnapped at knifepoint from her own slumber party at age twelve. Thousands of people search for her and the TV news plays a central role. The police happen upon her suspected killer when his car gets stuck in the mud, but they let him go. They later discover the little girl has been strangled. We report the breaking news. They find the suspected killer and I report it on TV. These kinds of stories become the bread and butter of my working life.

Within three months I am named bureau chief for the East

Bay. Or, more accurately, they move me to Oakland, and I am the lone reporter in the bureau so by default I name myself bureau chief. Brad is starting business school at Berkeley, so it brings us closer. I report for three solid years. Really get my arms around the job. I tell Brad I am confident we are going to be married. He says he feels like he is the guy, but I think my attitude kind of scares him. We drive all over California in his Honda: Sonoma, Napa, Tahoe. I tell him I'm in California because of him. He is running his own business, so he's busy. We never live together: That's the way I was raised. My parents visit and we clean up any signs he even stays there.

We are low-drama people. So one night over dinner I tell him I feel like he's about to propose. He is. It's like a dance between us until he does. Then fast-forward a year to 1995 and there are 135 people on my parents' lawn in Smithtown and it's ninety-eight degrees and scorching hot. I am in a white bead gown. My mother is slightly annoyed that I'm not wearing panty hose in church but okay with Brad refusing to wear a tux. The crowd reflects what my life is becoming. Bob and Jeanne are both there and my colleagues from California fly in. My adult life is standing on the lawn of my childhood home all dressed up. Brad had been living in Menlo Park and I leave my apartment in San Francisco. We get our first apartment together in the East Bay on Mandana Boulevard right on Lake Merritt. I am loving being in Oakland and loving every minute of my life. I am suddenly very happy.

· CHAPTER FOUR ·

FINDING MY VOICE

Oakland is the second-most-diverse place in America, and when I move there it's also the momentary epicenter of crack cocaine, rap music, and earthquakes. My bosses never expected me to move there, but Oakland is the place I have to go live if I'm going to cover the community like Jeanne has taught me to do. This is the kind of place where interesting stories are happening, but there is definitely a sense of amazement from the higher ups that I want to live there. One day the East Bay Bridge is out and all the execs complain about how they have to drive through Oakland to get to work. I'm supposed to be covering the community objectively and my bosses look down on the inhabitants. It feels slightly racist, but it's more like a division based on class. The fact is, many of these people are poor. I speak up. I remind everyone that the people who live there are the people I'm covering. They roll their eyes.

Even so, I walk into my own apartment every night and glance into the living room to see if my TV is still there. The neighborhood is wonderful, but it's also rough. I am glad I can live in it because it helps me understand my community, but it's complicated. I walk outside and love the chaos of cultures coming together at one moment. I cringe when I see them clashing fiercely the next. I am here for a reason. They can call my beat whatever they want, but I am covering poverty, life in the inner city, the punishing existence of the have-nots, the many injustices heaped on vulnerable people by urban life.

A guy wearing a pink dress knocks over a Wells Fargo truck and I'm leading the news with the report. He has guessed correctly that people will only remember the dress. Children scream as they are pulled from their parents by Child Protective Services. I am there to do a story. Fires rage in the middle of the night. I am there. This is what much of America looks like, but it is nothing like my cozy little suburban Smithtown. For so many people in this country who look like me, this is real life.

Oakland is like any one of a number of American communities that flower in darkness. The folks who drive through it see only urban ills, but there is immutable beauty left behind from another time. Towering redwoods were replaced by racing streetcars and sprawling rail yards that gave way to suburbs. Little villages sprouted up when immigrant groups from China and Latin America planted their flags. Where some folks see modern ghettos taking root there are also leftover redwoods and the timeless lake in the park. I love the cultural stew of the people. I jog around the waterfront and wave at Jerry Brown. I feel the bay breeze lift the heat and catch the smell of flowers.

At KRON, some reporters see poor people in poor neighborhoods behaving like animals. A number of people are saying the station's best days are slipping by and it's stuck in this lazy pattern of reporting stories off press releases and staged photo ops.

I catch one every day or get sent out overnight for the latest fire. I do the live shot on the familiar serpentine roadways that guide people past the slums. I want to get into the neighborhoods where families wage battles for safety and education and basic services. But I'm a young reporter practicing her live news delivery without the clout or wherewithal to sell those stories effectively.

Meth labs are everywhere in Oakland, or at least that's how the KRON assignment desk makes it feel. I cover meth labs and meth busts and meth fires. Methamphetamines are a gross drug. They trick the brain into overproducing dopamine. To make them, people cook nasal decongestants with ephedrine using toxic chemicals like lithium they get from batteries. The process produces powder, little rocks called "ice." It's so easy that kitchens and garages become drug labs. The problem is these labs can suddenly blow up if you mess up the process. I find myself covering lots of these fires. The methamphetamine rush is not a poor people's rush. It's a rush craved by anybody who wants to escape life's downs. It's cooking in Oakland but it's an equal opportunity American high. The reporting makes clear we don't effectively treat drug addictions or try to lift people out of the lows that accompany life's burdens. But we enforce our drug laws with the ferocity of hungry lions. Police hold press conferences announcing their latest bust like gladiators holding high a severed head. I feel like there is much more to this story.

KRON is not the kind of station that does stories about the plight of poor people. Most local stations are not. We cover the police, the schools, the missing children, and crime. I try to make the point at KRON that we need to do more than report the latest tragedy. Lecturing people is always a bad idea. I get nowhere and I'm still too young at my craft to just do it on my own. Those stories intrigue me but I have no idea how to tell them or pitch them or do them. I have no mentor close by. I feel lost and angry some days. People who deserve more from their local TV station surround me.

The neighborhoods of Oakland divide by class more than race. Or at least it's easier for people to divide them that way. It's part of America's ambivalence about the poor, the struggle over whether to pity or despise someone who is down on their luck, especially when they lash out. There are middle-class black people who hate poor people, working-class Latinos who hate poor people, and so on. The poor get layered. There are the working poor and the criminal poor and pecking orders within each. People are so much more multidimensional than how much they earn, but it counts for a lot in a place like Oakland. It counts for everything to people watching Oakland from outside. I want my reporting to explain why police disproportionately focus on the guy cooking up crap in a meth lab but won't prosecute the middle-class cocaine user who goes to work each morning.

I feel the limits of my abilities and it is frustrating. I need to get there. I'm too young to hurl my anger at anyone. I just carry it around until it turns into frustration. I get really pissed off by what people at work say. But I don't explode. I try to save my fire. I know if I lose my temper then people will begin to work around me. I rephrase my arguments but I end up outside yet another fire, yet another murder. I concentrate on the stories. I practice getting better. I am getting better but I need to get good, really good.

I feel like I come into my own as a reporter during the teachers' strike of 1996, a five-week walkout that begins over salaries and class sizes. At first over 80 percent of Oakland's fifty-two thousand schoolchildren and nearly 70 percent of its teachers stay home. The schools try to stay open by hiring strikebreakers, scabs in the eyes of the union. The strike is heartbreaking. The teachers are so obviously underpaid. The kids are being taught in oversized classes. They are some of the worst performing students in the country and the schools have no money to teach them? The result is teachers not teaching and kids not learning, a standoff that paralyzes Oakland.

I camp out and bring donuts to both sides. Neighborhood kids with nothing to do come spend time in my office. I buy them books from the local store and several tell me they have never owned a book before in their life. The parents try to teach their kids in churches and community centers. Oakland plays tough and bans them from public buildings. Teachers begin teaching out of their homes. This is where living in the community pays off. This meltdown is happening around me. I can see the parents racing around in the morning, trying to figure out what to do, fretting that their kids' subpar education has been replaced by no education at all. I see the teachers trying to survive making $30,000 a year. For the first time, I am dug in deeply enough with both sides of a story and feel confident enough in my skills that I get beyond just reporting a headline. I report a nuanced story of the politics behind why education is failing urban kids. The contract settlement hikes minimum teacher pay to $30,524. This is a story where no one wins. The story of the Oakland schools is the story of so many urban schools, underfunded and understaffed and searching for ways to teach the kids. Parents will ask the question here and in so many places around the country: Why is it too much to expect to get a basic education at my local public school?

Meanwhile, I feel stuck at KRON. The news director is clear I'll never get a chance to anchor. I feel like I am one woman too many. I am frustrated because I am not growing my skill sets. It is 1996 and I am wrapping up my time as the KRON Oakland reporter, when a six-year-old black boy is charged with assaulting a Latino infant with a stick. He is taken to juvenile hall even though he is so little. I keep asking people why he's there when he's so young. The answer is always technical, something about the rules and no other place to send him.

The first time I see him, he is wearing big brown shorts that are down around his ankles because they are too large. The clothes are meant for a teenager. He clearly doesn't belong there but he clearly has problems. He walks in the courtroom one day and waves at the sketch artist. "Who are you drawing?" he asks, whispering politely. "You," the artist tells him. He is pleased and surprised. He wants to see the drawing. He is clueless. He doesn't realize this is all about him.

The boy is charged with attempted murder and burglary because he entered the house with twin eight-year-old boys to rob a big wheel. The baby is four weeks old, Ignacio Bermudez Jr. He has skull fractures and bleeding in his brain. The prosecutors say the six-year-old knew what he was doing. I interview the father of the baby. He and his wife, Maria Carmen, had taken their other children to get groceries but left the baby behind because he had a cough and the night was chilly. The father is soft-spoken and deliberates before choosing his words. He feels for the parents of the children who have been accused. It won't make things better for their lives to also be lost in all this. It amazes me that his calm tone never falters. I search this man's eyes for anger, but I can't find it.

I do live shots and a group of black people shout behind me. It's stunning. They are not yelling at me—they are just yelling. They scream about the white media. They don't mention either boy. There is nuttiness to these big crime stories. The sideshow has a rhythm to it. I am the morning reporter. They want me to use the elements I have—sound and pictures from the night before—to leave a story for the afternoon. The story changes so I have to report some more. Then everything changes for the next morning. I feel like I am always aiming for good enough because there is no time for being particularly thoughtful. We chase the newspaper reporters, who dig in a little deeper. Like all the reporters, I search for a reason. Even the kid's own lawyer says it is impossible to get at what the boy had or had not done. He is just too young so his account keeps changing.

It is not shocking to me that a little boy ends up being defined by an assortment of social ills familiar to Oakland. He is a six-year-old redoing kindergarten. His neighbors and teachers say he is somewhat hyper, though mostly a regular kid. His mother is a twenty-six-year-old single child-care worker. His home is described as a crack den. His father was shot through the head and killed when the boy was four. The family is very poor. A granduncle trashes him to the media as a child demon. He says he obsessively played with Teenage Mutant Ninja Turtles. He remembers the boy standing outside late at night while screams erupted from inside. The family is disturbingly dysfunctional, almost beyond analysis. I can't fully relate. I want to understand what happened and why, really why. But I can't. The boy is sent to a group home for disturbed children after they find him incompetent to stand trial.

A year later, the baby can't sit up and suffers from seizures. Ignacio, the father, still refuses to place blame. The saddest thing about this story is that none of the people involved have the emotional energy to scream out about the miserable situation that surrounds them. That is the awfulness of America's poorest communities, that sometimes what's most horrible just becomes the norm.

In 1996, NBC launches MSNBC, a twenty-four-hour cable

competitor to CNN with a tie to Microsoft. The Internet is the presumptive news provider of the future. A year later, David Bohrman comes to California to set up an MSNBC studio. He is a gruff, hairy guy with a big smile, glasses, and the demeanor of the friendly bus driver who used to transport you to school. He has a very long list of female reporters he is interviewing to anchor a tech show. He figures he'll pick the most energetic of the group and pair her with a serious guy who gets technology. For some reason my name is on his list. David figures he'll meet me as long as he's in town. It is not cool for him to be swiping employees from one of his network's affiliates so we have a secret breakfast meeting at the Clift Hotel. He is enthusiastic from the get-go and discards the idea of me needing a male coanchor. He offers me a job anchoring *The Site* for MSNBC from Silicon Valley. I'm thrilled. Among other things, David is a sweet guy. He seems to think I'm terrific.

Two days before we're on air, David is crawling around the floor assembling the control room. He is one of those people who believes you have to do things yourself for them to be done well. I move to an industrial section near Potrero Hill. I can watch the fog consume San Francisco in the distance. I can walk to work and I often do. Third and Cesar Chavez streets bound the neighborhood. It is tucked away from the highways. Waves of immigrants built this land. They were drawn by a gold rush. I feel as if I too am mining a piece of America. Brad is working at J.P. Morgan in downtown San Francisco. We have a sixth-floor penthouse apartment with a giant deck. How good is life?

Focusing on high tech, I am away from the tough stories of Oakland, but I am not done with them. I just have a few other things to learn about TV. I am anchoring. I do spots for the Discovery Channel, too. I have to interview guests. I don't know much about technology, which turns out to be a good thing because I can ask questions like a viewer. The downside is I can sound like an idiot if I'm not careful. David creates this cyber guy to help me out. My coanchor is not even a person; he is a virtual geek played by Leo Laporte, who is a tech expert on the Web. There are so many new gadgets. I keep telling myself to boil it down, boil it down. Boil it down. I don't know a thing about technology. David keeps celebrating my energy and enthusiasm like a proud parent. He is thrilled that I can carry a whole show on my own. It goes really well.

I keep hounding the people at NBC. I send tapes. I am interviewed several times, on the phone. Mostly I keep asking David what I'm doing wrong and right. I feel like NBC is where I should be, like I am on a trip away from home. TV is driven by events. You can never get used to the rhythm because then something happens and everything has to change. For me that something is the death of Princess Diana. I am anchoring a West Coast tech show. MSNBC launches into rolling news coverage and I'm dead, too, metaphorically. They realize this story and rapid-fire news coverage draws more viewers than my tech show, which just fades away. They keep paying me but I have no job. I sit in my apartment. I am told not to go to work. I can see a dire ending so I push for another job. They offer me the MSNBC weekend morning newscast, *Morning Blend*, back in New York. They tell me I can be a correspondent during the week for the *NBC Nightly News*. The three years at KRON have paid off. I'm on my way home—to do big things.

This time at NBC, I'm a grown-up. No one is cutting me any slack. I'm anchoring for MSNBC, but during the week I have been dumped on the *NBC Nightly News,* and part-time as well. The producer is David Doss. He is tall, smart, and handsome and not particularly friendly. I've been handed to him. But he doesn't really need me so he seldom puts me on air. I anchor weekends but during the week there is not much for me to work on. There are plenty of stories. There is a whole slice of America that is not getting on anyone's news shows. I can't get their stories on air if I can't get me on air.

The weekends are better. The executive producer, Rod Prince, is black. He gives me opportunities to do important stories. He hands me over to a senior producer, Kim Bondy, who is also black. There always seem to be plenty of people of color working on weekends trying to move up. She makes me laugh. I want to be her friend. She has these terrific shoes and always looks fantastic, not business dress fantastic but stylish and outgoing. She smiles and has a quick tongue, these piercing dark eyes, and a way of entering a room like she has completely thought through what she wants to say. She acts like she can own a conversation in a bar as easily as she can in a boardroom. I trust her instantly.

There we all are on the weekends when it seems that none of the network executives are watching what we are doing. Rod and Kim use me. They put me on TV and push me to grow. Kim has a great attitude. Tell me something I don't know, she asks. Rod tells her to watch out for me. And she does and she will for the rest of my career. I have another Jeanne. The thing a woman most needs in the workplace is a good friend. Rod invests in Kim. Kim invests in me.

I fill in for weekend anchor Brian Williams. He is the heir apparent to Tom Brokow. It sounds like a big deal but a lot of people get to do it. Rod makes sure I'm one of them. I get noticed. After years of operating on my own, I finally have allies and mentors in positions of influence. But it's not enough. I'm just not busy enough. The viewers are friendly and I have plenty of fans, but it feels a bit part-time.

MSNBC pulls me to cover the Pope's visit to Cuba. Monica Lewinsky happens and we get derailed. It's Princess Diana all over again. My big shot at international reporting has been shut down by an intern who had sex with the president. But I am in Cuba, the place my mother fled to find a better life. A lot of America's immigrants get to go back and touch home plate every few years, remember why they left or savor what's left behind. Not the Cubans. Politics has separated us from our past.

I realize on this trip how much of my mother's past I've lost. My Spanish isn't strong enough to chat fluidly, but people come up and try to talk with me anyway and I feel dumb. The food is wonderful, if you can find it. There is an ease to this place, a beauty to Havana that even its crumbling walls can't obscure. I am an uptight American. I feel like this is a part of me I want to restore. I love the way the music pulses through the streets, interrupting the night frogs and crackle of the ocean. I love the warmth of the people, their good manners. They make an effort to work hard even when there is so little work to be had. I watch the old cars bounce by and walk the exact streets my mother saw as a restless preteen girl. The island has all these little places that smell of burnt tobacco and ocean mist and the occasional whiff of rum.

I've been in no other country where everything feels a bit like a lazy evening in my grandmother's bedroom. I am suddenly surrounded by people who look like me. I am connected to the past by the red in my hair. My father's mother used to call my mother "la Russa" when the colors lit up in the summer sun. I look around at them and see my toothy smile, tight nose, and freckly features.

My cousin has a son named Orestes, who sits on her lap wearing a red and gray tracksuit. I can tell the death of my uncle Orestes has made a mark. My little brother, my favorite, is Orestes, too.

These are the children from the stories of my youth. My mother never talked much about Cuba beyond them. I can now see why. I am in Cuba during *"la crisis,"* when everything is in short supply. I feel incredibly uncomfortable meeting my cousins, who have nothing. They hug me and pinch my face but there is a tone to their voices that sounds something like resentment. Their house is buckling. They have crowded into too small a space. I have no way to help them and they need everything. I sit there as a symbol of what could have been if they could have left like my mother. My relatives aren't allowed to visit me at my hotel, which stings of humiliation. I am not a product of the politics around Castro; my mother left before he arrived. I don't even think about the swirl of controversy around what he has done. But in their smiles and laughter and feeling of home, I feel a connection and lament that I am not more a part of the Cuba that bore my mother.

America gives you the freedom to hold on to the past, even if it lives somewhere else. I can be Cuban in the United States because part of being American is bringing your culture to bear on the new land of your people. I suddenly understand something about my mother's culture now, her race and ethnicity and roots that feel more visceral than intellectual. I know that this place feels familiar because it lives in me. I have the power to apply the forces of my immigrant roots to my American experience. Every time one of us chooses to do that we enrich the America around us. I go home and begin to study Spanish once again.

———

It's 1999. I go to *Weekend Today*. I anchor with Jack Ford. This is the pipeline show to *Today* with Katie Couric and Matt Lauer. Jack is the first of three coanchors I'll have. This is a big deal. We have millions of viewers. I'm suddenly a celebrity. I didn't think I could be Katie Couric but I really admire her. I earn more money each year than my parents earned in a year combined. My weekends begin with one big serious interview. Then the show segues into cooking and fashion. My job is to continue the brand of *Today*, the most powerful morning show on American TV.

Elian Gonzalez floats ashore on a raft after his mother dies escaping Cuba by sea. A public battle ensues over whether he should be sent back or remain with his distant Miami relatives. Federal agents seize him in a predawn raid. I go on the air right away with my hair pulled back in a ponytail, still wet. I apply my makeup in the commercial breaks. Kerry Sanders is the reporter on the Elian story. He reports live, doing interviews on the fly. Passions flare on both sides—Elian should stay; Elian should go. I don't relate to this story. This is not about the Cuba I know. Plus, the anchor job is a different job. You're like the hub, the air traffic control, not the pilot. I manage the story; I don't report it.

The space shuttle *Challenger* explodes. I go and stand at a location and hold on to it until Matt Lauer arrives on Monday for the big show. I interview guests and keep the story moving. Everything is top-notch, very controlled, where everything back at KRON was pure chaos. The reporters run around me and bring in facts. The anchors, well, we anchor. I miss reporting.

David Bloom becomes my coanchor. We have good chemistry, friendly and competitive. We are like brother and sister. We have dollar bets riding on everything. We race ice bikes on the

Rockefeller Center rink. We have a dunking contest. He brings in a ringer who is a softball champion. We have a Mardi Gras parade and host concerts on the plaza outside. We invite Isaac Hayes to be Santa Claus at Christmas. We invite performers from Broadway shows, which I love.

Brad, meanwhile, is working for Morgan Stanley. He's stressed, busy, and climbing the ladder. I'm having a lot of fun. I have a mental list. Get pregnant and have a baby are next, so I get pregnant. Complete strangers come up and grab my stomach as soon as I begin to show. I do a story about trapeze school. People tell me they love it. I like the praise but it feels a little hollow. I don't want to be famous for doing a story on trapeze school. I do a show on Navy SEALs training and do the first underwater interview on *Today*. It's a hit but no one is going to say that story changed anyone's life.

In 2000, as I am pregnant with Sofia, it is bothering me that I have never graduated from college. It's not like I need the degree, but something inside me feels like I should get it. I am just a semester away. It's like low-hanging fruit and it's annoying the heck out of me. Kim sets me up to speak at events and I'm introduced as someone who "attended" Harvard. With a baby on the way and a job as a network anchor it feels like this has to happen now or it never will. I sit down with Kim every so often and we list our goals. Mine go something like this: graduate from Harvard, get pregnant, have baby, and so on. I'm pregnant already and I have no degree. My life is out of order.

My big sister Maria comes to the rescue. I am doing a weekend show. I just need to be in Boston for a few days to go to class. She lives in the suburbs of Boston. So I hop on the train from New York to Boston Sunday nights and move in with Maria until Wednesday. Brad is working constantly so we barely miss each other. Maria is a full-time professor at BU with the first five of her seven kids at home. I arrive exhausted, spent from being pregnant more than anything. Her kids surround me with their youthful exuberance and we play around in Maria's big house with its oversized everything. I brush their hair and let them play with my makeup. I am the fun aunt who gives manicures and facials. I keenly watch how Maria parents in search of tips.

I have awful morning sickness. I call Kim on the phone and complain about throwing up, as if she can manage this for me. I call her from the plane once and ask if I should get off. She's like, "I don't know." I am huge, really quite big. I have cravings like Lucille Ball expecting Little Ricky. I eat Kozy Shack Rice Pudding every day and search menus for fried oysters.

I face classrooms full of people much younger than me. I walk through Harvard Yard and fantasize about paying someone $20 to crash in their dorm room. I am back at school but this go-around I have money, so I can eat lunch in actual restaurants and pay for cabs. The money gives me this raging freedom. I see shoes I like and I buy them. I do things I never thought I could do. I can help people and fix problems. I feel good and proud and accomplished. I'm also in my second trimester so I've stopped throwing up. I feel like a normal person again, just a big one.

The funny thing is, when I get it, the Harvard degree feels uneventful. I have it framed and hang it on my wall but not anywhere anyone can see it. People in my family rarely go to graduations. At Harvard, the tickets are so limited we couldn't have all gone anyway, and our lifelong philosophy is it's all of us or none. When I get my set of tickets I talk about selling them on eBay until Kim talks some sense into me. "The anchor of *Weekend*

Today does not sell tickets to her graduation on eBay," she says. Brad is so busy he's happy to not go, but I can tell he's really proud of me by the way he makes no big deal out of it. That's the way he is. But Kim is all excited so we plan a girls' getaway to Italy. I am big as a house when I get on the plane and we spend a week traipsing through Venice.

In the fall of 2000 I deliver Sofia. It's a quick and easy delivery, but it's a game changer. For the first time in my life of rushing, I feel trapped. I have entered the land of the great American equalizer, motherhood. My child is so darn cute I race home to be with her. I want to be with her all the time. I'm in love like I've never been in love with anyone, not my parents or Brad. I also want to run. I can't tell if she is a tough baby or if I have no idea what I am doing. Motherhood is really difficult. She is a lazy eater. I can never tell if she's fed. She falls asleep nursing. I call my sisters constantly and tell them I can't do this. I tell them I've lost all control. They tell me I am right on schedule with motherhood. I have the perfect gig for having a baby because I'm basically working a three-day week. But I feel like I have no time! I suddenly feel a kinship with everyone who has ever given birth. I smile at total strangers. She falls asleep. I clean. I fall asleep. She wakes me up. I feed. I clean. She falls asleep. I can't fall asleep, so I clean some more until she wakes up and wants to eat all over again. I clean.

On weekends, Sofia is with Brad, who is so calm and level-headed as a parent. It's unnerving. I walk through the door and pick things up as I go through the apartment. But at the end of the line of empty bottles, spent Pampers, and assorted clothes, there he is rocking her gently. She is basically his clone in all ways. The child looks nothing like me, except for maybe the temper. The whole thing is insane, but sixteen months later I give birth to Cecilia. She has pitch-black hair that is frizzy and sticks straight up. Over time it will turn curly blond. She smiles at everyone and has a sunny disposition.

I am so tired I'm dizzy. I can't even tell if I'm happy, but I feel like I must be because I have two kids who are crazy cute and this husband whose devotion fuels me. All my partners in life are so on my side. Kim is my executive producer at *Weekend Today* and she is my pal, a ball of energy and ideas. My family is rooting for me weekly, sitting down in front of the TV set as if Edward R. Murrow himself is about to do a segment on fall fashion.

It is a gloomy time in my adopted city, after planes lance the Twin Towers like spears. My positive energy feels a bit out of place. I was walking down the street running some errands when the whole thing began to unfold. I ran home a few blocks and turned on the TV. Brad calls me, and we watched the second plane hit together. I'm called into work to report on the triage center set up along the West Side Highway. The ambulances are lined up and ready to be dispatched at a moment's notice, but the reality is brutally clear—there aren't that many people to save. I'm one of the fortunate ones. I really didn't know anyone who died in the World Trade Center towers. I didn't lose anybody close to me, but I looked out on my city and hurt and knew there were others who had lost so much that day.

After that, a little bit of me feels like I'm ducking reality, losing myself in my kids and the comfort that my family survived the shocking destruction of September 11. We are doing so well. I thank my God. We are a family religious enough to know it's not just luck. But the noxious cloud that hovered around downtown Manhattan has never left our country. I report it on air every day in so many ways. Ours is a country where people often fail to forge a link, like some frustrating puzzle. Then all of a sudden something unites us and we come together to form this picture. I just wish that unity wasn't forged so often by our tragedies. In the aftermath of 9/11, America looks like a nation stricken, gray and black. We claim boldness when we're all feeling a little broken. I push back at the sadness around me. The world is spinning in the wrong direction. I sit on my desk and report stories that have nothing to do with morning news—funerals and flight plans and almost endless stories of individual grief with a live shot of a burning pile of American steel continually showing in the background.

David and I have to keep a tone that is morning TV comfort in the face of all this. I walk in after the attacks and he and I reset each other's mood. He has twin girls and a baby daughter. His wife looks like an anchor's wife is supposed to look: gorgeous and fresh-faced. We can relate to what we're each facing at home, keeping life moving for small children when so much around us seems uncertain. On air, we look like an all-American team, me with my multicultural persona and him traditional like apple pie.

The anchor duo is a relationship only understood by pilots and figure skaters and other folks in symbiotic work relationships. You can't fake TV chemistry. If you hate each other, everyone can tell. When David and I go on air it's a continuation of the conversation we've been having overnight as our morning show came to fruition. We lighten the mood. It's a weekend morning. And slowly we lift ourselves, and others, ever so briefly, from the tsunami of bad news that rolls in over 2002 and 2003. We find each other interesting. We're like a couple that just woke up and are starting their day, except we have a million kids watching us racing around in our pajamas. As coanchors we laugh and fight and bicker and banter.

The only time there is a hint of tension between us is when assignments roll in that we both want. We argue like siblings. His hefty reporting credentials often win. He has done his share of hurricanes and biting investigations, won an Edward R. Murrow Award and an Emmy. He covered the president. He's steps ahead of me in the credentials race. He is also eager to do stories that downright scare the crap out of me. He is practically in his Kevlar vest when war breaks out in Iraq. NBC has this great idea to strap a satellite dish to an army tank so David can charge into Baghdad with the troops and report on the advance. I am sad when he goes and I'm also immensely proud of him. I talk to him through the airwaves but he sounds so far away, so unreal. It's April and spring is consuming New York. In Baghdad David's reporting is remarkable, and I'm worried about him. I wish he'd come back. His wife and kids miss him. The viewers miss him and I miss him. We are a good team.

David calls his wife, Melanie, one day and says he is on the border of Baghdad. He whispers because they're fearful of an ambush. He is sleeping atop his tank and she demands to know why if they think someone might come shoot them. He complains that his legs are cramping up and he wants to stretch. The flights from New York to Kuwait are endless. He talks to doctors by phone and tries to find ways to make himself feel better. They don't have enough water and they are riding in the back of a tank, unable to move for hours on end. I watch him on air with his hair pleated by the desert dust and his cheeks cracked by sunburn. He looks bold and dashing, like the hardworking war reporter making huge sacrifices. His face looks red on the screen but I barely notice—is it sunburn or a dust storm or poor reception? I still want him to come back and race me across the ice rink on live TV.

It's April 6, 2003, at one a.m. I am the weekend morning anchor so I'm just two and a half hours shy of waking up for work. The phone rings that way phones sound when someone calls at an early hour: jarring. It's the NBC operator asking me to hold for the boss. The first thing I think is that all our predictions about a Saddam Hussein chemical attack have come to pass and David has been hurt. "Soledad," Neil Shapiro says, "David is dead." A blood clot has traveled from his cramping legs to his lungs. He is thirty-nine years old with three young children. He is the 153rd journalist to die in this war we are waging abroad, cut down by his own body.

I walk into work like a zombie to join Matt Lauer reporting on our own colleague. This is a guy who used to bring his little girls to play around on the very set we're sitting on. We have a half dozen two-dollar bets still unresolved. He had written a letter to his wife just a few hours before talking about how his love of his family and his God outshined his work. I sit on the set, our set, untethered and all alone, a half orange stuck in a half skin. The energy has been sucked out of the newsroom. The cameramen are openly weeping; the production assistants are sobbing in the stairwells.

There is a memorial on the third floor of NBC—near *Nightly News*—showcasing journalists who died on the job. There is gear from Don Harris, a reporter who was shot at the Jonestown massacre in Guyana in 1978, and a few others. David's helmet gets added to the stuff in the glass case. He died joining Americans together for life's most climatic moments. With David, the viewers traveled to the ravages of Bosnia and Somalia, the agony of

Ground Zero, the clashes in Israel and Pakistan. He was on a mission. He had something to say.

I come in each weekend now heavy with his memory, feeling like there must be more to life than this. I think of all those Sunday mornings back in Smithtown when my parents would pack us in the car for a 7:30 a.m. trip to church. We were so lucky in life and it was time to say thank you to God, then have chocolate-covered cream-filled donuts and milk and a lazy afternoon with our parents. David relished life and risked everything to make his full and important. Somehow his death put the value of all that into sharp focus. I run home to embrace my kids more tightly than ever. But I couldn't go back to work and sit on our half-empty set anymore joking about relay races on Rockefeller Plaza. Something was missing in more ways than one. A few months later I am offered a job anchoring *American Morning* for CNN, a hard news program where the anchors spend a lot of time digging into stories in the field. I push away from a fifteen-year career at NBC and an anchor desk that's missing an anchor. I want to go out and report on the world.

CHAPTER FIVE

An Ax to Break Out

$\mathcal{M}$y plane cracks through a bank of clouds. We descend into Baton Rouge, Louisiana, on September 2, 2005. The sky is silent, hot. The air is rich. I have enough baby wipes to wash with for a week. Rain jacket, pants, boots. A cap. PowerBars. Water. Plastic everything. I have all I need to slog through the receding waters of Hurricane Katrina—except maybe the stomach for it.

A wall of wind and rain had fallen on southeast Louisiana on August 29. There was a last-minute call to evacuate. Chaos erupted. Levees failed. Much of New Orleans went underwater. So did a slice of the state of Mississippi. People died by the hundreds. The deluge of water unleashed a flood of evacuees. They raced up I-10 from New Orleans by the tens of thousands, arriving in Baton Rouge.

I am landing a few days later in a city unhinged, kneeled not by a storm but by its aftermath. The airport terminal resembles an enormous indoor campground. People of every race, class, and age roam around lost. They seem to be looking for a way out. The air rumbles and squeaks from the sound of roller luggage. I walk through crowds that move aimlessly in four directions. The airport employees have their mouths half open, their hair askew. The air smells like laundry left wet in a broken dryer. Old black ladies who look like my mom push through the crowd. Handbags dangle from their wrists. Kerchiefs clamp down their hair. Loud military planes push warm air down onto the runway as they land one after the other. An evacuation is under way. People board planes bound for unknown destinations. I wonder what is in their tiny bags. What do you take when you leave behind a lifetime of belongings that is underwater? I look at their eyes. They are too tired to cry, too dry for tears, swollen, purple, pained.

The hurricane hit on Monday. It's Friday. This all makes no sense to me. By now this place should be abuzz with rescue services, with government relief from a storm. I feel like I am in another country. All week I'd seen the images, seen the pain as I anchored from New York. This is what an American city might look like the day after a storm. But now it's four days later. How can this be? I see the fear, the panic. Anger rises into a tight knot behind my forehead. CNN has set up a live location outside the airport. A tent tries to block the sun but the wind off the runway blows it over every time a plane lands. I join a clutch of exhausted CNN staffers. No one says more than they have to. I begin to report.

I left NBC in July 2003 because I wanted to be a serious news reporter again. I become the coanchor of *American Morning* on CNN. Everything I want as a journalist comes together at once. I'm at a place that values hard news and lets me report on people left on the sidelines of life. I also get to anchor the big show. Sitting next to me is Bill Hemmer, a wheat-fed bespectacled guy with a sunny disposition. He looks much younger than he is. He has a patch of gray hair on the back of his head, but from the front he's boyish. He is also devoted to being out in the field. Bill had covered Kosovo and done marathon live shots from Tallahassee during the 2000 Florida recount and September 11. He adores his family. We have our family ties in common. Bill is from Cincinnati and he oozes Midwestern charm and good manners. Little Sofia is in love with him and calls him "Bill-hemmer," as if it is one word. I ask her why she loves him so much and she says, "I don't know. I just love Billhemmer." I am buoyed by his niceness; it gives our show a friendly feel that is totally genuine. But that is not enough. The network also wants more viewers.

CNN has been in perpetual news mode since it launched in 1980 in hopes of tapping into America's need for constant information. Our viewers are like people eating peanuts, unable to resist but sealing the can every so often because they think they've had enough.

My show rides the news highs and lows. When there are lows, the fallback position is always more hard news. The stress level rises constantly. Then I do something that makes things even harder. I get pregnant again, with twins. I race to the restroom to throw up during breaks as Bill sits there smiling away in my absence, picking up my reads on the TelePrompTer. I insist on keeping up the same pace I had before the pregnancy, faster even, in this ridiculous effort to prove it makes no difference at all that you are carrying two babies in your belly. I move about slowly. I am the size of a zeppelin.

Then one day, as the summer is nearly ending, I deliver Charlie, who smiles and cuddles like a puppy, and Jackson, who looks like a duplicate of his father. They are perfect. I am utterly in love and uniquely overwhelmed. I cry almost every day from exhaustion, fear, and panic. I suddenly have four children under four, a reality that is so amusing to my colleagues. I get a full-time baby nurse until I realize she is raising my boys, and I ditch her. I walk out one day with four kids stuffed in a double stroller—two are hanging off the back—and I realize I'm truly acting like a nutcase. I buy my way out of all sorts of problems, but money can't buy a good night's sleep.

Brad is as driven in parenting as he is at work. His point of view is we need to just set a high bar for behavior. We have full-time help, but when we are not at work we are going it alone. Brad is a big believer in limits. We take all four kids to restaurants with us. It works sometimes, but they are all still babies so it often doesn't. They mesmerize me when they are all good at once. But mostly my life is a blur of chaos. I feel like I am constantly responding to one emergency or another. And then a real one rolls in. One day Bill and I are smiling from atop the anchor desk; then suddenly I'm off to Phuket, Thailand, to cover the tsunami, and everyone is watching. I leave Brad with four small children racing around untethered. But his eyes light up and he says "Go go go. This is a big deal; this is a big opportunity." I head out the door.

December 26, 2004: A plate shift deep in the sea has caused a mountain of water to slap the coastlines all around the Indian Ocean. Countless people have died along the shores. The world turns to CNN for news. I sit aboard the plane bizarrely relaxed, able to get more sleep on this ride to human disaster than I'm getting at home. In Phuket, a massive watermark about a mile inland separates the living from the dead. The smell of decomposing bodies makes me wretch. This is my first experience of a major international disaster, on the ground for CNN. They deploy scrappy reporters and technicians from around the world, everyone arriving alone, just like me, and regrouping like a small army. We gather at a chaotic, smelly, hot hotel, where people surround us expecting news of missing relatives.

CNN is remarkable at these disasters. Every hour resources seem to appear from out of nowhere—from no food, to bad food, to packaged food, to water and PowerBars, and crates of medicine and fans to fight the heat. We sleep on a wood floor in sweltering heat with images of death swirling inside our foreheads. But there is something impressive about the international relief effort, about the united nations of rescue groups corralling survivors, organizing the searches, feeding people, and dropping supplies on remote places like Banda Aceh in Indonesia mere days after such an enormous disaster.

We set up a live location in the middle of the chaos and suddenly I am anchoring *American Morning* from the other side of the world. My insides are in agony when I'm asked how it feels to me as a mother to be seeing so much grief. I can't even answer that because the heartache is inconceivable. The 6:00 a.m. show is on at 6:00 p.m. local time, so in the morning I grab a cameraman to go off and report. My photographer is from our Bangkok bureau but was in Phuket vacationing with his wife and baby. The morning of the event they had been spared because they'd moved inland when the baby got sunburned. That saved their lives. We head off to the center of town, where people are posting photos of the missing, and it seems to be a version of what happened near Ground Zero after September 11.

A man shares a story of how he lost his grip on his three-year-old son as the waters rushed through and lifted them through a thicket of palm trees. He shows me the picture of a cute, blond, chunky little boy and recounts over and over again how he shifted his hand to get a better grip on him, then lost him when the boy, slathered in sunscreen, slithered out of his hands. His face is etched with grief and guilt. My frustrations with being a working parent suddenly seem embarrassingly idiotic. I tell myself I have to get a grip on what is important.

I take a small boat for hours out to Phi Phi Island, where a mostly Buddhist population is gathering its dead on pieces of rock, tin, and wood. Robin and Ingrid De Vries had come to Phi Phi because their twelve- and seventeen-year-old daughters had fallen in love with the sandy beaches outside the Kabana Hotel. Isabelle, the younger daughter, had seen the tsunami rolling in at them in the distance. Ingrid called the girls in from the beach. The girls ran but they were laughing because they thought it was an ordinary wave. In an instant, the wave's pace quickened and swallowed the girls. Isabelle stayed afloat at first but Dominique panicked. The parents were also torn apart by a second wave that wrenched them from the balcony of their hotel. They were forced through the sliding glass doors, across the room, out the back door and under the water, where they gasped for air.

Ingrid remembers thinking that if her daughters had died she might as well surrender to the water, because the lives she valued had already ended. Then, in an instant, the wave pulled back out and left them all separated. Isabelle, injured, swam to an offshore boat. Ingrid, injured, found her way aboard a crowded rescue flight. Robin stayed until darkness searching for his family. The three of them ended up in different hospitals. As soon as the three were reunited they began looking for Dominique. Family members came in from Holland, along with a Dutch forensics team, to help in the search for her. They were hopeful that

Dominique was lost, injured somewhere, unable to speak. The response from each country was that precise. I channel their desperation and report on them as a microcosm of everything that's unfolding around us.

One day Dominique's body is found lying in a Buddhist temple, identified by her dental records. There is no data on how she arrived there, just another soul recovered by the legion of desperate searchers gathering the loss after the storm. It is devastating, but a resolution for the family. I am becoming more unglued with all the individually painful stories. I am fine during the day, but I can't get to sleep. I call Brad at 10:00 p.m., which is 10:00 a.m. his time. He tells me he can't start his days with these stories, so I call a girlfriend every night instead. I feel as if I'm floating away from everything around me those last days in Thailand, released from my reality.

My return to the U.S. feels like an electric shock. I walk through the door of my home to a chaotic mess, Cecilia's hair large and dirty, Brad haggard. Sofia races over screaming "Mommy" and we embrace. I am overcome by a sense that I lack gratitude for everything life has given me—I take that feeling and press on.

My show experiences some upheaval during the summer of 2005. The bosses want Bill to stop anchoring and offer him the job of White House correspondent. He wants to anchor and field major stories. He suddenly leaves for FOX News and the network brings in Miles O'Brien, who had been anchoring from CNN's base in Atlanta during the day. He is this gentle man with thick dark hair and warm eyes. He is generous to a fault, smart and self-sufficient, a solid anchor and writer and human being. People look at us and say, "Oh, the O'Briens! Are you married?" And he says,

"Yes, and so is she." I smack him. "Oh, not to each other," he adds with the silliness of my father. He calls me SOB, which becomes a joke around the newsroom, then adds that his wife Sandy is the other SOB. He understands the meaning of being on a team so much that he apologizes when he gets more airtime.

On Friday, August 26, Miles is sent to hunker down in Baton Rouge to wait on Hurricane Katrina while I stay behind to anchor the show. The storm makes its first landfall over the weekend and is devastating. There are predictions it will hit the Gulf even harder. Having him in New Orleans feels like we are really both there.

Kim Bondy, my producer at NBC, has preceded me to CNN. Her work on weekends at NBC has paid off, and she's now Executive Producer of *American Morning*. We are working together again, and she is sitting in the control room at CNN on Monday, August 29, when the storm makes its second landfall in Louisiana. While I had been going up the ranks, she had become a vice president at CNN, and she has taken the reins of my struggling show. Between her and Miles, I feel like I'm doing a show with my family. Kim has become one of my closest friends. She really wants this to work. This story is both thrilling and frightening for her. Kim is New Orleans born and raised. She loves the place so much she bought a house there in May 2001. Her brother had evacuated to Texas with his wife and two small boys a few days before the storm hit.

By late August 2005 there have been ten storms, so we are up to K in the year's storm alphabet. The rest of Kim's family, like everyone, has storm fatigue. Her mom and stepfather decide to stay in New Orleans to ride out the storm. They live in Kim's house. She's told me a bunch of times how fabulous it is. She couldn't buy a one-bedroom in New York for the price of that house. That's the house where she'll move home someday. Owning a home is a staple of American life; it grants you a future, plants a flagpole in the American dream. Kim's is a mile from Lake Ponchartrain. She's bought her parents a generator. They're all set.

The Monday show unfolds and all the reporters in the field tell me Katrina is a strong storm. A Red Cross spokeswoman confirms there are eight thousand to nine thousand people seeking shelter in the Louisiana Superdome. There is only generator power but it's fine. The spokeswoman worries aloud about the levees being overwhelmed. But the consensus is that they are fine. Kim calls her mother, who says she is waiting out the storm at her house. She says, "It's fine," and asks if it's over. The word "fine" is repeated a few more times. Our weather reporter, Chad Myers, tells Kim there should be another wave of rain; then it will be fine. This storm is driven by wind. The house is strong. It has never flooded. The whole thing feels like a near miss. Kim explains to her mother how to "text" so they can keep in touch.

We start reporting that NoLa has dodged a bullet. It feels like we have moved past the latest storm drama on TV. Then all of a sudden reality splits in two. For the next few hours, there is the official story and there is Kim's story. Her brother calls from Texas. Their mother calls. She says the sunroom in the back of the house is flooding. She is moving furniture inside. The brother calls again to say Kim's car is underwater. We call our reporters. It's hard to reach anyone. Official reports say the storm is passing. We say it again. NoLa has dodged a bullet. Most of the city evacuated. Kim's brother calls again. He is crying. He has heard his house is underwater.

I stay on air past the scheduled hour of my show. "Good

morning. Welcome back, everybody. Welcome to a special extended edition of *American Morning*, August 29, 2005, where we are tracking Hurricane Katrina, which has made landfall about forty-five minutes ago." I debrief Chad Myers, who draws a line with tape and shows how the storm took a last-minute turn. He repeats what he said to Kim about New Orleans having seen the worst. I push him. Chad says this storm didn't overwhelm the levees. If it had, "those pumps would have been bogged down and water could have been in New Orleans for eight months before they could pump it out. And this is not that scenario," he says. Kim insists we put people on air who are in the city. We talk to a local reporter. He says pieces of the Superdome are flying off. The rains can get inside. There are no lights. There are thousands of people in there seeking shelter. We talk to Governor Kathleen Blanco and Michael Brown, head of the Federal Emergency Management Agency. Everyone says the same thing. Bad storm. We've got it under control.

The day before the storm hit, I had kept reading and rereading the research. The storm had grown to a category 5. It grew in size in the Gulf of Mexico. Today, warm waters have increased the wind speed until the size and strength of the storm is record breaking. The extended show winds down. This was such a big storm. It still feels as if New Orleans has dodged a bullet. It's not that bad. But this isn't over. Every one of Kim's relatives and friends is calling. It is *that* bad. Something is wrong. There is so much water.

What no one yet realizes is that fifty drainage and navigational levees are breaching one after the other throughout the day. Water pours into 80 percent of the city. Mississippi's beachfront towns go underwater. The rush of water undermines entire structures and unmoors boats. Waves carrying rafts of debris crash through neighborhoods. The whole thing is like something out of a science fiction movie. I just keep staring at the TV screen all day. There are no pictures. It's like radio. I walk in and out of Kim's office a dozen times. She is always on the phone. She rushes from her office to the CNN newsroom more than once. Every time a friend calls from New Orleans she transfers them into the control room and they are live on CNN. Kim's brother calls again. He got through to their mom. She and her husband are on the second floor of Kim's beautiful house and the water is rushing in. They say to send help. They are scared.

I don't like danger. I don't like the feeling of electricity curdling the air just before a lightning storm. Rising waters make me want to run. When a crowd begins to swell with anger, I want to leave. This is one of the tough things about our business. We are initially propelled by the excitement of being at the center of a big story. But we are human beings. We get scared and overwhelmed by the cruelty of what's around us. Some reporters thrive on danger. I am not that kind of reporter. I don't find danger exhilarating or exciting. I will face it, headlong, with purpose. I will stick it out and do my job and tell people what's going on. I will suck my fears deep into my gut until the danger passes. But I do not find it exhilarating. To me, when the trucks with the megaphones roll by asking people to get out of the way of the storm, the logical thing to do is pack it up. I don't get the guy who hunkers down with his video camera and a six-pack of beer.

At CNN, I sometimes feel surrounded by heroic action figures. A natural disaster hits. A reporter throws an arm into a cherry red windbreaker emblazoned with "CNN." Grab a bag. Jump on a plane. Find a position just close enough to not get killed by the oncoming storm. Wait until whatever it is hits—the missile, the hurricane, the oncoming plague. Bombs fall behind Christiane Amanpour's head. A gust of rain and debris shoves Anderson Cooper to his knees. I am in awe. But that's not me. I don't feel triumphant when the storm slinks away and I've survived. I just feel lucky, in a professional sense—and a tad dumb for being there.

It's probably the nerd in me. I was born with a deficit of bravado. I don't crave excitement. I crave good conversation. I want to be there, in the aftermath, figuring out what went wrong. I don't need to see the wind pick up a trailer full of children and toss them to their death. I feel no thrill at watching the last-minute rescue. In life, we are all passengers on a plane. You get to choose exit row, window, or the aisle. I like the aisle. Let the superhero with the cape make the call on when to wrench open the door. I'm just fine organizing the departure of the passengers.

CNN tries to get more reporting teams into the area the moment they appreciate the severity of Katrina. There are no planes, no cars, no power or water once you land, no safe place left to hide from the storm. We have reporters descending on every corner of the disaster the same day it hits. I start to make preparations to join Miles. I operate in a dazed slow motion. I don't know when I'll go, but I know I'll go. Kim gets a text at nine p.m. from her mother. All it says is, "I'm okay." It's the last time she hears from her for days.

Then that evening, the first night after the storm has hit, the CNN reporter Jeanne Meserve goes on air and suddenly the two realities come together. Jeanne is in the thick of it. She is beleaguered and upset. Her photographer has broken his foot. They've boarded a small boat and gone out in the darkness. They can hear stranded and desperate people. They see dogs wrapped in electrical lines, still alive and being cooked. A boater pulls out a woman with a severed limb. Jeanne is reporting on air what Kim has been telling us all day. That an enormous human tragedy is unfolding and there is not enough help. Jeanne sounds as if she has been crying. She has just turned back from trying to go out to where people are trapped on rooftops. "You can hear people yelling for help. You can hear the dogs yelping, all of them stranded, all of them hoping someone will come.

"But for tonight, they've had to suspend the rescue efforts," Jeanne reports. "It's just too hazardous for them to be out on the boats. There are electrical lines that are still alive. There are gas lines that are still spewing gas. There are cars that are submerged. There are other large objects . . . the people who had the boats couldn't get to the boats to bring them to the scene to go out and rescue the people . . . as the boats went around through the neighborhood, they yelled. And people yelled back."

She talks into the night. The anchors barely interrupt her. At CNN, we all listen, riveted by what she is saying. Voices cry out from the darkened rooftops. There is no one out there to rescue them. We know this but somehow government doesn't? We are broadcasting this on live TV. Where are the police and the firefighters, the military, the cavalry that is this country's pride?

One of the lessons I've learned from being a journalist is to count on no one. I'm not a cynic. I'm a generally optimistic person. I trust in people, particularly friends and family. I even think that most of the government actually has the best of intentions most of the time. That said, there is nothing wrong with storing a few cans of tuna in case the world betrays you.

Here's the thing. When people dial 911, help doesn't always come. It's just a fact. It's at the heart of so many stories I've covered—the dashed expectation that some institution has your back. If you think otherwise, think again. I'm here to tell you that fire alarms sometimes go off and the fire trucks don't always pull up minutes later carrying spotted dogs. I've seen it happen many times. America seems particularly disappointing when it fails you because the pile of promises is stacked so high. There is nowhere that you can escape the reality that help is not always on the way. The places hit by Hurricane Katrina couldn't rely on regular services; they required a massive national response, a cavalry of forces only our country can muster. Yet the cavalry didn't arrive. To survive, you had to be ready to help yourself. If that makes you angry, it should. It makes me angry, too. But anger doesn't get you pulled off the roof of your house when the waters rise.

I admire the folks in New Orleans who kept an ax in their homes to break their way out of the attic. I applaud the parents of small kids who hightailed it to a hotel they couldn't afford. To the folks who board up their windows and insist on taking their pets, I say good move. I opt for living life like the Boy Scout motto. Be Prepared. I don't understand why more folks don't. I've met so many people who carry an umbrella even if the local "meteorologist" says the chance of rain is just 30 percent. So why wouldn't you get in the basement when they declare a 10 percent chance a tornado is going to slice you to pieces? I'm not for a moment suggesting I don't feel for folks who refuse to live life preparing for the worst. I'm just saying I don't refuse. I am ready. I don't trust anyone to come when I call. That is one of the main things Katrina taught me, plus this: If you survive because of your own wits, you have the right to be angrier than you've ever been, to rage, to roar, and to demand accountability. That is where I come in.

Night pours into Baton Rouge like ink into a glass. I am fuming. CNN doesn't want us to go anywhere without security. It's September 2, the Friday after the storm has hit, but they insist security guards need to come from New Orleans to get me. Kim says people are looting, there are carjackings, the highway is eerie and dark. I eat. I wait. I reposition my gear several times. I want to get into the city already. It's remarkable that conditions are so bad four-plus days after the storm. It's bad in Baton Rouge, and this is what people are fleeing toward! Kim says no, to wait.

I had interviewed her brother just that morning from my anchor desk in New York. He had been roaming around the Astrodome in Houston hoping their mother had been evacuated there. That wasn't the case. When the water rose, her stepfather had jumped in and brought them out in a little boat. They had camped out at a college. Kim was fearful they would end up at the Superdome in New Orleans. The place had swelled with evacuees. Water had penetrated holes in the roof. There was not enough food. It was hot and awful and dangerous and the images of people in wheelchairs slumped in the heat frightened everyone. As it turns out, that's exactly where her mother was headed. She got off a line for buses to the Superdome when she saw reporters and waved down an NBC crew. She told them she was Kim Bondy's mother. They took her to CNN. Kim's mother had narrowly escaped the worst. After that near miss, Kim was not taking chances with anyone else.

Four security guys finally arrive. We drive to the NoLa air-port. The sixty-mile drive takes hours. Buses blow by us. There aren't a lot of people on them. There are tens of thousands of people trying to get out, but the buses seem half full and there is no one organizing the evacuation. The city is shut down when we arrive. We talk our way through six police checkpoints to get in. It is strangely quiet until I take my place at the New Orleans airport. It's dark. The Federal Emergency Management Agency has turned it into a field hospital. The Delta Airlines terminal is a triage center. Old people sit in wheelchairs, waiting. People sleep anywhere they can. Entire families sleep on the baggage claim carousel.

I talk to an ambulance driver who is resting from a day of rescues. "Here's the lesson," he tells me. "Keep supplies in your own home. Now you know no one's coming for you." No one has come. I'm arriving six days in and I feel like a first responder. I make a mental list of what everyone needs. It gets so long my head begins to shut down. I tell myself I'll stockpile things at my house for the rest of my life. Water, granola bars, canned food, cash. Everyone is rushing to nowhere. FEMA is bringing more people in, folks who were camped all over Louisiana. This will be their "hospital." They say they've set up as many as five of these in past hurricanes. Here, they set up forty. There are FedEx trucks coming in as rolling pharmacies. No one here seems to have any relationship to the actual airport. The counters are closed. The tarmac is empty. Nothing is working. The quiet in some places is disturbing. The place is uncomfortable, smelly, crowded, and awful. I'm on TV by morning:

(September 3, 2005, anchoring CNN's *American Morning*): This, of course, is the Louis Armstrong New

Orleans International Airport. You can hear the choppers over my shoulder. They've been coming in all morning. Kind of a little bit of a lull during the night. But really starting up again in the last few minutes. Right now, no firm numbers on the number of people inside of this main terminal. About four thousand is what they're guesstimating at this point. But it's very strange, as I'm sure you noticed yesterday, the departures level, where you normally go to get on a flight and get out of town, is full of elderly people in wheelchairs, many of them evacuated out of the hospitals.

The downstairs level—that would be the baggage claim—literally sitting on the baggage claim carousels are thousands of people just camped out, some of them ill, some of them getting help from the medical teams assembled here, some of them lying on cardboard boxes with their small children, just grateful to be out of the City of New Orleans.

We drive into the center of the city just after the show goes off the air. It feels quiet and empty. Most of the tall buildings are missing windows. I have never been to a war zone, but this is what a war zone would look like. There are military vehicles circling and people rolling through with everything they own in shopping carts. The NOPD has cordoned off the street and is stationed outside the Sheraton Hotel.

On September 5, I go live from Bourbon Street, the place America often comes to party. I have always loved Bourbon Street, where an amalgam of cultures and experiences blend in this crazy way. It's often throbbing with youthful American energy. The streets are full of happy drunks who broke away from schools and jobs to listen to music or celebrate Mardi Gras draped in colorful beads. Today, the only energy comes from a stack of massive generators bringing lights and air-conditioning back to the Sheraton Hotel. That is the craziness of capitalism, that a business can power up days after a cataclysmic storm but government can't figure out how to hand out bottled water. They have Porta Pottis on Bourbon Street outside the big hotels but people are peeing in unlit hallways of the Superdome.

The water line is still visible on the sides of the buildings but the true damage is away from this tourist zone. The water is still high in low-lying areas. The quiet is disturbing. The rescue effort is winding down and the focus is on all the bodies, but survivors keep turning up. A town known for the beat of jazz music and the hilarity of raucous parades has been bowed. Every person who walks up to me seems to explode with rage. Why did the rescuers take so long? Why were the bridges shut during the evacuation? So much has been lost by the pathetic response in the aftermath of the levee break. I interview Mayor Ray Nagin and channel the anger of the people around me:

"There are people who say your evacuation plan, obviously in hindsight, was disastrous," I tell him.

"Which one?" he responds.

"Your evacuation plan before—when you put people into the Superdome. It wasn't thought out. You got twenty thousand people in there. And that you bear the brunt of the blame for some of this, a large chunk of it."

"Look, I'll take whatever responsibility that I have to take. But let me ask you this question: When you have a city of five hundred thousand people, and you have a category five storm bearing down on you, and you have the best you've ever done is evacuate sixty percent of the people out of the city, and you have never issued a mandatory evacuation in the city's history, a city that is a couple of hundred years old, I did that. I elevated the level of distress to the citizens.

"And I don't know what else I could do, other than to tell them that it's a mandatory evacuation. And if they stayed, make sure you have a frigging ax in your home, where you can bust out the roof just in case the water starts flowing.

"And as a last resort, once this thing is above a category three, there are no buildings in this city to withstand a category three, a category four or a category five storm, other than the Superdome. That's where we sent people as a shelter of last resort. When that filled up, we sent them to the Convention Center. Now, you tell me what else we could have done."

God, even the mayor sounds desperate in this town. New Orleans is cut off, and to pierce the American consciousness they need to get their story told. But one night on Aaron Brown's show *NewsNight* the evacuating families are called "refugees" and, in an instant, they are reduced to foreigners searching for aid. Kim is furious and tells me repeatedly to report on the people like they are taxpaying Americans. These were people like her family, people who were caught unaware, folks who made a bad decision to stay, home owners whose lifetime of savings had been wiped away by rising waters. The viewers are seeing black folks massing at the Superdome and white politicians ignoring their plight. A slow rage is building and race is part of that equation. But on the ground I see a storm that did not see skin color. St. Bernard Parish took the most direct hit from the hurricane. It is 88 percent white. Everyone has been put in the same terrible situation.

I travel to St. Bernard Parish on September 8 to punctuate

that fact. I am with the U.S. Coast Guard. Where there has not been flooding, there has been looting. They have rescued nine people already just this morning. We follow the winding path of the Mississippi, and immediately the vastness of this disaster is clear. We spot a family on their porch. They don't look desperate, just depressed. We see another porch, another resident, a man who doesn't want to leave, even though his street is a lake and a toxic mix of sewage and oil and debris that is black and crunchy and stinks. There are chairs and a sofa alone on a rooftop, an indication of another rescue. I can see the Superdome in the distance surrounded by mounds of festering garbage. The highway leads nowhere, an off-ramp descending into a sea of sludge. The repairs on the 17th Street levee, the critical failure that flooded the city, are clearly visible.

It is September 8 and water is finally flowing back into Lake Pontchartrain. Yet a mile north, we come upon water up to the eaves of the homes. The damage in St. Bernard takes your breath away, even after days of touring this disaster. Everywhere I look, I see homes lost, cars sitting on rooftops. An army of amphibious military vehicles goes door to door marking the homes empty, evacuated, or chronicling the number of deceased. We come up to a family standing on their driveway with a sign that says they are okay and plan to stay. I look around at this murky pool of debris that used to be the neighborhood and I wonder what they're staying for. A sign on one lonely rooftop just says "HELP US." The coast guard has performed 3,689 rescues here in its fifty years. This week alone they've done 6,584. I do a live shot that day from about three or four miles from the Superdome and show how the on-ramp to I-90 is underwater. As I recount my day, the rescuers drop off people pulled from their homes, leaving them to high ground. Then they go back toward the stench of decaying bodies in hopes of finding more.

The days for us CNN staffers begin and end with the issue of the boots. The muck around Katrina is mixed with oil and toxic debris. We go out each day with new boots. Then we circle back to a drop-off spot in the evening, where we literally step out of them and into a car in our sweaty socks. There are piles of foul boots left behind. Our central location near the NoLa garden district faces a house that had its front ripped off. It resembles a dollhouse with all the furniture neatly set up inside. You can see a little boy's toddler bed in the shape of a car. In the building across the street, we have satellite equipment and supplies balancing atop metal filing cabinets, banks of phones and computers. CNN has built its own command center. If you didn't know better, you'd think we were running New Orleans in crisis and this was City Hall.

I arrive with my producer, Justin Dial, a guy who always has something lighthearted to say but today can't think of a thing. He is young and energetic and a master of details and logistics. But today his brown hair cut in the swoosh of the moment is matted with dirt. We both seem to have receded into our CNN caps and grungy clothes. We fall into this odd rhythm together where we just say what's necessary, then throw each other supportive glances. We don't even have to discuss what to cover because everywhere we look disturbs the senses. There is so much to tell. It's like being trapped in a haunted house.

We eat at the command center, Cajun food from a local cook who drives in supplies from Baton Rouge. Then we go sleep, at first in a car, then we get upgraded to a recreational vehicle, and later a hotel. I sit at the headquarters one afternoon on a satellite phone trying to get my twin boys into a preschool at the last minute. I am trying to sound relaxed and charming and I am hoping the admissions officer I am talking to can't hear the sirens wailing behind me. The connection to back home makes me realize how far a distance I've traveled from what is sane. There is an enormous disconnect in my head between what surrounds me and what America should be.

The situation in New Orleans is unacceptable, ridiculous. Every reporter is screaming that into microphones, yet no one seems to be listening. The city is nearly 70 percent African-American, and the images of chaos can't be separated logically from the government response, yet class is the biggest divider around us. Money divided where people lived, their ability to escape, and it will surely divide them when it comes to rebuilding. If it isn't about race and class, why do we not see the difference?

I feel an anger inside that projects while I'm on TV. I have trouble watching what I say. A part of me feels like I am following a great American tradition. One great thing about this country is its loud mouth. We're people who can't hold their tongues, who explode from an existence of prudence when pushed too far. I feel like I should tamp down my emotions or I'll lose my credibility, but it's very hard. I think often of interviewing people outside the Superdome. A line of people angled for the mike, black people who had been humiliated and humbled in a town they own. They did not fall to a natural phenomenon but were let down by their country's inability to help them out. Now they've ended up standing in ninety-degree heat, half naked, hoisting their children up for the cameras and crying out for attention. People can only wait so many days before they begin to snap. I feel some moments as if I may snap myself, like when the tenth person asks me where the buses are to get them out and I have no answer. "Just go here," I tell one poor man, mad at myself that I don't know and even madder that there may be no buses on the way.

The story of America has always been that we help each other, but Katrina is a moment when some folks were just left out there on their own. When they called for help and no one came. When a human dividing line was drawn in the midst of crisis. This was a moment when people had to decide whether they'd become the looter or the volunteer. The grotesque water pooling everywhere reflects the image of the lost and weary. They walk about like these dark green figures, absent race or class or any perceivable difference. They are just people left abandoned with a choice of what to do next. Police officers are caught stealing things, yet two cons are released the day of the storm and spend forty-eight hours rescuing people from rooftops.

I ask Mayor Nagin what he's been promised by the federal government in the wake of a visit from the president. The mayor is black, born in Charity Hospital to poor parents, raised as a reflection of the possibilities available to someone like him in the city of New Orleans. Now he looks drained of life. His eyes are dark with anger and frustration. He recounts pressuring the president and the governor on Air Force One to come together to make a decision about what to do next, to step off the plane and promise that more help is finally on the way. He says they told him they needed twenty-four hours to think about it.

———

I go back to St. Bernard Parish, where Sheriff Jack Stephens is at his command center. He is working out of what is basically a floating houseboat. He's sitting in an easy chair with folding card tables around him. He has walkie-talkie radios and cell phones lined up on top of everything. He is a good old boy, white and big and friendly, out of central casting for a movie about New Orleans. He is presiding over the safety of a nearly all-white community of seventy thousand that felt the brunt of the storm. Justin notes that the small number of black people in the parish seem to have gone suddenly missing, segregated even in the midst of chaos.

Sheriff Jack takes us to St. Rita's nursing home, where he believes thirty people have died. There are still three feet of the maybe ten feet of water that consumed the place. Cars have landed willy-nilly around the lot outside. Sheriff Jack says he believes nearly fifty people were able to get out, but no one can answer why the staff left these folks behind. A refrigeration truck pulls up and removes people's grandparents to a morgue as choppers stir the hot air above. There is still a rescue going on and we keep bumping into folks who've just been pulled from their homes. One is an eighty-nine-year-old attorney who complains of being forced to leave.

At Chalmette Slip, which the locals call Camp Katrina, Sheriff Jack breaks into tears recounting how people died there waiting to be rescued. His officers took some three thousand people there but not all of them survived the wait to be evacuated. It is heartbreaking for his officers to rescue people just to see them die waiting. I ask him to estimate the percentage of the parish damaged by the storm. "One hundred percent," he says. I ask him what he needs. "Money to pay my officers," he says. A national tragedy is unfolding that requires local police to abandon their families and undertake hazardous rescues, and no one in the federal government has thought to help the city make payroll.

One thing I learned in New Orleans is that ours is a land of individuals, not institutions. The grace of this nation is that people rise up above what surrounds them. Angela Cole is a public health nurse who lives in upstate New York and works for medical marketers. She is not a rescue worker or a government official or even the type of person who gives up weekends for anything as organized as the Red Cross or the National Guard. A storm blows over a slice of our country, no one responds, and the victims send out a cry of distress. But there are people like Angela who hop in their SUVs and drive down to answer the call.

The wonder of Katrina is that there are scores of Americans like Angela. They drive solo into places the Army Corps of Engineers claimed it couldn't get to quickly. They paddle in small boats to waterlogged neighborhoods not found by the coast guard. They create tent cities of volunteers with construction gear and open hearts. They grab the hands of poor, dirty, distressed, and dismayed survivors and pray for a better day.

Angela Cole somehow finds a place called Pearlington, Mississippi, that everyone has overlooked. The community is so lost in the thick pine forests that it barely exists on a map. The downtown is one paved road with a cash machine, a church, and a convenience store—all flattened by the storm. The people have only their poverty in common. They are black and white, low on education and opportunity, yet high on resolve. Katrina blows in an ocean of salt water while the town holes up at a NASA facility on higher ground. The people emerge to see the landscape reorganized, the crawfish gone, a lifetime of savings for a tiny one-bedroom vanished in a flash. Angela drives in after the agencies on the ground tell her they will never make it to Pearlington. The town has no organized government to advocate for them. So Angela arrives with food, water, and clothes and immediately begins lobbying to get them help.

Until Angela, Pearlington's families are camping in tents and tarps. Then by some miracle of the American imagination, her appeal gets out there and volunteers begin to arrive. Christian missionaries erect tent cities and begin to rebuild. Volunteers transform an abandoned schoolhouse into a clearinghouse for donations and supplies. Angela's work is emblematic of an effort going on all over the Gulf. She sees people in need of medical care so she enlists a group of doctors to supply her with tetanus and hepatitis vaccines. She walks tent to tent giving shots and bandaging wounds. Her e-mails reached a Georgia couple, Suzanne and Reggie Lybrand, who send in a tractor-trailer loaded with supplies. I meet Angela on the day of one of her big deliveries. She is a fireplug of a woman with short hair and thin glasses, the kind of person who shoves her feet in a pair of hiking boots every morning and walks out with a sense of purpose. It makes her downright ecstatic to see supplies roll in that require no paperwork or lines for people to pick up.

Angela takes me up a dusty road and introduces me to the people she is trying to help as if they are her long-lost relatives. First up are Denise Martin and her four kids, crammed into a trailer provided by FEMA that smells of construction glue. The trailer is parked next to what used to be their house, a soaking little structure that looks like it was slapped by a wave. The youngest, Lisa, takes my hand and shows me where she sleeps. It takes me a minute to comprehend that she is pointing to the kitchen cupboard as her bed that she shares with her older brother. She sleeps on a shelf. The trailer is so crowded that her mother and older sister are still camping outside a full four months after Katrina. There is no plan to move them anywhere and the adults are seething with frustration. Angela has outsized dreams of someday building Denise a house, but they embrace her because she is the only person making any promises.

We meet an old man with skin the color of ink living out of a tent nearby. He kicks over cans with his cane as he tells us the storm has shortened his life and flattened his resolve. He looks haggard, like a homeless person. Angela promises to work on getting him on the list for a trailer. The whole scene would make loads of sense if she was employed by some relief agency, but she is just a nurse from New York, an individual who answered a call for help.

Angela turns us onto another story. There are 100,000 FEMA trailers housing families in the Katrina zone at an expense of a half billion dollars to taxpayers. I meet a guy named Paul Stewart, who has one sitting empty outside the wreckage of his home. He and his wife, Melody, moved into it shortly after the storm. But they wake up with this heavy feeling in their chests. They can barely breathe. Paul does some research. He discovers that the types of campers given out by FEMA have a history of leaching formaldehyde used to glue together the particleboard. He tells FEMA he is worried but they ignore him. So he tests the air in his camper. He finds a formaldehyde concentration of 0.22 parts per million in the air. That's more than twice the concentration several federal agencies say is unsafe. The EPA says anything over 0.1 parts per million can harm the respiratory system and may even cause cancer.

I walk through a nearby trailer park with Paul and some local environmental activists testing campers. The campers are supposed to be for camping, not for living in months at a time. Susan Saunders opens her door and shows us how red her eyes are from the fumes. She has a hacking cough. FEMA inspectors tell everyone to ventilate the trailers, but it is nearly a hundred degrees outside and no one wants to turn off the AC. Everyone keeps talking about the smell.

I decide we should conduct our own tests. CNN pays an independent lab to test the FEMA trailer of Denise Martin and her four little kids. Lisa is sleeping right on the particleboard shelf that contains the formaldehyde. The test comes back 80 percent higher than federal recommendations. The tests done by the group return high levels in twenty-nine of the thirty-one trailers where they take samples. We find a dozen home owners who have complained to FEMA about feeling ill. Gulf Stream, which manufactures the Cavalier trailers, warns people to ventilate but says they have had no complaints. FEMA says the problem is more nuisance than health hazard and offers Paul and Melody Stewart a new trailer. They take out a second mortgage on their home that was destroyed by the storm and buy their own.

I come back to St. Bernard Parish a year later and take a tour with Sheriff Jack. I see gutted houses and the fortified levees but not much other progress. An estimated ten thousand to twenty thousand of the seventy thousand residents have returned. Every so often you see an oasis of flowers, but mostly there are abandoned houses and piles of debris housing rats and snakes. A year ago, I had met Rachel Kestling while she was breaking down her door to get back in her house. Now volunteers have gutted the inside of her old home and begun repairs. It's far from perfect, but it is better. Sheriff Jack worries about anything that could drive the fledgling recovery away, a growing crime problem, ten-foot weeds surrounding abandoned homes. He claims the disaster has been liberating for him, that he no longer cares about his political career. There is still limited electricity and sewage and every rain brings a flash flood. Contractors gouge the residents with prices ten times the normal rate.

Sheriff Jack says he could go to three funerals a week for local residents, mostly seniors he says have died of depression. There has been a spike in attempted suicides and suicides. The schools are reopened but there are not many children. The value of homes has fallen to a quarter of what they were. Sheriff Jack feels like they are victims of government neglect. A year has honed his anger. He begins to list the communities ravaged by the storm—Mobile, Alabama; Gulfport, Mississippi; Biloxi; Long Beach; Waveland; Ocean Spring; Slidell; Plaquemines; St. Bernard; New Orleans; Cameron. All of these, he says, should be worth more than Baghdad.

The residents who are rebuilding are doing it on their own.

Christmas 2005 arrives in Pearlington and Angela becomes obsessed with making it a little less miserable for everyone. Lisa Martin is still sleeping on the particleboard shelf. She sometimes plays in the wreckage of her old home. She asks after the kittens that drowned in the storm there. The town has no way to pick itself up. The shrimpers have no boats and the muddy Pearl River is choked with sewage. Lisa's grandmother begins to cry when Angela mentions Christmas. But Angela has collected donations back in New York and brought in a truckload of gifts and supplies. Firefighters from Canyon, California, help her transport everything and medical students from Stanford unload it. She enlists Steve Horn, who came in from Carbondale, Colorado, to rebuild homes. He helps her figure out distribution. "You can't make that kind of connection with somebody in a situation that is so dire and then just say I did my part and walk away," she says.

The most consistent thing about this tragedy has been the resilience of both the victims and the volunteers. They prove over and over again that in this country you have to get up and do things yourself if you want them done right. Americans know how to be angry and make demands, but at their best they also know when it's time to just step in and fix stuff. Angela decorates a six-hundred-pound tree at what passes for a main intersection and sings mightily as a generator powers up a string of lights. The younger folks cry and give thanks but they can't capture a Christmas spirit. What, they ask, could they possibly be thankful for? Then the town's elder, an eighty-eight-year-old woman they call Mama Sams, yells at folks to come together. "They have fed us, they have clothed us, they have given us shelter, and we want to thank the good Lord for them," she says to the volunteers. For them, at least, they can give thanks.

A few months after the storm I come up with a plan to monitor the wound that Katrina has left on people. I give out digital video cameras to eleven students in the NoLa school system in January 2006. I go with Spike Lee to hand them out. He has made a documentary called *When the Levees Broke* and is something of a rock star in New Orleans.

At age twelve, Sophie Boudreaux is the youngest of our group. She seems quiet and shy, until she suddenly blurts out something incredibly thoughtful about her goals for telling her story. She wants to explore why people have forgotten about New Orleans. Sophie used to live on Florida Street in St. Bernard Parish, a street where I spent a lot of time reporting right after the storm. It's a street where some of the homes were blown off their foundations; the hurricane resembled a tornado on one corner. Florida Street is also where we've returned to do more stories lately. Some home owners have been coming back and rebuilding, in some cases without any insurance money to help them out. Sophie says she wants to show people exactly how she survived the storm.

When I ask if their stories would be "overwhelmingly hopeful or overwhelmingly negative," I am surprised at the quick response. Fifteen-year-old Deshawn Dabney says "overwhelmingly hopeful," and all the other students murmur in agreement. Deshawn lives with his mother, grandmother, and uncle in a crowded, run-down two-room apartment around the corner from the destroyed house his grandmother owns. Money is tight; repairs are going brutally slowly. The family is currently relying on church volunteers to patch and paint and wire their home. Still, he is hopeful.

Spike asks the kids if they saw the president's State of the Union address. They all say, "Yes." Deshawn complains that the president "didn't say anything about the hurricane, nothing about building more levees or sending money down here to help rebuild the Gulf Coast. He didn't even mention us, not one word."

Arianna Cassar, seventeen, tells me she wants to retrace the steps she took when she was evacuated. She lives near Baton Rouge, Louisiana, now, and her parents drive her to and from high school in Chalmette, Louisiana. That's about a 130-mile round trip. Every day.

Darold Alexander, fifteen, tells us he already knows ten or fifteen people with Katrina stories he wants to tell. Brandon Franklin, nineteen, says he wants to "show guys what I used to do, prior to Katrina, catch all that, as it is now, you know, still shut down and nothing popping."

These are kids, but they're old souls, even beyond Katrina and the recovery. Jerell Edgerson says, "At times, it feels like I'm sixteen and I'm on my own." She says she and her mom are very close, but her mom stayed in Atlanta, where there's housing and stability. Jerell felt it was important to finish high school in New Orleans. She's living with a family friend and was chosen for a Mudd jeans ad for what she wrote to the company about Katrina. She calls the modeling work a "blessing" of Katrina.

My producer Michelle Rozsa falls in love with the kids and methodically documents everything they do. She allows me to chart how their lives are challenged in the aftermath of the storm. What will their video stories reveal? What lies ahead for these kids who are so hopeful, and yet, at times, seem so worn out by all they've been through? The tape will tell. Sophie, our twelve-year-old, says she wants to show us her home, which they're in the process of rebuilding.

A month later, in February 2006, I get to see the first results. Eighteen-year-old Amanda Hill sits on a plastic lawn chair in a gutted home, talking straight into a camera. She looks shell-shocked, as if she has survived a war, and in a way that is exactly what has happened. Amanda and her grandmother lost their home and their livelihood as a result of Hurricane Katrina.

"I know what it is like not to have the finer things in life," she says, "and I don't need that to be happy, but I wake up at three a.m. to hearing my grandma crying because she doesn't know if she'll have money to put milk in the fridge or bread on the table." Amanda speaks these words on the first tape she sends to us. She tells us her grandmother, Dolores, has mentioned suicide. "All I could say was it's going to be okay, when in my heart I don't think it is." Dolores has raised Amanda since she was eleven years old. That was the year her mother died from cancer. Since returning to St. Bernard Parish, east of New Orleans, Dolores has tried to support the two of them while working at McDonald's.

In early spring, fifteen-year-old Deshawn Dabney confides to his camera, "I don't want to be dead at fifteen. I have dreams, a whole life to live. I want to be this huge entertainer . . . and there is no way I can do that if I'm dead." He has reason to be concerned. He is speaking just days after a neighbor, seventeen-year-old Anthony Placide, was killed by a gunshot wound to the head. The shooting happened only a few hundred feet from Deshawn's front door.

On another tape we get a few days later, Deshawn is interviewing Anthony's fourteen-year-old brother, Jamell Hurst. "I was shocked," Jamell tells Deshawn about his brother's murder. Seventeen-year-old Shantia Reneau talks about her inability to afford the college of her dreams, Southeastern Louisiana University. All of the family's extra money is going toward rebuilding their damaged home in the Ninth Ward. They're living in a FEMA trailer in a parking lot. "I really want to go to Southeastern, but if not, I'll have to stay down here," she says while walking along her damaged street. "I didn't want to. New Orleans has nothing to offer, nothing, not a thing."

Nineteen-year-old Brandon Franklin is looking outside New Orleans, too. He wants to go away to college to study to become a band director. But it may be a tough road for him. He is raising a one-year-old with his live-in girlfriend, Ivorionne, and they have another baby on the way. "I feel like we're a little bit too young for the responsibilities we have," he tells the camera in a strong, confident voice. "But I feel like I can do anything I put my mind to." Seeing and hearing him, you want to believe it. Amanda, Deshawn, Shantia, and Brandon are among the approximately thirty thousand students who attend public schools in Orleans and St. Bernard Parish nearly two years after the storm, down from more than seventy-five thousand before Katrina hit. Their stories will be seen on TV.

With all that hope coming from young people, the adults of St. Bernard Parish seem hopelessly in competition for scant resources. The storm aftermath had been punctuated by moments of bald-faced racism, roads blocked off to black people, and survivors left behind. It had also unified everyone in mysterious ways. There was a shared agony, a common enemy. But in the slow, painful rebuilding the parish fought to make sure the low-income, working black families would never return. The efforts were so blatant that a federal court would ultimately find them in violation of the Fair Housing Act.

St. Bernard Parish was listed as 88 percent white before the storm destroyed nearly all its homes, including Village Square, a collection of a hundred buildings inhabited mostly by low-income African-American renters. The parish leadership fought against rentals and multifamily housing units. Craig Taffaro Jr., the president of the St. Bernard Parish Council, promoted a "blood-relative ordinance" that forbid anyone from renting there unless they were relatives of home owners. The white population already owned 93 percent of the housing before the storm.

Two years after the storm, Sheriff Jack, who keeps getting elected, tells me just a third of St. Bernard Parish's residents have been able to return. The place still lacks a fully operational sewer system, enough schools or fire stations. Weeds grow up through the cement, threatening to overcome the city. Sheriff Jack figures he has spoken to twelve sets of representatives from the Federal Emergency Management Agency, each with a new set of rules. One set asked him to prove his deputies worked overtime in the days following the storm. "We were sleeping on cement slabs. We didn't have cars. We didn't have boats. They want us to produce sheets for the deputies to justify the overtime. We didn't even have toilet paper, much less paper to fill out trip sheets," he shouts. The new FEMA administrator confirms they made the request as if it meant nothing. Meanwhile, the sheriff seems to have abandoned his promise to be done with politics and is running again.

When my series on Katrina is over, so is my job as the anchor of *American Morning*. It happens suddenly after weeks of flagging ratings. MSNBC simulcasts Don Imus and their ratings rise 39 percent compared with the previous year. It's a slow news period and we are down 6 percent. We are nearly tied with them and both of us are suddenly being overshadowed by the personality-driven *Fox and Friends*. The hope had been that teaming me with Miles would overcome these challenges but it's not working. We are told that we are great reporters but not magnetic anchors. He will move on to covering NASA and I will do long-form documentaries, which I've never done before. It feels like I'm being fired and rehired the same day. In our chairs will go John Roberts from CBS and Kiran Chetry, freshly hired from FOX. The news is painful to hear and the coverage biting. One report even mentions that I have a lot of kids.

I feel suddenly I have nothing to do and nowhere to go. I have a job but nothing to shoot and no stories to tell. I am anxious because I don't know what lies ahead. I am just sitting around, enjoying my kids, taking yoga, and running like someone is chasing me. I feel very different from when I started at CNN.

In a way—like they say in church—I've been changed. After I lose the pace of the *American Morning* gig, my brain loses its main distraction and begins to replay the last few years. I have daily crying jags. I feel like I'm losing my mind. Pictures of bodies facedown in water or rolling by in trucks pop into my head when I'm on the treadmill. My work feels so much more important, but it feels like it's killing my head and making me a little bit insane. I care so much that I feel like I have to hop on another plane and get the word out. I cannot lose that platform. Technically I have been rehired and promoted. Part of me wonders if the new job I've been given is a consolation prize. I have four lovely kids who need to go to college, but for me it has never been about the money. The salary is only the half of it. When we walked out of the airport for the last time after Katrina, people spotted our CNN hats and stood up and applauded. I am overwhelmed by how many African-Americans walk up to me and urge me to tell more stories.

My last day on the anchor desk of a CNN flagship show is April 3, 2007, and a week later I'm invited to the anniversary gala for Dress for Success, a group that collects business clothing for disadvantaged women trying to enter the workforce. I decide to go. I have just turned forty a few months earlier and I slide into a fitted cream pantsuit and leopard-print heels. A young reporter nervously introduces herself and says she has landed a job at FOX News. "Great! Good for you! How old are you?" I ask her. "Twenty-two," she says. "Awesome—that's perfect!" I tell her. "If you're not a little bit scared, you're not doing it right." I am the last person to leave the red carpet that evening. I have so many more stories left to tell.

CHAPTER SIX

WORDS TO CHANGE A NATION

I peer out the car window and see the glint of razor wire coming up on the right. Michael Eric Dyson leans out and sees it, too. His eyes fill with water and he takes a quick breath. I steady his arm. Michael has a doctorate from Princeton. He has published over a dozen books. He rose from the ashes of ghetto Detroit to become a celebrated social critic and sociologist. He is one of the people we turn to to understand the world, a top intellectual voice of black America. Yet, he is about to cry in my rental car. We are on our way to visit his brother, Everett, who grew up with Michael under the very same circumstances. But Everett is now serving a life sentence in a federal penitentiary—for murder.

I have just begun to report a two-night, four-hour special called *Black in America*. I feel excited but I'm a bit overwhelmed. It is my first major assignment as anchor of CNN Presents, a long-form unit that makes news documentaries. There is no way to cover an entire people in a documentary, much less a group whose American experience has been historically underreported.

The task feels enormous. But I am thrilled. This is the kind of reporting I have wanted to do all along. This is a great opportunity to give voice to so many important stories in the African-American experience. I hardly know where to start.

I am eager to tell the Dyson brothers' story. I've heard it so many times, yet don't often see it on TV. African-American men are 14 percent of the general population, yet they represent 40 percent of the prison population. In the United States, nearly one in twenty black men is in prison. It is typical in this country for many African-American families to be fractured by the criminal justice system. It is a consequence of bad law, bad discrimination, bad circumstance, and bad behavior. The end result is brothers divided and family life flattened. Dyson and his brother are an opportunity to take a human look at that harsh reality.

Dyson dresses in a sharp suit. His white shirt is ironed flat. He has trimmed his goatee. We are staying at the same hotel, so I know he's been up since dawn getting ready because I have seen him. He can't visit Everett very often. He is anxious. He is excited. He is sad. He misses his brother. Dyson is usually a firecracker. He is accustomed to talking like the preacher and professor he is. He pushes the limits of the common vocabulary, ignites controversy and passion. Today he is quiet. He takes two bites of a powdered donut and seems to forget he is hungry. His forehead looks sweaty and it's not even hot. I walk quietly next to him. I have two brothers. I can't imagine the agony he is feeling, much less how to record the measure of this pain throughout an entire community. He turns to look me straight in the eyes.

"My brother didn't do this," he says.

We walk into the penitentiary and settle down in a small room. Since we are media, he is taken to a nearby office, so we skip the usual searches. But the place is dry and institutional, belted by razor wire and depressingly quiet. My producers put up cameras and lights.

"Evil is real," he had told a congregation in Detroit the day we began filming his story. "It's not a metaphysical projection. It shows up when folk won't let you have the job you know you should have. It shows up when people won't give you acknowledgment for who you are. It shows up when you work twice as hard to get twice as far behind and still keep going. Evil is real." His dark eyes scan the prison guard.

The last thing I said the day I lost my job as anchor of *American Morning* was the same thing I'd said every day when I signed off: "We are out of time on this *American Morning*." I certainly was.

When the storm of Hurricane Katrina hit in August of 2005, it rearranged the television universe as well. The public was outraged. They wanted reporters to ask hard questions, not just spin in windstorms clutching their microphones. We stood in the muck alongside survivors, with not a single public official in sight. Anderson Cooper, Wolf Blitzer, and I, the whole team, raged at the people in charge. The viewers cheered us on by elevating CNN's viewership to 3.7 million, celestial numbers for a cable news network.

By November, those viewers were slipping away. CNN replaced Aaron Brown and his 10:00 p.m. show *NewsNight* with more of Anderson Cooper. Anderson's stature had grown immensely following the storm. By April 2006, as our *American Morning* numbers began to slip, my good friend and boss, Kim Bondy, also left CNN. But, more important, she left me! *Ameri-*

can Morning was averaging 330,000 viewers to *Fox and Friends'* 836,000. Kim had joined the show with 551,000 viewers, taken it upward with the news; then she had seen it go back down.

American Morning is a hard news show, and when the news out there is soft, a lot of people tune out. Kim was perfectly capable of solving that issue. But she faced a far greater life problem. Her parents had been plucked from a balcony during Hurricane Katrina. The home she'd financed with a lifetime of savings was awash. She suffered the damage daily of feeling like her future was unmoored. She just wanted to heal, and go back to New Orleans to rebuild. CNN was covering one of the biggest tragedies in American history, while Kim was living it. She was a typical Katrina survivor, marching around her property in tears, constantly trying to regroup and shake the memory of her mother's agonizing days in the storm. Yet she spent much of her time sitting in New York physically exhausted and emotionally distracted. She feared she was letting me down by leaving. The storm had changed both of us, except she was still drowning in responsibilities and stress related to its real-life damage. CNN fought to keep her, but she was determined to go focus on rebuilding.

There are these little moments in life when your friends need you to let them go. I knew the newsroom would feel empty without her. She needed to go home to New Orleans and deal, so I bid her good-bye. She was and is my toughest critic, yet she always had my back. Her departure only deepened our friendship, but suddenly she wasn't there to pull me aside and give me the 411 on a story, office politics, or the stress of the day.

Kim leaves, our ratings suffer, no one on staff takes vacation. We take the stress of 2005, carry it into 2006, reignite our frustrations with the Katrina anniversary, then fall headfirst into the fall as election coverage begins to wind up. I am so tired I can barely put two sentences together. At some point the blur becomes even blurrier when they move our show an hour earlier to 6:00 a.m. I am flat out running but making no progress, in motion but going nowhere in particular but as is always the case I quickly regain focus when a great story rolls in.

Before I leave the show, an opportunity comes from out of nowhere. We are approaching the fortieth anniversary of Martin Luther King Jr.'s assassination. The King family and Morehouse College offer me an exclusive opportunity to review his private papers. His words have become the treatise of our country's civil rights movement. Whenever people cry out for justice, they quote King. "There is a new Negro in the South."

I get to hold King's papers in my own hands at the Robert W. Woodruff Library at the Atlanta University Center, to see what he crossed out and what he added. I get to read the little annotations in the margins and they are spellbinding. I see the books he read and the parts he underlined. I get to see where anger gave way to hope, where optimism prevailed and dreams emerged. His speeches were like music and I am getting a peek at the notes. He had taken our nation on a journey from Birmingham to Selma trying to wash away the stain of racism. Yet his writings reveal a regular man, young and smart but mostly present when the moment called, steady when most sane men would run. He is poetic and values words. But it is obvious his writings come from a man inspired by a moment. That is what sets us apart in this country, how you rise up after you're kicked down. He makes me feel like just about anyone can do great things.

"After one has discovered what he is called for, he should set out to do it with all of the power that he has in his system. Do it as if God almighty ordained you at this particular moment in history to do it," he wrote. So, he does.

It is 1954. King is twenty-five when he writes his first sermon on four pages, back and front, of lined notebook paper. They are the simple words of a young preacher talking to folks in Montgomery, Alabama. But a year later Rosa Parks takes one of the ten seats reserved for whites in the front of a bus. She refuses to budge. Civil rights leaders want African-Americans to boycott the bus system. King is plucked from obscurity to be the voice of the bus boycott movement. He is chosen because he is a noncontroversial young man who everybody likes. He ends up articulating the philosophy of a movement. "This is a movement of passive resistance, emphasis on nonviolence in a struggle for justice."

I interview King's former aide Andrew Young and Parks's lawyer, Fred Gray, who recall how frightened Dr. King was by what came next. "Listen, nigger," an angry caller told King. "We've taken all we want from you. Before next week, you'll be sorry you ever came to Montgomery." His house is bombed. He steps outside and talks down an angry crowd. He tells them God had suffused him with instant courage. Gray tells me that King believed he'd found a cause worth dying for. No one was taking the bus after that. That was the "new Negro in the South" he had spoken of, people who would rather walk in dignity than travel in fear. Young said King was hardly the leader type, more interested in chatting about his new baby than strategy. Circumstances called for a leader and he rose up and answered.

His notes betray how unprepared he was for living in fear. He and his staff begin to write in code. He is Jack Kennedy and Birmingham is Johannesburg. He is arrested for marching. His jailhouse notes are focused on how much he misses his family. He calls the isolation a living death. His lawyer, Clarence Jones, sneaks in paper for him to write. He is composing his "Letter from a Birmingham Jail," where he says, "when you have to concoct an answer for a five-year-old son asking in agonizing pathos, 'Daddy, why do white people treat colored people so mean,' then you will understand why we find it difficult to wait." I see where he's added the words "in agonizing pathos" at the last minute, as if he had conjured up his child's own face. Those three words make a world of difference. He is not just telling the story of the black community; he is evoking a painful image that any parent can absorb.

King's private library includes a copy of E. Stanley Jones's *The Christ of the American Road,* where he has underlined the part about how "America is a dream unfulfilled, a place where race and birth and color are transcended by the fact of a common brotherhood." In the book *Horns and Halos,* he pencils the note: "A dream that did not come true." I can see that he is in warm-up mode for the "I have a dream" speech. He makes a speech in the late 1950s imploring folks to "confront your shattered dreams." He goes further in an address to the National Press Club in July 1962, but crosses out the paragraph on dreams. An idea is germinating; he is collecting his thoughts. I can see the epic line of a movement coming together.

The night before the march on Washington in August 1963, Andrew Young remembers giving King notes as his advisors pushed him to come up with a new message. But President John F. Kennedy is so concerned about the march he asks the activists to tone down their speeches. King titles his speech notes "Normalcy—never again." The word "dream" doesn't appear anywhere in that early draft. Witnesses said he turned his notes over in the middle of the speech and just gave himself up to the moment. "I have a dream," he said in the defining words of our country's civil rights movement. "That my four children will one day live in a nation where they will not be judged by the color of their skin, but by the content of their character." They are just words but there are people around the globe and in our country who can recite that speech to its end. They speak of the promise of our country and of promises unfulfilled.

A month later, four little girls die in a bombing at a Birmingham church because of the color of their skin. King delivers the eulogy and writes this:

"The innocent blood of these precious children of God say to each of us we must substitute courage for caution." And this: "No, we must not lose faith in our white brothers." He is asking people to tamp it down at exactly the moment when rage can win the day. I look at the notes from a speech he gave years before the Birmingham campaign titled "Loving Your Enemies," and I can tell this has always been a part of his philosophy. The lesson for the rest of us is clear—don't let anger win the day, anyone's anger. "Throw us in jail and we will still love you," he wrote long before this awful bombing had been conceived. "Bomb our homes and threaten our children and we will still love you," he wrote. "We will wear you down by our capacity to suffer. We will win our freedom." He had no idea of the suffering that was still to come.

In February 1965, state troopers would fatally shoot twenty-six-year-old Jimmy Lee Jackson, a Baptist church deacon, in Marion, Alabama, while he was trying to stop troopers from beating his mother, Viola. King wrote of Jackson:

"He was murdered by the indifference of every minister of the Gospel who has remained silent behind the safe security of stained glass windows. He was murdered by every negro who passively accepts the evil system of segregation." Jackson died in Selma, the starting point of the marches to Montgomery, which led to the subsequent attack on protesters on the Edmund Pettus

Bridge by police that became known as Bloody Sunday. Blood was shed to fulfill the words he said at the Capitol that day. King cried at the White House when President Lyndon Johnson signed the Voters' Rights Act of 1965 and said: "We shall overcome."

King died planning a poor people's campaign. He came to believe that bigotry imposed black poverty and that poverty perpetuated inequality. He was looking ahead at the time where we live now. He tried marching with garbage workers but some youths broke store windows. He pledged to do it again without the violence. He came to Memphis on April 3, 1968, and stayed at the Lorraine Motel. He had a scrap of paper with him that said: "Gandhi speaks for us. 'In the midst of death, life persists, in the midst of darkness, light persists.'" Then King wrote:

"We are today in the midst of death and darkness. We can strengthen life and live by our personal acts by saying no to violence. By saying yes to life." He used it for a speech that night. He focused on death. "I don't know what will happen now. We have got some difficult days ahead. But it really doesn't matter with me now," he said. "Because I have been to the mountaintop. So I'm happy tonight. I'm not worried about anything. I'm not fearing any man. Mine eyes have seen the glory of the coming of the Lord." Andrew Young told me they had a silly pillow fight in King's room the next day. King seemed happier than ever when he walked out his door and into the sights of a killer.

I got this rush from having reported on the King papers. My show may be going nowhere but I feel at least I am doing important work. On this *American Morning*, I have an exclusive look at a man at least half the world admires. I feel like what he is saying speaks to me and I am honored. I am energized, a new member of the quarter million people who joined him on the Mall, and a new recipient of the grace he handed out in Selma.

Then, out of nowhere, the Reverend Jesse Jackson calls with an invitation to meet and talk, and it brings my reverie to a halt. We greet warmly and sit. A young, clean-cut security guy hovers nearby. He stays close enough to be summoned for a quick question but not close enough to overhear. I notice the china is clinking, but like really good china. I have four small kids so I never hear that particular sound. We're in a nice restaurant on the first floor of a famous hotel.

The Reverend Jackson begins talking in his strong Southern accent. His voice is very low. He says, "Call me Jesse," but that's something I feel like I cannot do. I am confident he doesn't remember the first time we met. It was my job in 1989 to escort him through his live shots at WBZ-TV around Boston during Nelson Mandela's historic visit to the United States. I was his "babysitter," the one making sure no other media plucked him away. He was our contributor. He whispers something. He is speaking so low I can barely hear him. I strain to get closer.

Even though I am not sure what he is saying, I can tell he is angry. Today he is angry because CNN doesn't have enough black anchors. It is political season. There are billboards up sporting Paula Zahn and Anderson Cooper. He asks after the black reporters. Why are they not up there? I share his concern and make a mental note to take it back to my bosses. But then he begins to rage that there are no black anchors on the network at all. Does he mean covering the campaign? I wonder. The man has been a guest on my show. He knows me, even if he doesn't recall how we met. I brought him on at MSNBC, then again at *Weekend Today*. I interrupt to remind him I'm the anchor of *American Morning*.

He knows that. He looks me in the eye and reaches his fingers over to tap a spot of skin on my right hand. He shakes his head. "You don't count," he says. I wasn't sure what that means. I don't count—what? I'm not black? I'm not black enough? Or my show doesn't count?

I was both angry and embarrassed, which rarely happen at the same time for me. Jesse Jackson managed to make me ashamed of my skin color, which even white people had never been able to do. Not the kids in the hallways at Smithtown or the guys who wouldn't date me in high school. I remember the marchers behind me at the trial about the black youth who beat the Latino baby. The folks that chanted "biracial whore for the white man's media," even they didn't make me feel this way. I would just laugh. Biracial, sure, whore, not exactly, white man's media, totally! Whatever. But Reverend Jesse Jackson says, "I don't count"?

I am immediately upset and annoyed and the more annoyed I am, the more upset and pissed off. If Reverend Jesse Jackson doesn't think I am black enough, then what am I? My parents had so consistently pounded racial identity into my head that the thoughts of racial doubt never crossed my mind. I'd suffered an Afro through the heat of elementary school. I'd certainly never felt white. I think my version of black is as valid as anybody else's. I am a product of my parents (black woman, white man), my town (mostly white), multiracial to be sure, but not black? I feel like the foundation I'd built my life on was being denied, as if someone was telling me my parents aren't my parents. "You know those people you've been calling Mom and Dad—they aren't really your parents." "What?" The arbiter of blackness had weighed in. I had been measured and found wanting.

It knocked me off my equilibrium for a bit, the first time that had happened to me since that guy in a bar back on the West Coast pinched my butt during my first live shot. After two weeks of stewing, I sit upright one day, angry at myself for not telling this man he is wrong. I am a product of my own life. That's one of the wonders of America, you have the right to define yourself regardless of what little box someone wants to shove you in. He is certainly right that CNN doesn't have enough people of color on the air, even the bosses say that and spend their time trying to fix it. But "You don't count"? Screw that. Of course I count. Who is he to say that? My experience is not universal—no one's is—but it is legitimate. I get to be who I am outside and in.

I was embarrassed that I didn't call him back and ask what he meant. I (like my mother) like a good fight. So I should have called him up and said, "What the heck does that mean?" But I didn't. I slunk away. Annoyed. And more annoyed that I never forgot his words. I look at other mixed-race people now and wonder. Did their parents slam their identity into their head as mine did? Or do they not even get a category? Jesse Jackson caught me off balance.

But that day I couldn't say a word to Reverend Jackson. I run into the man all the time. We are invited to the same events. We kiss at functions but still I say nothing. I see how deeply people respect him. Al Sharpton tells me Jackson taught him civil disobedience. Roland Martin credits him with paving the way for Obama. Jackson sat at lunch with me telling me how he hates always being asked to talk only about black issues, hates to be tagged as only the black expert, never the guy negotiating peace or brokering deals with Wall Street. He lashes out at people who define him by the color of his skin. It matters that they don't see inside him. It mattered to me that he didn't see inside me.

It wasn't until recently that I called him and reminded him

of what he'd said to me that day. I had done four documentaries on race in between the two conversations. He was totally surprised and barely remembered the details. He had not known I was black! He said he honestly did not know, that when he said I didn't count he was alluding to the fact that he thought I was a dark-skinned someone else. That is how precise the game of race is played in our country, that we are so easily reduced to our skin tone. That even someone as prominent in African-American society as Reverend Jackson has one box to check for black and one for white. No one gets to be in between. I thanked him for his candor.

Soon there would also be one less black anchor, whether I counted or not. The story of King's papers was my last major story as the anchor of *American Morning*. I did the show not long before I lost the job. Reading those letters, though, had rendered my own inconsequential losses so silly. I decided I knew nothing of real adversity. I carried the project over to my new job, which had felt like a consolation prize but now seemed like an enormous opportunity.

I did an hour-long documentary on the King papers. As it came together, I realized that mine was a very real promotion, a chance to grow as a journalist and contribute powerful reporting, I was going to report long-form journalism, thoughtful documentaries that could go beyond the news of the day. I could do stories that give voice to the voiceless. I was being named the go-to reporter on race and ethnicity at a time of high viewer interest in both topics. CNN had taken my anchor slot while at the same time had loosened the leash that a more structured show has. I had never had professional aspirations much higher than rising through the ranks of journalism. Now I dreamed of telling un-told stories, of making a small difference in the way we all view each other. I had the option of looking at my firing as the anchor of *American Morning* as one of those backhanded opportunities, like many we get handed in life. I can seize this and run with it or get bogged down in feeling lost and bitter. We can all rise up to the occasion in our own small ways.

I walked away from the King papers with the gift of clear vision. I also brought with me one particular thought he wrote: "The major problem of life is learning how to handle the costly interruptions. The door that slams shut, the plan that got side-tracked, the marriage that failed. Or that lovely poem that didn't get written because someone knocked on the door."

CHAPTER SEVEN

BLACK IN AMERICA

The door swings open abruptly at the penitentiary and in walks Everett Dyson. He is wearing an orange jumpsuit. He limps from a leg injury. His face is sullen, almost snarling. He sees his brother and the sourpuss cracks. He is nearly smiling when they fall into a strong embrace. They look so very much alike.

Michael and Everett were raised on Firwood Street in Detroit. Michael was a gifted public speaker as young as eleven. He dreamed of writing books. His buddies called him "the professor." That's a lot of dreaming for a kid raised in a place consumed by violence and poverty. "When you look at the reality of being poor and black, it is psychically depleting; it is spiritually exhausting; it is emotionally enervating; and it just does something to your morale. It's a wonder that more poor people don't misbehave," he said to me on a visit to his childhood home. The brothers say they are separated by the choices they made. Everett says Michael is a symbol of what could have been. Michael was on the front page of the *Detroit News* when he was twelve: "Boy's Plea Against Racism Wins Award." "A teacher told him he had taken all the talent out of the family." Everett remembers riding his minibikes and playing in the dirt. "I'm not articulating anything great. I'm not talking about saving brotherhood," he said.

Life was equally unkind to them both. Michael was on welfare and raising a son by the time he was eighteen. Michael remembers how he was treated when he went to apply for welfare. The unemployment counselors would shout: "Have you been looking for work?" "Oh, my God. And it was so loud," Michael remembers. "And 'Are you working? Are you trying to work?' 'Yes, I really am.' I shoveled snow. I did sodding with my father. I painted houses. I worked as a manager trainee at Burger King, and I did everything I could to make ends meet. And then finally, I decided I've got to go to school. My son has to have a better way of life."

Meanwhile, Everett figured the marines might be his way out of poverty. But he was discharged after going AWOL and found himself back on these same streets, selling dope. Michael went to college. He gathered degrees. He tasted sweet success. In 1989, Everett says a wounded man stumbled from a drug den. Before the man died, he uttered Everett's name. Everett says that dying declaration led to his conviction for murder. Twenty years later, twenty years he has spent in jail, both brothers still insist Everett is innocent. There is no telling whether that is the truth, but it is clear both brothers believe Everett doesn't belong in jail. Everett acknowledges that he was living on the wrong side of goodness. Michael says the biggest difference between them was their skin color. Everett is much darker than Michael.

"I saw how the differential treatment was accorded me, little curly-top, yellow Negro child. I'm not dissing any yellow Negro children. That's who I am. I'm saying that being a dark-skinned black man has a kind of incriminating effect to many people. And

I'm not even getting to white brothers and sisters yet. I'm talking about within black America. And I'm saying to you, many darker-skinned black children don't get the opportunity," Michael says. I tell him that plenty of dark-skinned black children are very successful. Both the brothers take a beat. Everett responds for both of them: "It takes a keen eye to look beneath the rough exterior of a person and see the beauty that's within."

Then Michael heads off to a book signing in Canada. His brother, Everett, heads back to his cell.

Racism was very clear when I was a kid. The racism of forty years ago in this country was of the can and cannot. My mother couldn't marry my dad. There were places people couldn't go. Those concrete boundaries were replaced by the social discrimination of my youth—the nasty kid in the hall who tries to pickpocket your self-esteem. America now suffers from a wound that won't heal because you can't help but pick the scab. Black folks can go anywhere they want, do anything they want. But we have to have the resources and the wherewithal to do it. American racism now has less to do with a lack of access than with opportunities denied. So much of the African-American community is victim of this great pile-on, this mountain of injustices so high they can't bring themselves to climb over it. Families are divided by who got a shot at something better, and who just got shot down.

The Centers for Disease Control and Prevention once began a campaign to try to teach black children to swim because so many die of drowning. The reason was simple. Generations ago slaves weren't taught to swim so they couldn't escape by water. Then the pools were segregated so few had access to pools and never learned. Then some folks just thought blacks couldn't swim. Today, three times as many black children between the ages of five and fourteen die of drowning as white kids, largely because they can't swim.

But there are no longer people keeping us out of the pools. Is there a point where the psychological damage ends and the obligation to just pick up and get on with it begins? Now that the National Guard has escorted us in, shouldn't we just sit down and crack the books? Or are we too hampered by the journey to get past the spitting morons at the gate? I learned to push ahead, keep steady forward motion. But I had two loving parents, with jobs and a strong education. One of them is white. The other is my immigrant mother, who grew up absent the history of American slavery and desegregation. She separated from her own history by traveling across the sea.

We ended up wrapped in suburban middle-class comfort, bound for college from the time we first picked up a book. My white dad and Latino mom had the backbone to look us in the eye and say, "You're black, don't let anyone ever tell you you're not black. Don't let anyone ever tell you you're not Latino." I could never figure out who "they" were, but I was prepared if they were to show up. They drilled into us that both identities were things to be proud of. I filled up a deep reserve of self-esteem of immeasurable value.

I am in no position to judge someone for whom the wall was built too high. I can only tell their tale. That is my way of helping push them forward, by getting their story out, by sending out a cry for understanding and accountability. By urging them on with the sentiments of my own family to push forward, push ahead; rise up. I am still living my life of perpetual motion, and when I am in a position to tell stories that aren't being told, it is helping me propel my work. The very least I can do is bring some folks along for the ride. Is it reasonable to expect that my work can help build bridges of understanding about race and racism, or at the very least motivate a few people to open doors? I'm not sure. But I can try.

I find it hard to tell if reporting a documentary called *Black in America* means doing a documentary about a race—the black race—or racism. Those things are so inextricably interwoven in this country it's often hard to pull them apart. So trying to report this documentary unfolds as one of the hardest projects of my career. My producers feel the strain as well. There is perhaps nothing more challenging than reporting on race. CNN adds four producers of color to my team, which helps bring some fresh perspectives—two black men and two mixed-race women who are part Latina and part black. We also have several long-form producers who are accustomed to assembling these far-reaching surveys.

I can tell instantly that everyone is feeling the strain of getting this right. One of the biggest challenges to this project is its name, that it is called *Black in America*. Because the very title seems to promise a survey of all things black, and that is impossible. There is also a presumption out there that it will somehow magically make up for the lack of thoughtful coverage in the babble of overall news reporting, another impossibility. I can't possibly cover every black experience, even in four hours over two nights, nor can I hit every social issue. I'm a little worried and the ideas flowing in from my staff are great, but mostly contradictory. Some of the team wants to tackle all the social issues facing the black community, while others want to provide new, more positive images. What we need are great human stories that unveil a community so often reduced to nothing more than the sum of its problems. We need keen eyes to look beneath the rough exterior of a person, not to mention a whole people.

I fly across this great land several times a month. I am on this crazy mission to tell the story of what it means to be *Black in America*. I crisscross the country, entering people's lives to tap their lows and highs. I crash an enormous family reunion in Lodi, Texas, the tentacles of a line of black folks who turn out to have a very distant white ancestor. I unite them with their white distant cousins. I tell the stories of various members of the family, the black women who can't find soul mates and black men who can't find jobs. The stories will be worked together as our first night on women and families.

Then we plan to devote a second night to men. I follow around a hyper-successful advertising executive who worries that people see his race rather than his smarts. I talk to celebrities like my friend Spike Lee, who included me in his Katrina documentary. I am like this bird, migrating so I can feed. I want to tap into some of the crisis of the black community without dwelling on their sorrows. I want to show the striving black middle class, the plight of the single mother, to give a snapshot of where we stand as a people.

In my effort to spotlight men, I go visit Little Rock, Arkansas. I meet some of the children of desegregation, the graduates of the class of 1968 of Little Rock Central High School—kids who entered the school more than ten years after the U.S. Supreme Court forced it to accept blacks. They are celebrating their fortieth class reunion, so it makes sense to see where they are. I begin to follow the lives of four of them, all men, and their sons and grandsons.

Little Rock Central High School is a mirror of our country's ambitions for its children. The building cost $1.5 million in 1927 and was trumpeted as a rosy model for America's future schools. Every time I pay a visit, I experience a chill. The school is impressive with its towering brick facade and reflecting pool. To this day, the academic achievement here is notable. The school frequently ranks among the top in the nation, gathering armfuls of awards and recognition for its science and sports achievements. There has always been plenty going on in this building that a black parent would want for their kid. So in 1954, when the U.S. Supreme Court ordered American schools to integrate, black families wanted in to Little Rock Central High.

Perhaps no moment better reflects the ugliness of American racism than when the federal government had to use U.S. troops to escort nine frightened black teenagers into class. The grandchildren of these brave pioneers now attend a school that memorializes the standoff. Little Rock is one of those fault lines that have fractured America's promise of equality. No black person in this country can watch those children braving angry white racists without believing that the promise of America's possibilities has its limits. I am aware that history has moved on, but they can point to experiences like that in their own life. They know those angry white people standing outside are not dead; they're not necessarily even altered. They're just a part of our history. They are real live obstacles to unity. I followed the men who graduated from that school ten years later because I wanted to see what an average man can do with that heavy weight on his shoulders.

One of our Little Rock Central High class of 1968 graduates is Donald "Duck" Gray, who is remembered by his classmates as a fast talker and a bit of a hustler, labels he's not quick to shake. Duck, as his friends call him, fathered ten children and raised none of them. He acknowledges his brushes with crime and drugs and womanizing have left his children bitter. "I was a drug dealer. I was a pimp. I mean, you name it, I damn near done it," he says. Today he is a contractor who says his life is back on track. Every time we visit Duck he's lounging around in a one-piece painter's suit. He seems attached to his battered pickup and pint of beer. The man is drop-dead charming, still a fast talker, and he's obviously recommitted himself to hard work.

We track him as he paints one home, re-pipes the next, throws up some drywall in another place, then rips out old carpeting and redoes a floor. He has two grandsons living with him when we meet and is determined to do better by both. "Sometimes I sympathize with him. Sometimes I understand him. Sometimes you want to beat the hell out of him," Duck says of one grandson. He is funny and swift. I can totally see spending a hot afternoon on the front porch sipping a cold beer with this guy. It's hard not to like him. He is, however, the farthest back we can go among the living to where this sobering statistic began: Nearly 60 percent of all black children are growing up without a father in their home.

Duck's daughter Tina Smith seethes with resentment over her father's lack of concern for his wives and children. She sees what he's doing now as too little, too late. She is a social worker and she knows all about men who create and foster social problems. I go to her house. It is small, white, and looks like it is slinking into a mountain of earth. Gates and trees and the slope of the land separate it from the houses around it. There is an angry pit bull slobbering and snarling next door and a lot of cars parked in awkward directions on her neighbor's lawn.

It's clear Tina has drawn a line between her home and whatever is going on around this neighborhood. The floor inside her house slopes and sinks and there are boards missing, but there is something tidy about the setup. She is broad but moves quickly. She has pretty eyes that her head and shoulders follow around as she picks up the mess left by two boys, her husband, and her sleepy daughter, who emerges from her bedroom to wrap her arms around her mother's waistline before shaking off a nap.

Tina offers water and we open up foam cartons of barbecue. She has an easy smile, but Tina is a woman on the defensive. She is at war with a list of social ills and my team and I have the potential to be another headache. Her youngest son, Braylon, looks and acts just like her. She tells us he is mad inside, just like her. One in three black men will have a criminal record in their lifetime. That makes Tina just crazy with regret. Braylon was charged recently with assaulting a police officer who was frisking one of his friends. "The police officer told me stop. And I stopped. I turned around and he came and grabbed me and I hit his hand the first time. Then he grabbed me again and I just hit him in the face," he told me. The day Braylon's mother, Tina, walked him into court, she feared she would lose her son.

"The kind of things I was afraid of was I would never see my child again," she said. Braylon could have gotten a felony conviction and served time behind bars. Instead, he was sent to juvenile rehabilitation to deal with his anger issues. Now he's back home. Tina believes this experience might be an eye-opener for him, or his undoing.

"You are a young man. You're an African-American man. You already have a strike against you. But, no matter what people say or what people do with you, you can do anything that you set your mind to doing," she tells him.

Braylon is going back to school soon and says he's scared enough of prison to control his anger. He talks about his temper as if it is another person he can't control. He says he wants his temper to go away. He wants to feel less angry. I ask him what he's angry about. He is not even certain he knows. He just knows that when he saw that police officer grab his friend, his temper paid him a visit.

I hear about this anger from so many of the young black men I interview. The anger crosses the lines of class and education; it is shaped by fear as much as temper. It has the potential to lance even the most solid lives. I hear it most often when black men talk about their interactions with the police. The feeling is reflected in statistics that show 75 percent of black men feel they are treated more harshly by the criminal justice system. I hear it from the TV comic D. L. Hughley when he recounts how he coaches his son on handling any interaction with the police.

"When you're black, your skin color is always in the equation," D.L. tells him. "He already knows, and he has learned from the time he was twelve years old how to speak to the police, what to say, what not to say, to view the police differently than everybody else."

His son, Kyle, recites his father's advice without hesitation. "If they ask me a question that I'm uncomfortable answering, I say, 'Officer, I respect your job, but I would appreciate it if you would just call my parents and I'm not saying anything else.'"

I hear the same story from Professor Ronald Mincy of Columbia University, who has made his career studying African-Americans as a renowned sociologist. He says he has taught his sons to fear encounters with the police. "If a police officer approached you, you cower," he says with a hint of emotion in his voice. "You cower."

Ellis Cose, whose books on race have become primers for black folk looking to understand the strains on our culture, says these experiences cannot be divorced from the negative social messages they get about education.

"Young black men are much more likely to get a million messages directed at them that tell them you can't succeed in school; you're not supposed to be in school; that's not what young black people do," he said. Those messages sabotage their self-esteem and stunt their future.

"It comes from all of this concentrated poverty, all of these people who don't have models of people who are doing well, who are getting a college education. . . . And you also just have, in a thousand ways, from rap music, to television, to just what people see in the streets, these messages that get sent that education is not really a black thing."

Which gets me back to Braylon Smith, who dreads his return to Little Rock Central High, an institution desegregated by his own family. He fears walking the halls his grandfather, Duck, walked to the delight of a string of girlfriends in 1968.

Tina hated going to school there, too. She remembers just being tagged as another of Duck's loser children. She walked away from it to a solid career. When her first husband left her to raise her eldest, Brandon, she tried to create a stable family with her new husband, Calvin. They had Braylon together, and Calvin was a responsible and loving father to both her kids. Then Braylon mixed it up with a police officer and she suddenly felt her son slipping away.

Braylon says being in rehabilitation was maddening. He is not a big talker and every day he had to talk about his anger. But the institution eventually felt comforting. Returning to school is like stepping into a pressure cooker. He finds Little Rock Central High overcrowded and uninspiring, with temptations to get in trouble around every corner. He feels like he'll return carting around this albatross of having gotten in trouble with the law. Teachers will view him differently. No guidance counselor will track him for college. They will be watching him intensely to see if he screws up. We follow him the day he goes back to class and he couldn't be walking more slowly.

"What I believe has happened is generational, because it's been passed down," says Tina with her eyes full of tears. "This is what my parents grew up with. This is how I raised my children. And it's just being passed down from one generation to the next."

That Sunday she takes her boys to church, where she sings in the choir. The boys' shirts are pressed and she is wearing a spectacular red suit with a sharp hat. They walk in with a pride and enthusiasm that is absent from the way they walk in the rest of the world. The Pew Forum on Religious and Public Life did studies of American religion that show how central historically black churches are to black family life. Congregations are concentrated in the South, serving mostly working-class people of all ages. The people who usually don't get more than a high school education and are less likely to marry. They report that their religion is central to their lives, that they want bigger government and more services. Most pray every day, regardless of whether their prayers are answered.

Whatever is going on in Tina's house, in this house she walks in with a high head, accompanied by her sharply dressed young men into a place of pride and stature. She ascends the altar in shiny black heels and leans over the microphone with a booming voice as her sons kneel down to pray. Calvin is a preacher at the church, when he isn't at his day job as a school custodian. She feels that her sons have been affected by the lack of male role models in their lives, even though her husband is present. It is hard for any one man to make up for a legion of men who make poor models—Tina's father, brothers, so many of the men on her own block.

Professor Mincy says the damage done to families when a father goes absent lasts many generations and is not easy to repair. He also says that it has done harm to the entire African-American community because having children outside marriages has become the norm.

"These men don't marry their babies' mothers. And those mothers have found a way to live without them. We have figured out a myriad of ways to enable young women to raise children in the absence of fathers. And I think that's a huge problem," he says.

"History has a lot to do with it. Slavery did do major damage to gender relationships in the African-American community, and, in addition to that, shock. We have had renewed shocks over time."

Professor Mincy charts a progression of social and economic ills that have beset black men from slavery onward, obstacles that have made it very difficult for them to raise families. He points to high rates of school dropout, unemployment, and incarceration.

"It is very difficult in this society for a man to marry, to sustain a family, to sustain a relationship with a woman, children, etcetera, if he can't fulfill the provider roles," says Professor Mincy. The lack of male role models has led to low expectations for black men throughout the community. A lot of women, says Mincy, have usurped the power to make decisions about whether to have a family. Many move ahead with families with no expectation that men will play a role and every expectation that their community will support them. The stigma of the single mom has all but vanished in much of black society, says Mincy, and, while well intentioned, that's not necessarily a good thing.

Brandon, Tina's older son, scoots around the church that morning, handsome and well spoken. He has no relationship with his father, although he is friendly with Calvin, his stepfather. He has a child with his ex-girlfriend Sherita and another with his most recent girlfriend. He dropped out of school to become a security guard. He says he is trying to contribute to his ex-girlfriend so she can raise their daughter, Salia. But he is detached and overwhelmed and his new girlfriend wants help with his son, Jaden. Tina finds the responsibilities he has heaped on himself dizzying, but she is trying to help him in any way she can, including setting up a first birthday party for Salia with all the trimmings.

When the day arrives, the house where Salia lives with her mother is a flotilla of balloons and relatives. Tina and her husband and Braylon arrive early, all smiles and presents and helping hands. Then Tina begins a solid hour of waiting for Brandon to arrive. A stream of children surrounds Salia and games begin. Tina stands at the doorway checking and rechecking her watch and mumbling that this is his daughter's first birthday and he should have been early. Brandon's stepfather fumes on the front lawn. Even Braylon expresses his anger and calls his older brother's cell phone numerous times. Salia is restless and her mother is saying out loud that Brandon always disappoints.

Brandon walks in just after Salia has blown out her candles. She cries when he picks her up. He mumbles something about having the wrong address. I ask him if he isn't abandoning his daughter the way his father abandoned him. He vows to break four generations of fathers abandoning children. "I'm going to change it up," he promises. "Traditions are always willing to be broken."

Yet four months go by and Brandon doesn't visit Salia. Just as I'm wrapping up shooting on *Black in America* I decide to visit Brandon. His story is so depressing. I don't just want to put it out there with a downpour of sociologists' excuses on top. I take him to see Salia and her mother, thinking maybe I can interview them together. We arrive to a surprise. Sherita is pregnant again, this time with twins and by another boyfriend. The animosity and anger between her and Brandon is obvious. I end up feeling like one of those television marriage counselors.

"Could you contribute more?" I ask Brandon. "Yes."

"Would you let him do more?" I ask Sherita.

"Yes. I mean, I don't stop him from doing it now. I mean, I look at it as a—I mean, I know there's times when I have an attitude problem, but I have a reason to, because of what all I have done by myself with Salia," she replies.

"Can he be a good father, if he tried? Can he be a good father?" I ask her. She stares at Brandon almost as if she's about to re-ask my question. "I think he could. But the thing is, will he?"

"Will you?" I ask. "Yes. You know, it's—yes."

These two people are not yet twenty-one and between them they are about to have four children, a tangle of animosities, and minimum-wage jobs. Brandon has obtained his GED. Sherita says finding work is nearly impossible but she will continue trying after the twins are born. She fully expects her boyfriend will marry her. I leave the two of them chatting amicably but don't know really what profound things to draw out of their story. These young people live on the dark side of that statistic on African-American men creating babies they feel little obligation to raise. Sherita lives there, too, boosting her self-esteem by making babies, creating a job for herself where there is none.

I struggle to tell this story. It feels like it's the story we hear about African-Americans every day, and I wanted to say something more profound, something different. So I rely on Professor Mincy to give me context. But I also sweat the fact that I've managed to heap onto the overall image of black America yet another anecdote of our struggle and shame.

Professor Mincy urges me to take a look at the other half of the statistic, "then you will see my theory play out," he says. The black American family is fractured. The reason black children are being raised without their fathers is because the fathers have detached from their responsibility to women and family life. That commitment is what lives on the other side of the dividing line.

Which brings me to Kenneth Talley, another graduate of the class of '68.

Kenneth Talley remembers Duck and the stress of Little Rock Central High. Where Duck remembers being a player, Kenneth was about hitting the books and fearing the overall stress of desegregation would upend his plans for success. His family made all the difference.

"I have been fortunate enough to have been raised in a middle-class home with a father who was a positive role model. A lot of these men didn't have that privilege. You know, they came from homes where the father was absent. Some of the fathers are drug addicts. Some are in jail. And, so, they didn't have a good example. They didn't know what it was to be a father, because they didn't have a father," Kenneth said of his classmates.

Today his father mentors kids in Little Rock and Kenneth works in the black community through his church. He faced every single obstacle life could throw at a young black man, yet kept his head above water. After high school, Kenneth joined the marines and went to college for a few years until he could no longer afford to pay. He got a job with the Department of Commerce and worked there for about five years. And then he lost everything after he was the victim of a layoff.

"So, that was what started my descent into the ranks of the working poor. Let me just say this. It was the lowest point of my life," he recalls.

Just like Tina, Kenneth turned to his church. His church helped him find work as a freelance photographer. He soon married his girlfriend, Pamela. They both continued their education and got solid jobs; Kenneth is now an editor in the Bureau of National Affairs in Washington, D.C. They threatened to cut his job at one point and he accepted a demotion to keep working. He and Pamela planned their family. Sakia and Xander attend religious schools. Xander is autistic and needs special education, so Pamela concentrates on him while her husband works long hours to make sure they have a stable financial life.

To look around their home is to see what struggle has built. Not a shoe is out of place, pictures of family events line the mantel, and food and toys are plentiful. Kenneth and Pamela are all teamwork, one of them feeding Xander, whose many challenges require boundless energy, while the other helps Sakia with her homework.

"When I see what has happened with children in the underclass, and the pain and suffering that they're going through, and think of my children having that same fate, it inspires me to make every sacrifice," Kenneth says.

His home is a place where hope thrives. Kenneth is warmhearted and nonjudgmental. He missed his high school reunion this year because he had to work. He wishes he had seen Duck but doesn't really care what happened to him after high school. He laments that someone with such a quick tongue and easy charm didn't use it for something better. His strategy is just to push for-

ward. Not let anger pull him down, and draw deeply from the re-
pository of love he felt as a boy growing up in Little Rock, where
his father never missed a school event no matter how insignifi-
cant. Desegregation didn't just mean mixing with the white folks;
it meant grabbing the opportunity to achieve right alongside them.

Kenneth Talley's mother taught the white kids at the school
and remembers the painful divide she fought to erase. She
wanted Kenneth at Little Rock because she thought the academ-
ics were superior. To this day she laments having risked his self-
esteem. He has few fond memories of walking those hallways and
also wonders if his life would have been better if he had stayed in
the black school. But today the Talleys live in mixed-race Prince
Georges County, Maryland, in a nice home surrounded by play-
grounds and friendly neighbors of all colors. Kenneth is certain
his parents' insistence that he stick with Little Rock Central High
School taught him that education is valuable enough to fight for,
no matter how many times it feels out of reach. His resume lists
every single time he tried to go to college and was thwarted by a
lack of money. He kept going until he was able to afford to complete his degrees. It also gave him an opportunity to remake the
American landscape for his children.

Kenneth is a serious guy, a shy man. But his face lights up
when he talks of his own little girl, who never speaks of race and
attends school with a rainbow of children.

"Sakia, she does not see the color of skin. She just does not,"
he says.

It is hard when reporting on America's racial and ethnic minorities
to not see life as a fistfight. Every person of color who has achieved
something seems to have fought for it. I never thought of myself as

much of a fighter, but I see a lot of fight in me. I am my mother's daughter and she was born a woman of battle. Fighting for opportunities. Fighting to learn. Fighting to marry, to raise her kids in an unwelcoming suburb. Fighting to preserve opportunities.

When we speak now it's often by phone. There are expectations but she doesn't cast too many judgments. But her questions are full of advice. What did you eat today? Are you tired? Did you enjoy that? Some people's lives are formed by their family dramas. People get sick, they die, they divorce, things fall apart, great things happen, then un-happen. My family is remarkable for how average we are. Our sanity is reassuring. Everyone loves each other. We study hard, succeed; then we make new families of our own. Some families pass around problems; mine distributes solutions.

I never realized how important my family was to me until I became a reporter. I meet people raised without that family tie. I realize my family makes me what I am. My mother's perseverance and my father's steadiness lift us. Together we are unstoppable. We walk around with a firm set of values and concrete sense of identity and purpose. It is appalling that not every child in our country gets that, doubly troubling that our country makes it harder. There are so many families that succumb to the turmoil around them, whose scant resources are not enough to get them through tough times. The fewer resources you have in this country, the fewer chances you have to get ahead. Life shouldn't be like a sporting event, winner takes all. You shouldn't have to be the first in your class to get a shot at college, especially when an entire family depends on your success. There needs to be room in this land of opportunities to try and fail and try again.

Black in America airs to record numbers of viewers. Students at Morehouse and Spellman and Howard gather together to watch, churches host viewing parties, politicians send out alerts urging people to tune in. Social networks are formed to celebrate the launch. Critics rave about the show in the newspapers. At screenings across the country, middle-class black folks tell me it is a call to arms, an alarming reminder that our community is being divided into those who have pushed forward and those left behind. I am lauded at historically black colleges and showered with invitations to speak on race and racism. The program even draws high viewership when it airs a second time. There are critics who say we shouldn't be airing our dirty laundry in public. Other people keep telling me they wish I'd included even more stories—gay blacks, Caribbean blacks, AIDS, affluence, health care, an endless list. Everywhere I go, people ask me when I'm going to do the next one.

· CHAPTER EIGHT ·

Not Black Enough

The sun rises over Washington, D.C., like a fluorescent light turned on slowly by a dimmer switch. It is cold, brutally cold, sub-zero when the wind whips across the Mall. Steam escapes from sidewalk grates and hovers in clouds above the lawn. The monuments look like ice castles. I have on so many layers I feel as if I have been wrapped in plastic. It is Martin Luther King Day, 2009. I arrive at our red, white, and blue election truck, a huge bullet of a vehicle with satellite capacity. My *American Morning* replacements look as if they are reporting from the tundra. They have no heaters and it's eight degrees out. Their "set" is a tiny perimeter of police tape and lawn chairs exposed to the wind. I have no desire to be one of them anymore.

I wrap myself up tightly, swallow hot chocolate, demand blankets and replace them on the big lawn. I am going to sit in this frosty wind tunnel at an awesome moment in history. Today we celebrate a man who rallied us to throw down racial barriers.

Tomorrow the U.S. inaugurates its first black president. This is about as cool as it gets.

"I'm Soledad O'Brien," I tell viewers from beneath my powder blue ski cap. "You are watching CNN's live coverage of Martin Luther King Jr.'s national observance, and the buildup, as well, to inauguration day. Barack Obama is going to be sworn in as the forty-fourth president twenty-three hours from right now." I am live on CNN for the next eleven hours. I am doing a live show on two seminal events in black history side by side. This marathon event feels like a wrap-up to my year of reporting documentaries on Dr. King's papers, his assassination, and the four hours of *Black in America*. I have become the go-to reporter on racism and race.

This is the day before the inauguration but tens of thousands of people have arrived a day early. They gather around me on the Mall. Roland Martin stations himself next to me. He has that great radio voice and knows everything about Dr. King. He is supposed to stay for a few minutes but he ends up staying hours. Andrew Young joins me. He is dizzy with anticipation. Then I interview Representative John Lewis, who spoke on the Mall the day of Dr. King's "I have a dream" speech. At one point we replay the entire speech.

Then Fred Gray arrives. I yell out to the growing crowd that he was Rosa Parks's attorney when he was just twenty-five. His presence is riveting. The crowds press in around us to introduce him to their kids. Cheers go up when he speaks. I'm suddenly hosting a parade of civil rights legends. I feel as if I am living history with them, standing in Times Square when the troops come home from battle. My mother used to always say she fought back against racism because America is better than that. I stand with this crowd knowing she is right. The crowd reflects America's new face. I see white people and black people huddled together behind unbreakable smiles listening to me talk about civil rights history as common history. Some pasty-faced guy named Jim snakes through the crowd with his flip cam and he lures me into recording us together, dancing against the wind on the icy Mall. So many people are stretching their arms into my live shot to take pictures it's hard to concentrate, but I can't complain. They all look so happy to be joining me in this bitter cold.

Brad calls and tells me he wishes he were there with the kids. Hours fly by. Brad keeps watching and calling. I wish I had my family with me. I want them to feel the cold air crackle with excitement, the coming together of so many different Americans on a day recalling great history. I am struck by how many people in the crowd did not support Obama during the election. This is not only about Obama; it's about what it means to elect a black man in an election where race was not the issue. I want my kids to experience this moment so they can tell their own kids about this day.

America is about to keep a promise it made of equal opportunity without regard to skin color. The content of our character is on full display. On this same lawn, people greater than us dreamed of overcoming bigotry. Now a black man is about to walk into the White House through the front door. I can hear the excitement in Brad's voice and everyone I talk to, regardless of race or background. This is the America I celebrate.

Barack Obama used the civil rights movement as a springboard for his candidacy. "I am running for president right now because of what Dr. King called 'the fierce urgency of now,'" he said. "This moment is too important to sit on the sidelines." Whether he can keep the implicit promise won't be clear for many years. He is young, low on political experience, serving

America as it faces an oncoming recession, two wars, and a lack of faith in government. Today he gets credit for having won the race, for being the black man who broke through. To this crowd, that is thrilling enough.

One day pushes into the next. People begin to fill the lawn before the sun even rises. They are heavily bundled. They shake from excitement and cold. They sneak around the barricades and fill the Mall, making little huddles until the spaces between them fill up and they become a vast blanket of humanity. I leave my hotel at seven a.m. to walk a few blocks to the Newseum building. I am supposed to be on the roof next to Anderson Cooper and Wolf Blitzer by ten a.m. I have three hours to go six blocks but there are now nearly two million people pressing toward the Capitol. I have waited too long. There is no way I'm going to make it there. I am going to miss anchoring the inauguration of a U.S. president, a lifetime opportunity for a journalist.

I walk a few steps into the crowd. This sea of humans consumes me. I get jostled, dangerously, from one place to another, going nowhere, turning back, pressing ahead and turning back once more. I introduce myself to the crowd. "Hi and excuse me, I'm Soledad O'Brien from CNN and I need to get to that building." The response is stunning. Person after person does a double take. "It's Soledad. It's CNN. Let her through. She needs to be there. Let her through!" There are mostly black people in the crowd. One by one, they push me through. For nearly two hours I make slow progress through this massive assembly. I am propelled by pure excitement. I'm suddenly at a rock concert, the Super Bowl of politics. "It's Soledad from *Black in America*! Let her through!" People shake my hand. They snap our pictures together even though we are squeezed so tight we can't move our arms. Then they push me along. It's almost as if the show can't start until I reach the anchor chair. It is insane and more thrilling than any red carpet I've ever walked.

It takes me over two hours to get to my seat next to Anderson and Wolf Blitzer. They look at me like I've cut it a bit close. David Gergen sits to one side of me. He has advised four presidents, representing both parties. He says the crowd looks like Mardi Gras in January. He can't believe the pep rally atmosphere they've created for a stiff inaugural event.

Obama's inaugural speech is not about breaking racial boundaries but about new challenges to our country's tradition of "hard work and honesty, courage and fair play, tolerance and curiosity, loyalty and patriotism." He tries to credit his successful rupture of America's ultimate racial barrier to our common good. The divisions in this country make it essential that he be right.

"This is the price and the promise of citizenship. This is the source of our confidence—the knowledge that God calls on us to shape an uncertain destiny. This is the meaning of our liberty and our creed—why men and women and children of every race and every faith can join in celebration across this magnificent Mall, and why a man whose father less than sixty years ago might not have been served at a local restaurant can now stand before you to take a most sacred oath."

The president being sworn in is the child of one white and one black immigrant, just like me. It's a commonality I don't think I'd absorbed until just then as I was watching it happen. It seems unlikely, but I don't really think of him or myself as being mixed race. I see him as another black man who may have felt like he didn't quite belong in any camp. That's the mind-set that a life-time of exclusion creates. Now he's standing up there as a symbol of having breached this great divide.

The timing coincides with my chief objective as the reporter of *Black in America*. I spent my last year fueling dialogue about race. He is a booming voice in that conversation. He has drawn attention for discussing a topic many politicians avoid. No one wants to say the wrong thing. His candidacy has sparked a com-plicated dialogue about the state of race in America and Ameri-can racism. It allows us to consider the possibility that perhaps we are pushing past our history of racism. It frees us to consider class as the emerging divider, to consider that many white people haven't exactly had anything handed to them.

The crowd erupts the moment he closes and cannons explode in the distance. The United States has completed a respectful change in government during a very trying time. I sit up on an outdoor perch with my colleagues wearing suits under our wool coats because it is so bitterly cold outside, and we intone about what it all means. But in the vast crowd below us, and the line of Republicans and Democrats assembled by the podium, the meaning of this ceremony is clear. We are embarking on a new era of American history. We move on with cautious optimism that we are about to back off on our nose-to-nose confrontations over race, and consider the option of simply talking to each other. That's if we can all heal our wounds.

The complaints that I'm not black enough to report *Black in America* live mostly in blogs. You can find them if you hit the for-ward arrow a few times on a Google search. The site Fresh Ex-press: The Pulse of Young Black America criticizes CNN for not picking somebody blacker. "The same station with nary a black woman in any on-air position of substance. There's no black female Rachel Maddow on CNN. There's no chocolate Campbell Brown. Hell, not even a ghetto Greta Von Facelift. And no, Soledad does not count."

A site called the Secret Council of American Negroes posts pictures of me, of the actor Wentworth Miller, my colleague Suzanne Malveaux, and the major league ballplayer Grady Sizemore. We are praised for not trying to "pass."

Thestudyofracialism.org displays pictures of my kids and begins a debate over whether they are black. Then on Zimbio.com a blogger called Black Snob adds this to the debate:

> Can Soledad O'Brien embrace blackness while not looking black, not "sounding" black and not being married to a black man? Can she embrace it with blond, blue-eyed children? Have the rules of blackness changed, or are we still playing the same psychological mind games we've always played when it has come to race in America? I often say in America you are what you look like? But if you look white but call yourself black, what are you?

Black in America was a clear assignment. Mark forty years after the assassination of Dr. Martin Luther King Jr. by doing a documentary. Answer the questions: How far have we come? Where are we not making progress? The goal was never to examine the whole black experience. We were to tell the stories of a handful of people. Look at the impact of Dr. King's death on the community as they were coming of age. We chose some people who were wildly successful and others who were terrible failures. What did their lives say about opportunities for African-Americans? Have they been able to leverage those opportunities? The fundamental question at the center of the documentaries is, Where are we?

Yet suddenly I'm answering questions about me, just as I had much of my life. Was I black enough? No one was asking Christiane Amanpour, who was born in Iran, if she was Asian enough to cover China. I was neither surprised nor particularly annoyed. I got it. There was concern that if I wasn't from the community, I might not get it.

One big fear I had was that the story of black America would seem depressing and sad. It's undoubtedly the case that some of the stories are depressing and sad but you can't only tell stories that are outlined by statistics. There is a way to nuance the story so that the community is fully represented. Michael Eric Dyson is extraordinarily smart and articulate and is also one of the happiest and funniest people I know, even if this one personal story is heartbreaking. There has to be a way to present stories that is not simply either/or—that can't be reduced to good news/bad news, happy and sad. These elements coexist. This was the perspective I was supposed to bring to the documentary. That's what made me black. It was important I reflect that in my work, convey that sensitivity to the viewers.

Michael Eric Dyson and his brother say their lives were separated by the shade of their skin. But Everett was dealing heroin in his own neighborhood. He wasn't sticking it to the man. He was peddling dope to black children. He is serving a life sentence for murder. Whether or not he killed a man, he certainly made bad choices. He said that to me when I pressed him. Yet there is no denying his skin color is an issue. Light-skinned people get preference. I remember the photo store where the guy asked:

"Excuse me if I'm offending you, but are you black?" It was pretty clear then that skin color makes a difference in the way you are treated. He wanted to know if we were black before taking our picture. Ultimately I have had to learn to navigate this minefield, and I believe there is value in my perspective that is different from what another reporter might bring. I did this piece because I love highlighting the story of Everett and Michael and their two paths to unveil one reality of black life. But I also know that prejudices over skin color are our reality, not our excuse.

The big surprise for me about skin color is that it matters so much to black people. I am not afraid to be criticized. The feedback has been overwhelmingly positive and wallowing in self-pity has never been my strategy. I learned back in San Francisco that people don't have to like you. You can be successful even if no one wants you to succeed. But I refuse to just dismiss people telling me that I'm unqualified to be black. I want to understand the anger. The president is mixed race, yet he gets to identify as black. Except for when someone makes a point of telling me he is biracial or "as much as white." I don't know if they're revealing his true colors or finding a conversation starter about my own.

I find it funny. I grew up with people who never thought of me as white. I was so different from everyone else. I had an Afro. It seemed as if I wasn't attractive to them. I didn't fit. Now here I am supposed to be proving I am black! But I was a teenager back then. Now I am a grown-up. I get to have a clear view of who I am and where I'm from. I get to be more than just a skin color; I can be the sum total of my life experience. I can embrace the community where my soul lives. I report on Katrina; does that make me any more black? I report *Black in America*; does that make me more black?

Black is not a credential; it's not even a skin color. African-

American culture is so much more than that. I feel like it's important to say "I'm black." I'm proud of my roots. I am a bit Irish, too, by way of Australia. Should I not say that? I am certainly Latina. Latino is an ethnicity, not a race. Latinos can be of any color from any place. I can be Latino and also black. So why can't I have a father from Australia but be black when my mother is black? People looked at me all my life and saw black. And, I am thoroughly proud of the black I am.

I host big screenings for the *Black in America* documentaries the summer before the president is inaugurated. I love the questions. The crowds love the stories. I get such hardy applause. But every now and then I am asked why I tell the sad stories. Why do I tell stories about poor people? Why the piece about the former drug addict? Why the guy who gets a degree in jail, then commits another crime after he is released? I recite the statistics on African-Americans and crime, incarceration and poverty. I stress that good reporting is about showcasing the range of stories that make up the black experience. I point to all the stories in the documentary about successful black people. The family at the center of my documentary is firmly upper middle class. The people attending their black family reunion came from solid homes with children going off to school, but the bottom line is I am a reporter, not a public relations specialist. I can't do a documentary about a community facing so many obstacles and not report about struggle. People in the audience applaud when I say that.

I tell them that there is an implication in American society that black people don't share American values. I would never do anything to contribute to that myth. I want to show the face of a community where character counts. I know folks don't only want to hear sad stories, but there is much to learn from failure; there are many lessons in challenges.

I begin to report *Black in America 2*, focusing on African-Americans finding solutions to pressing community problems. The conversations over the documentary have helped me understand why some people attack me for not being black enough. If I am black and I launch a discussion of social ills in the black community, then someone black has said we have a problem. If I am a white person, I am just the enemy once again putting people down. That is easy to ignore. There are some people who just need me to be white. That way what I'm saying won't count. I can be the enemy, too.

CHAPTER NINE

LATINO IN AMERICA

I enter the Latino Inaugural Gala right behind J.Lo and George Lopez. I wear a floor-length powder blue gown with tiny sleeves. J.Lo's dress begins at her chest, a deep blue gown pinned together with a big sparkling brooch. The red carpet is a sea of Latinos with standout outfits. There is no Hispanic ball so this is what passes as Latino night at Obama's inauguration. We follow each other into Washington's elegant Union Station as Spanish-language reporters ask us, one by one, when there will be an of-ficial Hispanic inaugural ball. It's what passes for an issue when there is nothing else to grab.

I pass the media scrum. I enter a big side hall reserved for celebrities and press. Applause breaks out as each of us walks in. "Soledad! Soledad!" the crowds yell out. Women grab me. I get pulled in for a kiss on the cheek. A few people talk to me in Span-ish. I can understand them but I don't have enough confidence in my Spanish to say much back. No one seems to care about my marginal Spanish. Latinos always claim me. That's the wonderful big tent of America's Latino world. As long as you or any ancestor has a "Maria" or a "Jose" sandwiched someplace in your name, you're in. Because Latino is an ethnicity, not a race, we get to be black or white or anything in between. Latin America is full of people who are half African or part German Jew, indigenous to South America or mixed with Chinese. Spain may have contributed the dominant culture, but Latin Americans are somewhat of a stew.

"Latino" is what happens once we all arrive here—the U.S. experience of tearing off roots from those twenty-one countries down south and joining them to American culture. Latinos are happy to include you, even if you're half something else. It suits us to play a numbers game. We have a deeply vested interest in being many. Our numbers ensure that we are the inevitability of "American" culture. We are the majority minority now. All minorities combined will comprise the majority by 2032. That is why I have insisted my next documentary project be *Latino in America*.

The chatter of two languages creates a happy hum in the room. I enter a roped-off VIP zone and J.Lo and Marc Anthony begin to offer me suggestions of ways to cover Latinos. We huddle in conversation as photographers snap and shout toward us. The faces in a Latino crowd are remarkable. Marc Anthony's skin makes his dark eyes stand out. A photographer leaning toward him has a thick Afro and black skin. I strike up a conversation with a cocktail girl whose sloping cheeks and almond skin could be stamped on a coin celebrating indigenous people. There are blonds, or wannabe blonds, with my husband's sea blue eyes. The range of ages here is distinctly Latino; when there's a glittery party, everyone gets to go. A child squirms around on a grandmother's lap. Teens huddle around fake cocktails looking big in their formal clothes. George Lopez, a Mexican American, and his Cuban-American wife shower me with story ideas and jokes.

George takes the stage to announce that we have just elected our first Latino president. After all, Obama is moving his mother-in-law into the White House. The crowd laughs. There is some excitement for the new president. But no one in this room is arguing that a black president necessarily guarantees good times for Latinos. There is a presumption that their enthusiastic voting for him will pay off, but nothing feels certain.

The community is at a difficult moment. A majority of Latinos, as well as a majority of everyone else, tells pollsters that Latinos have become America's most derided subgroup. A lot of Latinos have achieved personal wealth and newfound influence; they are enjoying an opportunity to choose between assimilation and remaking American culture all their own. But so many more are mired in poverty, stuck in failing schools, coping with immigration challenges, and struggling to adapt their values to a new home. The shared border means that immigration has never stopped. Latino is the one community that is constantly replenishing itself with cross-border newcomers. That means the entire community is often viewed through the prism of the immigration debate.

To illustrate the rising tension in the immigration debate we travel to a place much closer to the Canadian border with the United States than the Mexican border. Shenandoah, Pennsylvania, might be 1,800 miles from our southern frontier, but the issues surrounding the death of Luis Ramirez were as raw in Shenandoah as if the town sat in southern Arizona. As illegal immigrants from Latin America have moved into towns outside of the Southwest, the debate over their presence on U.S. soil has moved with them. The irony of Shenandoah's situation is that it is a town, like so many American towns, that was built by immigrants. In Shenandoah's case they were Eastern Europeans, who came to the area to dig out the anthracite coal in the late 1800s. The town grew to be a thriving community of 30,000 in the twenties but when the mines closed, this town born of immigration almost died from migration. The 2000 census counted 5,600 residents, a 10 percent drop from 1990. When we were there, the town often felt empty, on the brink of dying completely.

Shenandoah is a town withering from a lack of people but is at war with what newcomers there are. Not that it's a new phenomenon for an established immigrant group to be resentful of the wave coming in behind them. But Latinos' perpetual border crossing and tough economic realities seem to have combined in some heads as a toxic mix. There are towns like this all over the country that don't want anyone new. It doesn't matter if they take the most menial jobs, or even if they create new ones. The people who are already here don't want to see newcomers filling up empty housing if they are going to live ten to a room and gather outside. They don't want them overpopulating the schools, stressing out the teaching staff by learning English late in life. They just don't want them.

A young man from Mexico named Luis Ramirez ran headfirst into the pushback one night on a street corner in Shenandoah. Luis had come to Shenandoah from Mexico to look for work. There were plenty of jobs for him in Shenandoah despite the high unemployment rate and dearth of businesses. He picked cherries and fixed roofs and odd-jobbed his way through nights and weekends. Luis met Crystal Dillman, a local girl with a young biracial kid who lived mostly off public assistance until Luis came around. They had two children together and were planning to get married, which would in time have changed Luis's immigration status from undocumented to legal. The night of July 12, 2008, Luis was walking across a park on Vine Street in town with Roxanne Rector, Crystal's younger sister, when they were confronted by six white teenagers, football players from the local high school. One of the six tells Roxanne to get her "dirty Mexican boyfriend out of here." There's a scuffle. Luis walks away. Then witnesses report the teenagers began yelling "Mexican" this and "Spic" that and "eff you" as if the F-word itself is unseemly even in these circumstances. A fight breaks out—six against one—and Luis goes down under a barrage of punches and kicks. As he's on the ground, Luis's head is kicked repeatedly. Luis Ramirez never regained consciousness and was declared dead on July 14. The police report spelled out the motive: "Get your Mexican boyfriend out of here." The death was tagged a hate crime.

Crystal Dillman tries to teach the kids she had with Luis some of the few words of Spanish she picked up from him. I saw her trying one afternoon in the small white house she had shared with Luis. I speak a little Spanish to my own kids some days. Sofia and Cecilia take Spanish in school and a friend's babysitter tutors the twins at home. My mother never spoke Spanish to us back in Smithtown. She said it was because my dad didn't speak any and she wanted us living in the here and now. I want my kids to live for the future. When my grandmother came to live with us it was awkward because all she could say in English was "Hello" and "Bye-bye." We absorbed our *abuelita*'s presence not through conversation but through what she did. I loved to watch her stirring big pots of black beans and painting her long nails fire-engine red. I drank in her warmth. She smiled and laughed even if she didn't understand us. She was chatty. She lived to be surrounded by friends and food and music. She was a spark of life in our quiet little American suburb. *Abuelita* was our living link to Cuba, to the cacophony of that other place. It was sad when she ended up in a nursing home where no one spoke Spanish. None of the other patients or nurses could talk to her.

It was odd that my mother never taught us to speak better Spanish. She speaks three languages fluently and was a Spanish teacher, a woman who told us from the get-go that being black and Latinos was half of our immigrant stew. My mother was our cultural standard-bearer, the boiler of our rice. She enforced a strain of discipline and encouraged a social attitude that was deliberately Cuban. We learned that family came first, to mind our manners, to feel *pudor*, humility, even if we couldn't say it—to be aggressive but never to act aggressively. These are common denominators in Latino homes in our country. Things the most profound assimilation plunge cannot erase. Humility is the firmament upon which our unending cultural heritage was built. Family ties are what ground us. In some homes we connect through language; in others just by the way we use our words.

My home in Smithtown seemed so regular at the time, but in retrospect it was unmistakably Latino in nature. We heard our mother talking on the phone to distant relatives, in a voice she rarely shared with us. It was the voice of cultural connection, the language for who she was. She would always count in Spanish, balancing her checkbook of American dollars in a quiet math in *Español*. We ate rice every day: rice with chicken, rice with pork, rice with stew. She would occasionally plunk down a plate of boiled potatoes and indicate they were for our father. Otherwise, the food was a constant boil of rice. We learned to make *churros* and ate black beans and rice with our turkey for Thanksgiving. There was *carne asada* and *picadillo, natilla* and *flan, sofrito* from fresh peppers. But it's tough to keep those cultural ties when you never get to travel back home.

Cuba was our moment of disconnect. Until I was an adult, I never went. Even though it is ninety miles from Florida, Cuba is like some far-off island, a place you cannot go. What we knew of our culture we learned in our home. I am jealous of all the Latinos who grew up with a lifetime of vacations down south. They got to touch home base, to taste the food and culture of their ancestors, to understand the impulse of the journey to a different life. The infusion of this wonderful Latino culture was forever being renewed. They would come home flush with memories and souvenirs. I felt like my world opened up when I first went to Cuba. The visit made sense of so much of our life in Smithtown, from the vats of rice to the flotilla of happy children that were the center of every conversation. Seeing their poverty I understood why my mother left. I also saw the richness of their lives and know a part of her will never really leave.

I always wondered if my father deferred to my mother's Latino household because he knew she couldn't go back. She had to preserve her culture here.

Dad could take us back to Australia, and he did. Australia was the land far, far away, of lengthy plane rides and long stays. One of our visits lasted for so long that my little brother Orestes was born there and my siblings enrolled in school. Going to Australia taught me so much about my father. I remember traveling there when I was fourteen. My father's family was having a big reunion in his hometown in Queensland in a tent set up on a big lawn. My dad made sense there, surrounded by legions of relatives. I met my part-Japanese cousins, the part-Greek cousins, several who are part Italian. There was nothing odd in his family about marrying outside your clan. My father's people are all about big, colorful families.

We stayed with cousins who had seven boys and two girls, one for every age of ours, with some to spare. Their house was rambling, large, and open with lots of land to roam around. I played with a sea of O'Briens, all of our connected kin. Barbecue smoked in the background of every party: big slabs of meat and plentiful bread to go with it. We toured the family business, Defiance Milling, where the bread was made. Dad came alive in Queensland, chatting with his brothers and sisters, visiting with family and friends who wanted to meet his children. His accent sounded too American in Australia but people got his jokes. I made an embarrassing faux pas when I asked for a napkin and everyone laughed because it means sanitary pad in Australia. Now we're the ones with the funny accents. My father and his family did not see skin color; they saw people. A different nationality was a cause for celebration and exploration.

My father's family also practiced the kind of Catholicism that preaches a high measure of social justice. My father's twin brother is a priest; two sisters are nuns. His own life philosophy calls him to embrace the people standing right in front of him, to not pick and choose. That was clear in the way he and his family related to each other and everyone around them. When you look past people's complexion, you see their spirit. You get to meet a rainbow of humanity. His brothers and sisters and cousins were all like him, ready to give themselves to the vast world and all the different people in it. That's what the immigration experience meant to us, embracing new things and reaching out to new people.

Back in Smithtown, Mom and Dad decided we were to identify as black Latinos, prideful, studious, driven, and directed.
There was a hint of defiance in that, but mostly it was pride.
Though outside our home it was hard for us to talk in Spanish
or of Cuba or Australia or being Latino. Having any kind of immigrant identity out there in Smithtown was tough. I didn't know
other Latinos much less Australians, no one with whom we could
share traditions or explore our roots. We only knew the black
families we joined for barbecues and playdates. We were fortunate that immigration issues played no role in our lives. Anyone
can come from Cuba; it has a favored status because of the Com-
munism that took root after my mother left. My mother had no
barriers to coming to the United States; in fact, she sponsored
my father's visa, which also came easily. They were not escaping
something as much as they were moving toward something else. I
knew that my mother's family wanted to come here and couldn't.
That was a consequence of Fidel Castro's Cuba, not the United
States. But we didn't suffer the indignities and disappointments
of fighting for our immigration status.

I didn't suffer from being considered from someplace else; I
just didn't fit in to the place where I was. They'd catch me calling my mom *Mami*, which sounded a lot like Mommy, and tease
me in the halls. Outside that, Latino was something that didn't
really register. We kids had enough issues with skin color. People
focused painfully on our race; the color of our skin distinguished
us from everyone else. It was the thing burnt most indelibly into
our consciousness. Adding Latino would have only provoked a
"whuh dat" from the other kids.

I see Angela Cinqmani flash by in the halls of our high
school. I look toward her with a knowing smile. She was an outsider in the school, too, and somehow her presence gave me an

odd comfort. She is Latina; I am certain of it. And even more on the fringe than I. She is seriously chesty with all these deep curves, big black hair, and fragile eyes. Unlike me, she doesn't rush past a thing. Angela isn't like my shy friend Shevoy and me. She is all about confrontation. She shuts down her adversaries. She has a smart mouth and high spirit. There is something wild and racy about her. I have this image of her lancing into these big guys in the hallway like she was engaging in a fair fight. I sometimes wish I could break my trajectory and harness that kind of energy, stand up for something in the high school hall. But I rush past her, moving steadily forward. It's hard to want to associate yourself with trouble when your own positioning is at risk. She is in the thick of it, courting danger; I am racing by.

The trial in Shenandoah unfolded as small-town community dramas often do, in a bubble. The prosecutors, defense attorneys, witnesses, and the young men on trial all lived minutes away from each other, on the inside. The only person referred to as an outsider was Luis, who lived on the street where he died along with his girlfriend and three children. Brian Scully testified that he had known Derrick Donchak since they started playing Little League in the third grade. They played every other major sport together and shared a common history, a community pride. The high school teams were nicknamed the Blue Devils; the athletes were the Devils' pride. In Shenandoah it was unusual to date outsiders, particularly if they're black or brown. Crystal already had a baby with a black guy. Now this. Twenty years ago there were 504 white kids at the local high school, according to the U.S. Department of Education—and that was it. In 2007, there were 461 white kids, 12 African-Americans, and 56 Hispanics. Still, the town was described in 2009 as being 97 percent white and two percent Latino, hardly a deluge.

Inside the courtroom there was talk of murder and motive. Outside there was talk of immigration and outsiders. Latinos were coming to town each day and finding work. We met residents who told us that Latinos were taking jobs but at the same time they couldn't identify anyone they knew who had lost a job to a Latino. It backed up the research we were reading, like the 2008 study from the Kaiser Family Foundation that asked U.S. workers earning less than $27,000 whether they thought illegal immigrants were depriving legal U.S. residents of work. Nearly half said they did. Yet 80 percent of the same people reported that hadn't been affected negatively by illegal immigration themselves. Of course this is completely contradictory—both these things can't be true. But there is this sense of something being stolen but not what it is. There's a pattern here—better education, better jobs, less fear of immigrants. That's the story of working-class conflict.

I met many people in Shenandoah who ached for these kids, even as they conceded there was no excuse for this vicious murder. Brandon Piekarsky was a National Honors student who was on the varsity football team as a sophomore and worked part-time at Sears; Derrick Donchak was the Blue Devils's quarterback planning on attending Bloomsburg University that fall; Colin Walsh was a straight-A student who ran track and played football.Later Walsh would be the only one to express remorse and plead guilty in the attack. These young men were not so very different from so many young men I'd known back in Smithtown. They were remarkably average. They didn't know anyone Latino very well. They just felt someone had to be held responsible for so many frustrating things. At the trial, the boys had to testify against each other. Brian Scully, who was tried as a juvenile, and Colin Walsh, who pleaded guilty, both took the stand. The courtroom was never very full. Administrators from Shenandoah Valley Junior/Senior High School attended the trial to make sure none of the students was there, threatening to ban kids who went to the trial from graduation. Crystal Dillman sometimes went along with Gladys Limon, a lawyer from the Mexican American Legal Defense and Education Fund (MALDEF), a prominent Latino civil rights organization.

The trial described how the teenagers came across Luis and Roxanne on the street. Brian Scully told Roxanne, who was thirteen at the time, that it was late for her to be out. Luis answered in Spanish and Brian told him to go back to Mexico. Within seconds Luis is down on the ground. Colin Walsh testified that Brandon Piekarsky kicked Luis so hard when he was unconscious on the ground that his shoe came off. An out-of-town police officer testified that Luis's face was swollen and that he had a shoe print on his chest. Richard Examitis of Lost Creek Ambulance said he found what he described as "an assault victim." He was unresponsive and had "snoring respirations" and Luis never regained consciousness; he never reopened his eyes. It was said in evidence that Luis's brain was so swollen that it oozed from his head.

I go on a speaking tour after *Latino in America* airs. I have just released a book of the same name and schools are dying to hear my insights on Latinos. I speak at Hotchkiss shortly after the documentary is released. Hotchkiss is a private boarding school in Lakeville, Connecticut, with just under six hundred students, very diverse, yet with a traditional prep school affect. The lawns roll out into a golf course and fresh-faced kids hang out in khakis and button-down shirts. My screening is held in the main auditorium. The black and Latino organization invites me but the entire school is welcome to attend.

The room of teenagers looks entranced as they watch the stories of Latinos, rich and poor, enjoying great moments of triumph and terrible moments of hardship. The segments are interspersed with video shout-outs. Latinos of all backgrounds talk about their *quinceañeras*, about their family's flight from war, about the way their mother embarrasses them when she speaks in Spanish. The videos are funny, depressing, inspiring, and the stories that come afterward flesh them out.

A girl whose parents bring her to the United States as a child is arrested by the Border Patrol as an adult. She is raised fully American and has an American child of her own. A Venezuelan chef in Miami opens up a chain of restaurants and remakes the cultural landscape. I can tell there is excitement in the room.

Then they watch the segment on Shenandoah. A town is torn apart by the death of a young man. The story quiets a room full of anxious teenagers. Luis's picture flashes on the screen, beaten and bloated, near death. The town looks like any failing town, the kids like any kids.

Applause breaks out at the end. The lights come up. Hands are raised and questions come. I love the enthusiasm for the stories. How did you pick your stories? Why did you do this series? One kid with thick brown hair, a handsome athletic young guy, asks a question that is more of a statement about his opposition to illegal immigration. He is angry. He challenges me for not making enough of the fact that Luis was in the country illegally. He is angry that the Luis Ramirezes of the world are even here. He looks to be about fifteen years old and he is fuming.

I pause but I am not surprised. I keep waiting for the moment he is going to talk about his father losing a job to an immigrant but it never comes. The mood in the room has shifted slightly. "Why are you so angry?" I ask. I tell the audience this story is as much about murder as immigration. It's as much a story of a community in conflict as it is about why they are so upset. There is some part of me that doesn't understand his anger over the immigration debate. I have no dog in the fight. My parents' immigration experience most closely matches that of the Shenandoah miners. They came here legally, looking for opportunities. I understand the competition over jobs, the complexity of the economic debate. I see the obvious need to find solutions. I also know that race plays a heavy hand. Yet I still don't understand the rage. I look at this totally healthy, good-looking, privileged kid and just don't get it. He is at a prestigious private boarding school, a place where everyone is college-bound. He has nice clothes and food and rolling lawns to play sports, a battalion of friends, and a family making a sacrifice for his happiness. Yet he is fuming over a dead undocumented immigrant who used to pick cherries on some faraway farm.

His is just the kind of anger that leads to shouting that leads to nowhere. I don't understand how we can have a discussion about immigration or any other policy in this country if we are so angry we can't listen to the other side. Talking and listening are what builds consensus. Shouting is just a bunch of noise.

The Shenandoah trial centered on whether Luis Ramirez's death was the result of a fight gone awry or an attack, possibly with racial motivations. John Redmond, one of the six, said the boys had met up in a garage at Brandon's house. A police officer was there with the mothers of Derrick and Brandon, none of whom has ever spoken publicly about the events. The aim was to get rid of references to the racial slurs and the kicking of Luis. And also to the fact that the boys had been drinking. Brian and Colin said Derrick arrived in a Shenandoah police cruiser driven by Shenandoah police officer Jason Hayes, who is identified as the boyfriend of Brandon's mother. Officer Bill Moyer is also in the car. The boys talk about getting their stories straight.

At one point there is a suggestion from the defense that Roxanne and Luis were having a secret affair, and the story line becomes that the teens were imposing their moral authority. Roxanne even admits to it on the stand. Her sister Crystal doesn't believe it was possible for her little sister to be having an affair with her boyfriend who worked seventeen-hour days. And would that have made it okay to kill Luis? Then the MALDEF lawyer Gladys Limon discovers a picture on Facebook of Derrick at a Halloween party wearing a shirt with a legend on it reading "Border Patrol." There were three groups in the courtroom as the case went to the jury: the press, the teenagers' supporters massed in the center, then three people representing Luis Ramirez—Gladys Limon, a lawyer from Philadelphia who had come to keep her company, and Enrique Luis Sanchez, an official from the Mexican consulate. The jury got the case on May 1, 2009, a day when marches and rallies were held across the United States protesting for immigrants' rights.

The verdicts in the Shenandoah case came late at night. Brandon Piekarsky and Derrick Donchak faced decades in jail if convicted of murdering Luis but as the verdicts came—"Not Guilty." "Not Guilty." "Not Guilty."—the cheering drowned out the tears of Gladys Limon, the MALDEF lawyer. To Limon fell the task of calling Luis Ramirez's mother in Mexico to tell her the news. Piekarsky and Donchak were convicted of simple assault charges and corrupting minors by giving them alcohol. It turned out there was one holdout on the jury—the foreman, Eric Macklin—but the jury vote, 11-1 for an acquittal, came after two hours of deliberations.

Crystal Dillman was an outsider in Shenandoah even before she had met Luis. After he died, she lost her job, and Crystal was unhireable in that atmosphere. Even her own family stopped talking to her. She was holed up in her apartment through the trial, and now she locked her doors to avoid the people who chose to greet the verdicts by celebrating, driving through town with horns blaring like the local team had won a big game. There was a T-shirt that had been seen around town: "Fuck You, Crystal. Your Day Is Coming." Crystal would later start making plans to leave Shenandoah. Luis's mother wrote the judge a letter from Guanajato, Mexico. Luis was working to support his mother as well as his own family. He was undocumented—she knew that. "They killed a human being who was my son," she wrote. "I believe no one deserves to die like this simply because he was Mexican."

CHAPTER TEN

A Voice in the Debate

I wake up one morning at home and I feel as if I'm about to snap. I jump out of bed and fall into my clothes. I kiss everyone, head out. I rush off to another day of hair, makeup, coffee, airplanes, car rides, and questions with no answers. I'm exhausted. The spring and summer of 2009, I travel seven days a week. I make a speech, show a clip, go to an interview, huddle with my producers, fight, complain, nag, praise, and eat on the run. These documentaries are a massive undertaking. There is just one me and there are a dozen stories unfolding at once, each with a producer and photographer in a different place, a different airport, with different demands. I can't escape, but I am on the run. My feet ache. My back is stiff. I yawn constantly. My hair is wilting so I pull it back into a tight ponytail and slick it back. I am so tired from running but I can't bring myself to stop.

I feel so different from when I started at CNN. It's as though I'm not reporting stories anymore, but rather have been launched on this incredible mission. In the America where I was raised, I felt invisible—a light-skinned black girl in a white town. Now, my America is a kaleidoscope of people. I have permission to turn and turn the wheel and see all the different ways we can see ourselves. But I have to get it right.

In 1968, the National Advisory Commission on Civil Disorders, the Kerner Commission, once blamed bad media portrayals of the black community in part for fomenting riots. Black people on TV were too often depicted as poor, troubled, violent—as outsiders. That image affected how they were treated. Now brown is fast becoming the new black. A 2009 study by Pew Research Center found that Americans of all races believe Latinos face more discrimination in this country than any other ethnic or racial group. The National Association of Hispanic Journalists does surveys of how the networks cover Latinos. The biggest news is that they don't much cover them at all, except in a negative light. I want to do better. The U.S. Census is predicting that a quarter of the U.S. population will be Latino by 2050. The pressure is insane. I really have to get this right.

But in the midst of reporting *Latino in America*, an angry public debate erupts about whether CNN is using my work as an apology for community complaints about another anchor on the network, Lou Dobbs. Lou's is primarily a talk show of opinion and debate. He does not report straight-ahead news like the other anchors at CNN. And, he has a long-running series called *Broken Borders*, attacking illegal immigration. Latinos represent three-quarters of the country's approximately 12 million undocumented immigrants. Lou is a broad man, imposing, with a swath of brown hair combed perfectly into place. He jumps out of the screen and his booming voice gives him a certain gravitas. His earlier reports on NAFTA and the working class sparked lively debates. At first, his reports on immigration have that same oomph;

they are incisive, even scholarly. He speaks before the National Association of Hispanic Journalists in 2007 and gets some applause. But his tone changes and escalates over time. He doesn't just oppose illegal immigration; he calls it an "invasion" and gives voice to groups that are accused of vigilantism. Even when big news might be breaking elsewhere, his show often headlines with our country's immigration crisis, with a tight focus on Mexicans.

"Good evening, everybody. Pro-amnesty senators and the Bush White House tonight are struggling to sell their so-called compromise on immigration reform to both Congress and the voters," he says on Saturday, May 19, 2007.

"Opponents of that compromise say it would give amnesty to up to 20 million illegal aliens while doing virtually nothing to secure our ports and borders. But the supporters of the deal say it's the best chance we have." The show delivers five stories on immigration that day. Dobbs has a piece on a hole in the border security fence and another crediting immigration with a rise in leprosy. He then engages in a rancorous debate with two of his guests.

At first, a parade of Latino leaders debates him on TV. Eventually, most of them stop appearing on his show. They complain that his tone encourages xenophobia. They denounce him publicly. His report fuels the national immigration debate. He becomes a figurehead for anti-immigrant groups. He is the Harvard-educated founder of CNN Financial News, so his credentials give weight to opponents of illegal immigration. Two organizations are launched to ask for his head: Drop Dobbs and Basta Dobbs.

By the time *Latino in America* is in production, Lou has moved on from the *Broken Borders* campaign. The economy is spiraling downward. There is a new president. Lou reports on the "birthers," people who believe Obama wasn't born in the United States. This is Lou's new focus. The launch of my project has nothing to do with him. I lobby to do *Latino in America*. I had come off the heels of *Black in America* and wanted to turn the same eye toward Latinos. CNN is years into a very successful editorial effort to diversify viewership, reach new audiences. They give me the green light. I start to research and find a common theme. Latinos are dream chasers, a varied people breaking roots with twenty-one countries and three languages in search of a better life. I feel like I'm making some headway. But as soon as I begin shooting, Lou's opponents turn their attention to me.

"Unfortunately for O'Brien, her colleague Lou Dobbs has so angered Latino activists and bloggers that her quality work is at risk of being ignored," says blogger Kim Pearson.

"Will movement to remove Lou Dobbs overshadow Soledad O'Brien's *Latino in America* at CNN?" asks the headline in the Examiner.com.

"We believe that Lou Dobbs is the number one pusher of anti-immigrant hate and that has poisoned the environment for immigration reform," says Carlos Fernandez, a community leader in Chicago Now. "It's a good series. It's important and necessary. But four hours on the contributions Latinos have made is not enough to counteract what Dobbs is promoting."

Our *Latino in America* Facebook page poses a question: "CNN's Soledad O'Brien journeys into the homes and hearts of a minority group destined to change America. Is it the ultimate clash of cultures or the ultimate melting pot?"

The Latino author Adam Luna reacts on the Huffington Post: "CNN seems to have already answered the question. Airing about 260 hours of 'culture clash' TV every year, and just a couple of hours to tell the story of Latino families who are a vibrant part of the American experience."

The whole thing makes me queasy. I get excited every time I see articles talking about my project, then I realize they're really about this controversy. I can't get out in front of it. I feel like I'm standing in a field waving a flag in hopes of getting everyone's attention. I feel as if my effort is never going to get a chance to stand on its own. Latino community leaders are eager to spread the word about *Latino in America*, their opportunity to get wide-ranging coverage on national TV. They want to promote my work. They lavish awards on me and ask me to speak at their luncheons. But they can't resist the opportunity to talk about Lou Dobbs. He may have moved onto other stories, but they are not done with him. People used to thank me as I took the stage at community events. Now community leaders apologize as they stand to make a comment. "Soledad, I love your work," they say before hijacking my event. Their strategy is clear. They praise me and support the documentary, but they seize this chance to vent.

A central figure behind much of the organizing is Roberto Lovato, a former journalist who has emerged as a commentator and community leader. Roberto is one of those guys who are always smiling even when his rhetoric sounds angry. He can kill you with a friendly question. He has the shaved head, goatee, and bespectacled look of an activist.

"They [CNN] think that a few hours of serious reporting on Latinos by sunny Soledad O'Brien can make up for thousands of hours of anti-Latino extremism from the dark Lou Dobbs," he says in his columns. He keeps demanding meetings with my boss. At some point, we begin airing promotional videos for *Latino in America* and Roberto immediately hijacks them, does a reediting, and releases them on the Web. There I am on camera, all hair and makeup, with my multicultural smile:

"This October CNN will take an unprecedented look at Latinos in America. We have so many stories to tell," I say. Then brilliant bold letters flash across the screen: "BUT CNN HAS A PROBLEM." All I can think is, no, actually, it's *me* that suddenly owns this so-called problem! My promo has been intercut with Lou's voice repeating over and over again the words "criminal illegal aliens."

"Criminal illegal aliens are in the country including many murderers and rapists," his voice says. The video ties Lou's support of anti-immigrant patrols like the Minutemen Project to rising hate of Latinos, and even brutal attacks. There is a clip of Lesley Stahl on *60 Minutes* challenging the facts of his report that border crossers have caused an increase in leprosy.

"I can tell you this, if we reported it, it's a fact," he tells her. Lesley insists: "You distort the figures, you exaggerate." Then he faces off against the ultra-liberal Amy Goodman, who points out that he repeatedly says a third of prisoners in the United States are illegal aliens. Lou says he "misspoke." "Mexico has become our enemy," he says before a hail of images shows verbal and physical attacks on Mexicans. Then the video is done with him. But it is not done with me.

"Soledad understands," the narrator says, and they pull a clip of me making a commencement speech at a college graduation. "The worst thing you can do," I am telling a crowd, "is do nothing and say nothing and not act when your voice is needed." The whole thing makes me feel ill.

Lou doesn't take any of this sitting down. He says nothing on CNN, but on his radio show he calls Roberto a "bozo" and a "joke," a "delusional" liberal activist. "I'm just a dog and you're one of my fleas," Lou says. ". . . And the fact is, you wouldn't be accusing me of anything if I were supporting illegal immigration and amnesty, and you're not even man enough to admit that straight up. You are a typical left-wing activist coward propagandist, trying to use the Constitution that enables all of us to have free expression, trying to deny my rights."

I choose not to engage in the debate, either publicly or in print. My best contribution to a debate over the best way to cover Latinos is to cover them well.

"Occasionally at screenings I get asked a question or two about Lou Dobbs," I tell an interviewer at *Latina* magazine. "But you know, in my mind, going into this documentary it was the same as every documentary I've done. It's me. It's my voice. I'm fully one hundred percent responsible for the content of it. That makes it great for me, because I feel like my voice is really what you see and then sometimes it's scary 'cause it's my responsibility to make sure that these things turn out well. I think that, outside of the fact that we both went to Harvard, Lou Dobbs and I don't have a whole heck of a lot in common. I don't look to anyone else who works at this company who's not on my production team to be informed by anything. That's just how we do it."

Lou and I never discuss any of this. He never mentions my documentary or me in public. He is a complete gentleman the one time we run into each other in an elevator. I don't really know what to say.

I travel to Los Angeles to promote *Latino in America* before an audience of community leaders. I sit at the end of a long table with two personalities from our documentary, Lupe Ontiveros, a Hollywood actor who has played the Latino maid numerous times, and Edward James Olmos, whose productions put Latinos on center stage in film and theater. Ontiveros is this warm, delightful personality who squeezes me tightly every time she sees me. She is a ball of energy who could more appropriately be cast as a television aunt. She told me from the first time I met her that she recognized what I'd be up against trying to tell Latino stories. She has suffered a career of breaking ceilings. Her support and her fast smile mean so much to me.

"It'll be okay," she says numerous times. "Stick to your work." She is a star in the documentary, full of pride and promise, urging Latinos to not take anything sitting down. We sit there as the documentary plays. It wraps to ferocious applause. Then we begin a question-and-answer session. At first there are outsized compliments. The discussion is going well. Then, out in the audience, I spot a smiling Roberto Lovato. Lupe looks at me and rests her cheeks into the palm of her hands. She flashes the smile. Roberto goes on for a bit but the headline is clear: How can CNN launch a documentary called *Latino in America* and still air a nightly show attacking Latinos? The applause is thunderous. I pause before I respond.

"I think the strategy for me as a journalist has been this: To do good journalism and speak for people who want to support it. And follow what we do. I guarantee you that if people will watch our documentary and say, 'This is what we would like to see, fair and accurate reporting, storytelling of things that we have not seen.' At the end of the day it's about big numbers and people watching and someone will say, 'Wow, so there's an audience for important nuanced reporting, not puff pieces on people, but nuanced thoughtful reporting on everybody in every category.' And, guess what, that sends a very big message. I guarantee that. That's sort of always been my strategy on every story I've ever reported. To go and do good journalism. And what I've discovered is good journalism in the end wins out—it does. And people have to vote with their clickers."

That is all I ever say about Lou Dobbs. I say it again when we prescreen our material in New York and Georgia and at schools around the country. I say it at parties and events. I refuse to lose time on a debate about whether his reporting has fueled or furthered a growing divide in the immigration debate. That is for others to dispute. I have my own perspective to contribute, my own job to do, and I am going to do it if it kills me. And it just might.

My mother and father never talked to us much about their immigration. They looked forward, not back. Dad is the youngest of eight; Mom is one of five. They are the only ones who left. Dad is clear on why he left Toowoomba.

"There was nothing much going on in Toowoomba," he says. "It meant 'swamp' in Aborigine terms." Back home, he and his family had never even met an Aborigine, much less someone black. "The people there didn't know anyone to be racist to," he says. They had no reaction to him marrying my mother because they had no idea what reaction to have. He didn't even think of moving her back to Australia with him.

"When I met Estela, that made it easy to stay," he says. They got married just as Castro overtook Cuba. After that, Mom couldn't and wouldn't go back either. America was suddenly their home, their future. America was an unwelcoming place for a mixed-race couple, but it is a land of many options. Maryland had plenty of black people even if they didn't always treat them right. "I was too busy to tangle with the legal authorities," my dad says. "We couldn't eat in the white places, though the black places always let us eat there. I figured she was a good cook so we'd just eat at home."

Dad sees the racism as this annoyance, an inconvenience, and a shame on his adopted country that he alone cannot erase. He doesn't understand it. He just avoids it. My father has always had a gift for taking nothing personally. He is slow to anger, always calm. Rarely have I seen him mad. He was shocked to confront such a harsh reaction here.

"There is this stupid view of the whole racial problem," he says. He found Maryland a hostile place to interracial couples, but didn't pay it much attention. There were plenty of black people there, many folks in the same situation but he felt like there wasn't much he could do about it. He took a job at the College of Engineering in Stony Brook, New York, out on Long Island. He chose to move us to Smithtown for its proximity to work and good schools. It seemed like a place where his kids could prosper, but he didn't take my mother when he went to visit real estate agents. He likes to avoid conflict and he was not naive. This was the best town for his young family to live, but he didn't believe anyone would sell to someone black.

The only African-Americans on Long Island were slaves until after the Revolution. But slavery was shorter-lived than it was down South, ending entirely in 1827. Most of the blacks became day laborers or domestics, just like the Latinos of today. They established communities in the 1900s in places like Sag Harbor, Amityville, and Setauket. Some even married the Native Americans for whom the towns were named.

By mid-century, nearly every town had a suburb where the people were predominantly black. It wasn't until the period when my parents arrived that there began to emerge a black middle class. There wasn't the economic opportunity to form one. By moving to this nearly all-white section of Long Island, my parents became immigrants once again in some respects. They are new-comers in a foreign place, trying to find a way to fit in.

When Dad arrives in Smithtown, he tells the real estate agent his wife is black. There is no reaction, but he doesn't see any homes he likes. Then the agents introduce him to William Reed Huntington, a rich, progressive Harvard-educated architect with a big piece of land right near an inlet to the Long Island Sound. Bill Huntington is a pacifist and a devout Quaker. My mother and father like him a lot. Bill directs a camp for conscientious objectors in rural upstate New York. He spends his time with legendary civil rights activists who are white like him. My father remembers Huntington's stories about sailing on the *Golden Rule*. He and the crew used the boat to protest atomic testing in the South Pacific in 1958. They are arrested as they approach Honolulu. The confrontational act inspires future groups like Greenpeace. On Long Island, he takes a tract of land and builds a meetinghouse for the American Friends Society.

Huntington has a small house and rents it to my white father, black mother, and their growing mixed breed. Two years later, he sells them a large parcel of land where they can build their own home. "He sold to us at a good price," says Dad. "There was a lot of distance between neighbors and he was this big deal, out protesting things. So he built this little area with a Quaker house and us, reducing his own property." Dad built us a house on the land with a big green buffer from the rest of Smithtown.

Bill Huntington continued to travel the world fighting an array of injustices as my parents raised their mixed-race kids on his land in Long Island. Bill Huntington passed away in 1990. He was an activist to the end. At his fiftieth Harvard reunion, he implored his classmates to seize the opportunity to change the world for the better, in whatever way possible:

> I always get very excited and nervous attending powerful theater. As I take my seat for the final act, I cannot imagine how the author is ever going to make it come out right. But in my heart I know that it must. Somehow something or somebody will turn the tide. The grandchildren will live; Harvard and the world will go on. But in today's reality we are not just audience. If we are to applaud with joy and relief when the curtain falls, we shall have to help with the script and play parts on the stage, too.

America's history is full of people like Bill Huntington, who refuse to leave the world as they find it. Their touch is often light, but they make a difference in the way they touch life. The land he sold my father made it possible for us to grow up in storybook America. He made it possible for me to report stories about race. Bill Huntington's decision forty-five years ago is still paying dividends today.

"It would have been impossible for a black person to buy a home there," my father says. Impossible. Dad had no "rhetorical stance," as he would say, on the race issues blossoming around him. He was too busy building up the local university to be very political. He just wanted a place for his family to live. He wasn't the type to dwell on Smithtown's housing segregation. What he took away from the experience of our move was that Bill was a good guy. That is the America he introduced us to, a place where the kindness of a single stranger can change everything.

The Smithtown where my parents built our home was full

of descendants of Irish and Italians and Jews, some who would travel back to explore their roots. It makes no sense that they would have trouble with someone different. This nation doesn't naturally give you the option of living in a bubble. Our democracy forces participation in the world outside your community. You can't win in America without building bridges. We have public parks and public schools and public transportation that constantly force us to find new commonalities with total strangers.

That's what should have happened in Smithtown. Smithtown's resistance to things like Section 8 housing did more than rob a few folks of the opportunity to get access to better housing and good schools. A whole community was robbed of the chance to grow. We were supposed to be going to school with kids from a diversity of incomes and racial and ethnic backgrounds. Yet my family might not have even been there without a guy like Bill Huntington to make it happen.

My dad appreciated the impact this move would have on his family. He wasn't very political, but he felt his kids needed to make a statement of some kind about their race. It didn't matter that their father was white; they were to identify as black.

"I didn't have to go around telling people I was white," he says. "It was more important for them to say they were black." It meant something for us to stand up for ourselves, to embrace the identity others might scorn. That is one way in which my parents' immigration experience played heavily in our lives. They had not walked away from their provincial roots to see their children reduced by small minds. America gives you the option to redefine your world, to reclaim an identity that has fallen in disfavor. They had come seeking a chance at a different life, a place that affords them the opportunity to express their true self. They hadn't traveled across a vast sea, giving up their culture and severing family ties, to be told they don't quite fit in. Dad predicted that children like his might change the world, that education and pride and perseverance would take us forward.

We were to define the posture of the newcomer. We were to stand upright, proud of our race, and build an identity as achievers. The goal was to do so well that people looked past their prejudices and met you in a common place. That is the challenge of America, a country that is made up of so many moving parts. Immigrants arrive to ethnic enclaves and often choose to hyphenate themselves. But if we push past our differences we have the potential to become one America. The hyphenated identity—Italian-American, Pakistani-American, African-American—can be something to celebrate and explore, not something that divides us. We have the option to build coalitions with each other, to join together to face common problems rather than to fight over scant resources. We don't need to put other people down so we can feel big.

Years after we'd all left Smithtown, our area of Long Island would be torn apart by a debate over new Central American immigrants. I had no dog in this fight. I'm American born, and I'm a journalist who is accustomed to analyzing every debate from many sides. My parents had no immigration issues, nor do any of my relatives, even though I certainly know people whose lives are affected by their immigration status. So I am saddened by the acrimony but try to preserve my objectivity on the issue by keeping a distance from it. It is hard for my immigrant father to do the same.

"It is depressing," my father says. "The whole issue seems completely absurd to me, to treat people separately. I have no tolerance for how those people are treated. There needs to be a clearer policy, sure, but I don't see any reason for the reaction." He is an immigrant from a country whose relationship to U.S. immigration has always been friendly. His accent has mellowed. He has lived in this country for more than fifty years and he looks exactly like any retired professor on any American campus might look. All of that doesn't matter to my dad. These immigrant newcomers were just like him and his kids, people in search of opportunities to join the American family, if only given a chance.

The day that Judge William Baldwin sentenced Derrick Donchak and Brandon Piekarsky, he told them that illegal immigration was not the issue in his courtroom. A group of young athletes had beaten to death an unarmed man. The young men had no way of knowing whether Luis Ramirez was in the country illegally. The penalty for crossing the border illegally is "deportation, not execution," the judge said. But all he could give them for their assault conviction was seven to twenty-three months in jail. Colin Walsh, who pleaded guilty for the same crime, faced nine years in jail. He had the potential to be free in four if he cooperated with authorities.

Judge Baldwin tried to divorce the sentencing from the immigration debate raging outside his courtroom. What was happening inside the town of Shenandoah was altogether different. On the one hand there were people like Lou Ann Pleva, a former newspaper reporter whose grandparents had come to this country from Germany and Poland. Lou Ann had moved away from Shenandoah to raise her family and then come back. She believed the death of Luis Ramirez was more about ignorance of the outside world—a world she had experienced—than simple racism. Lou Ann worked to heal, helping out with a rally for the community, but she faced considerable opposition to her call for introspection in the wake of the attack.

She was out on her front porch one day, talking into our cameras when suddenly her neighbor Jaelynn Mackalonis emerges from her house. She is brimming with anger. She is a local bartender. She feels like the controversy around Luis's death is tainting her town. She waves her arms and whistles loudly, until she gets our attention. "We just want to let you know, the neighbors around here, it's not fair that one person is going to speak for us," Mackalonis insists. "This wasn't a racial crime." We roll tape on her, too, in an effort to get her perspective, but what we get is a window into Shenandoah's conflicts.

"I'm sorry; do I know you?" Pleva asks.

"I don't care if you know me or not," Mackalonis answers. "Do not say this town is racist."

"I didn't say that," Pleva says.

"Don't speak for anyone else," demands Mackalonis.

"I promise you, I don't," Pleva says.

"It's putting Shenandoah on the map for being a rotten town. It's not a rotten town," Mackalonis says. "I talk to people, and it's, 'Oh, yeah, you're from Shenandoah, where that illegal immigrant got beat.' Get your story straight before you go babbling anything," she tells Pleva. "If he wasn't here illegally, I think it wouldn't have happened."

Pleva doesn't understand her neighbor's anger toward her. She believes she is only trying to make sense of a tragedy. Our team made a dozen trips to Shenandoah. Each time we heard an alternate theory for why Luis died. Mackalonis raised the possibility that he was raping Crystal's little sister. She speculated that drug dealing was involved. My team of producers encountered many locals who blamed new Latinos for a spike in local crime. The police said there was little evidence of that. The most common scenario for what happened between Luis and the young men was that it was a fight that got out of control. Pleva insists the facts have been blurred because of an underlying anger in Shenandoah where 20 percent of the population lives below the poverty line. They feel the need to blame someone for what is happening to the economy in Shenandoah. Why not hate the people whose economic outlook appears to be looking up?

Derrick and Brandon's sentencing on simple assault and alcohol-related offenses didn't remove Luis's death as a center piece in the debate over the state of Shenandoah's soul. The pair had barely served out their sentences when a federal grand jury charged them with a hate crime for fatally beating Luis while shouting racial epithets. Both young men and most of Shenandoah's tiny police department were also accused of scheming to obstruct the investigation of the fatal assault. A conviction could send both of the teenagers away for life.

Shenandoah Police Chief Matthew Nestor, Lieutenant William Moyer, and Police Officer Jason Hayes face charges of witness and evidence tampering, and also lying to the FBI. Moyer and Hayes were the police officers allegedly coaching the boys in Derrick's garage the night of the attack. The three of them could serve twenty years in prison on each of the obstruction charges and an additional five years in prison for conspiring to obstruct justice. The indictment charges that the Shenandoah police were engaged in corruption even before Luis's death. Chief Nestor and Captain Jamie Gennarini allegedly extorted cash from illegal gambling operations from 2004 to 2007. Then they obstructed investigations of the scheme. They are even accused of holding a man hostage in exchange for cash.

By the spring, the two young men are living under house arrest and the police officers have resigned. One of their subordinates is made police chief, over the objections of a town board member who is the father of one of the officers. A bilingual Latino war veteran is elected to the town board in a first-ever show of political integration in Shenandoah. On May 5, downtown Shenandoah is festooned with piñatas. The Latino community comes out to play music and dance beneath broad sombreros with their kids. The Cinco de Mayo festival is sponsored by the local senior center at the Legion Memorial Park. A mural is being painted of flags of many countries. One of the senior centers even makes cupcakes iced with the colors of the Mexican flag. The Heritage Parade of Nations is scheduled to be held as always during the summer of 2010.

The furor over Lou Dobbs escalated, as CNN got closer to the *Latino in America* airdate. A small but vocal band of protestors marched in a circle outside a few of my screenings. At others they wore buttons begging CNN to "Drop Dobbs." The funny thing was that they'd stop protesting to welcome all the CNN people when they'd arrive at events. They were almost embarrassed to be disrupting my party. They kept telling me how much they loved CNN. They asked me for autographs and pictures. This clearly wasn't about me. They were upset because they didn't expect a news organization like ours to tolerate an anchor whom they heard as a one-note song.

I rarely was able to watch Lou's show during the peak of his immigration coverage. When I was an *American Morning* anchor, it was on at exactly the hour I got to spend with my four kids every night before going to bed. Then I was flying around reporting on ethnic and racial minorities. I knew what the show was about. I understood the uproar. But the thing that stuck with me most about the Drop Dobbs movement was not the impact of the show that went on every night. It was the frustration of people who felt voiceless. Lou Dobbs was the only person covering the impact of illegal immigration regularly. Whatever you thought of his views and how he expressed them, it was a platform on an issue of great importance to people of all races and ethnicities. If you had something to say about immigration, there was no other place to turn. The folks who agreed with him looked thrilled to have a stage. They were deeply angry over how illegal immigration had affected their lives. The people who disagreed with him could either subject themselves to confronting a master debater on live TV or have no voice at all. A full 40 percent of Latinos are foreign born; the immigration debate is a life-changing issue.

Latino in America was not just an opportunity to go after a TV anchor. It was a chance to get heard. That is what is so vital about preserving everybody's avenue to express himself or herself in this country. Change only happens where there is open public debate. When we put our heads together, we find solutions. I have yet to hear anyone defend our current immigration system as intelligent, right-minded, or humane. We're not getting anywhere by letting one side shout at the other. We're just creating a nation of young people, like that kid at Hotchkiss, who can't quite articulate what he is so angry about. This country has seen its share of nasty First Amendment battles, but this was not about free speech. We now have more ways to express ourselves than ever before with triple digit cable channels and the exponential growth of Web sites. The problem is not that people have no place to talk; it's that no one is listening. The flow of information is overwhelming and the quality is underwhelming.

Lou is one of a handful of TV people who ensured it was impossible to ignore them. His style and delivery were magnetic; his rage and lopsided debates were provocative. The conversation wasn't getting anywhere, but people were listening. At first his opponents just wanted in; ultimately they also demanded equal time. They wanted to be heard.

Latino in America, just like *Black in America* before it, was an opportunity to hear from everybody, to explore issues with nuance. That's why people could picket Lou but say emphatically that people also had to watch *Latino in America*. They weren't going to give up a chance for visibility and voice. Latinos had been some of the biggest fans of *Black in America*. They wanted their own program.

· CHAPTER ELEVEN ·

ONE CHANCE TO SUCCEED

I finished the main section of my book *Latino in America* with a fervent wish for one young woman I had met on my journeys for the documentary. "For her but also for all of us," I wrote, "I desperately want Cindy Garcia to graduate." Cindy Garcia was a seventeen-year-old senior at Fremont High School in East Los Angeles when I met her and she was about four weeks from graduation. I liked Cindy a lot and she was saying the right things about staying in school. But I knew she could go either way. Cindy was under tremendous pressure at home, working long hours to help out her sick single mom. Still, I was hopeful the support she was finding at school would get her over the finishing line.

Graduating high school is the minimum standard you must achieve to make it, the first predictor of future success below which the odds can be grimly stacked against you. In this economy, you need a diploma just to work in a fast-food restaurant. Over the course of a lifetime, high school graduates make on average $300-, $400-, $500,000 more than nongraduates, depending on which study you look at. (Of course, these figures escalate dramatically for college graduates and post-graduates.) In this country, you can't slip up when it comes to education. It's a deal breaker. The person who goes far without a good education is noteworthy, an exception, an asterisk in the American dream. Yet the Pew Hispanic Research Center reported in 2010 that 41 percent of Hispanic adults twenty and older have no high school diploma (versus 23 percent for black adults and 14 percent for whites).

The devil for a lot of Latinos in this country is that they often seem to get just one shot at success. If they trip, they fall. There is a large population of Latinos facing so many social ills that one mistake, one lost opportunity, one failure brings them down. It starts with the public schools. I travel to Los Angeles to take a firsthand look and arrive in time for an explosion of sunlight and violet flowers, the signs of oncoming spring in Southern California. I can't walk through any urban corner of this state and not think back to my days in Oakland, when pushing past the images of urban blight promised glimmers of true beauty. East L.A. bears itself in colorful walls of graffiti dedicated to Latino urban legends, growling serpents and bleeding hearts, thorny flowers and messages of hope. This is the town of *Stand and Deliver,* with its storybook promise that any lowrider can become the next math whiz. Yet Latinos have the highest dropout rate of any ethnic group, 22 percent versus six percent for whites. Some of the worst schools are graduating no more than 30 percent of the student body on time.

I visit Garfield High, where Jaime Escalante (who died in 2010) famously tutored students to pass the Calculus AP exam. The hall floors shine of floor wax and attendance is at 90 percent. The classrooms overflow with students but they are quiet and orderly. Garfield is one of the five largest schools in the United States. Garfield reflects all the overcrowding challenges facing L.A.'s schools. Portable classrooms have overtaken the parking lot. There are three daily shifts of class to accommodate everyone. The school year is short seventeen days even though classes are taught year-round to fit everyone in. They have neither found enough space nor enough money for all these kids. At the end of the year, no more than half these kids will graduate on time. California is number one in the country in funding prisons and dead last in funding schools.

I have come to East L.A. because *Latino in America* needed to shed light on what a huge number of Latino teenagers face in getting a good education. Their destiny is our national destiny. Half of all of the nation's students will be Latino by 2050, 84 percent of them U.S. born. Since 69 percent of all U.S. Latinos are of Mexican descent, the kids in this massive California school system reflect our country's future.

Latino kids, according to the Pew Hispanic Research Center, are most likely to attend schools with the country's worst student-teacher ratios and highest overcrowding. More than half of all Latinos are attending the largest public high schools in the nation with the poorest students. In California, 40 percent of Latinos go to large high schools full of economically disadvantaged people. From bottom to top the signs are ominous. Latinos represent one in five preschoolers yet they are the least likely to be in Head Start. Later on, they are absent from math and science classes, missing from Gifted and Talented programs; nearly half spend time learning English even though most were born here.

Language and how we use it have always been a deal breaker in this country. We are resistant to living a life in two tongues. The early immigrants came from so many places that foreign languages were reserved for ethnic ghettos or your kitchen table. English was less than a generation away. Latinos changed all that. They preexist the border. There was always Spanish being spoken in parts of the United States: the Southwest, South Florida, pockets of big cities and all of Puerto Rico. So the language took root when even more Spanish speakers came after the border was drawn and redrawn. Our shared border means that Spanish speakers will continue to revitalize the language even if the rising tide of immigration reverses course. A whopping 44 percent of all Latinos report being bilingual. The number of Spanish speakers concentrates in such huge areas that in many places it is easy to never speak a word of English. The language dominates the culture of places like Miami and L.A.

America prospers most often when it embraces changes rather than resists them. Yet it angers people of all backgrounds from coast to coast that so many Latinos have not learned to speak English. It doesn't matter that studies by the Pew Hispanic Center say that most Latino children will speak English by the time they are adults, even if their parents speak only Spanish. But the sheer numbers of Latinos struggling with the language in the schools sap resources and exacerbate conflict. Nearly half of all Latino children in U.S. public schools are learning English for the first time. Seventy percent of all Latino schoolchildren are speaking Spanish at home. L.A. spends about $8,000 a student yet is still laying off teachers and increasing class sizes. There are English teachers facing classes of 43 challenging kids, PE classes with 70 students, and guidance counselors "guiding" 650 students. People can burn with anger that an entire community seems disassociated from our nation's common language, but that won't get better with numbers like that.

There is something about the halls at Garfield High School

that makes it surprising that not enough learning is going on. The students seem so quiet and orderly, respectful and focused. I greet so many of them that day, my first of many visits to American high schools at risk of failing their students. There is nothing separating the Latino kids in this building from the white and black kids I meet in other places. They all need the building blocks to succeed.

Steven Perry, a Connecticut educator, built from the ground up a school that defied the odds. He did it with a racially mixed student body and faculty. I spent some time with him at Capital Preparatory Magnet School near Hartford. He walked the halls, pushing students to wear the school's official sweatshirt and keep the noise level down. He told kids to go to another school if they didn't see themselves as college bound. His is in one of the lowest-performing districts in the nation, yet he has a nearly zero dropout rate and sends everyone off to a four-year college. His key is setting high expectations for every student. No one is supposed to be at the bottom. No one is supposed to fail. He believes that the key to making it possible to succeed is making everyone in the educational process accountable for results—including the teachers and the students' own families. That means not accepting that something as intangible as the "system" is responsible for all the ills facing kids in public education. There has to be a point where the blame falls squarely on the shoulders of individuals, not systems, if even to hold people accountable for not expecting and demanding more than they are getting.

What maybe makes some Latinos different is that they live in a culture that venerates the family. The family is our way out, our backbone, our strength, the driving force behind our education and subsequent success. So perhaps it is the family that holds the ticket to helping Latinos overcome the challenges our schools throw in their way. I see how families propel kids to success, how they fight to get their kids into the best schools, fight to improve bad schools, fight against bad educators and budget cuts. They also have the power to establish high expectations, or not. I had two parents who were teachers. It went without saying we would learn. They both came to this country for the opportunity to study. That we studied hard is a logical by-product of that journey.

But studies show that a second generation away from immigration, Latinos lose touch with that commitment to learning. I won't allow my kids to do that, but I also have the luxury of sending them to excellent schools. These families fight not just the battle of teaching their kids the value of learning, but the fight to improve their schools. The world seems so out of their control. All they can provide is a basic family structure, the building blocks for perserverance and self-esteem, key ingredients to succeeding in school. But, as Perry might say, they have to at least do that. The moment family fails, or breaks under the pressure of the world around it, the kids almost certainly get lost.

I like Cindy Garcia the moment I meet her. She is seventeen and is friendly and enthusiastic. I meet her outside John C. Fremont High School, which is near Garfield. Her eyes are speckled and she is wearing typically Californian clothes that all seem to be made of T-shirts. A tiny ring pokes through her lip. Although she has about four weeks to go before she gets out of high school she is dangerously behind. Cindy forces smiles for me every time I ask a question, her optimism pushing through an obvious sadness. We are buffeted by the many urban stresses that haunt her life. Traffic chortles around us. Her school building explodes with the sound of too many students. Planes and helicopters thunder overhead. An occasional police car siren announces the pursuit of another crime.

Cindy notices that it's a pretty day, even though she is separated from success by thirty credits of school. She studies twelve hours a day plus Saturdays trying to catch up. She is quick to admit that she first fell behind because she skipped school so much in the ninth grade. She looks at dropouts working minimum-wage jobs and has her regrets. Her own sister got pregnant as a teenager, but Cindy still has hope.

Our country is full of kids like Cindy who keep pushing ahead despite facing ridiculous obstacles. Cindy's high school, Fremont, only graduates 29 percent of its students in four or five years. The school has three thousand students too many. Outside school, the rates of drug use, gang membership, and teen pregnancy exacerbate poverty. Cindy has sidestepped all those problems so far and she's still on track. What she can't avoid is what is going on in her own home. Her mother, who is from Guatemala, has lupus. Her father is from Mexico, his whereabouts unknown, as they have been for years. Her stepfather is in detention for something to do with an illegal handgun. Between attending her mother's doctor's appointments and her stepfather's court appearances, she practically works a part-time job as a translator. She also has to run the family store—a clothes and shoes store—when her mother cannot. She babysits for her sister's child and a cousin's three kids. All those things pull her from school on a regular basis.

Cindy's family lives life on the brink. Her mother's home, car and business are all being threatened by the banks. The whole day, Cindy races around like a fireball of energy, but she still misses her elective classes with regularity. When she gets home all she wants to do is sleep but there's always some job she has to do.

Her best hope is her school counselor, Marquis Jones, who remains ever hopeful, finding ways for her to make it, letting Cindy work in his office between school sessions. His own job is threatened by budget cuts, but he keeps focusing on Cindy. Just when Cindy needs a helpful voice like Jones's, L.A. cuts the $10 million Diploma Project, laying off nine thousand employees and depriving thousands of at-risk teenagers of counselors like Marquis Jones. He is spared, but he is doing a lot more work.

Cindy's route to opportunity lies through graduating high school but she is never in a position to put herself first. She doesn't feel that she can tell her mom she needs to be in school because her help is needed by so many people so much of the time. She's trying to blaze a trail but she has more resposibilities than any seventeen-year-old should have to bear. But what Cindy does next brings her efforts to a crashing halt—she gets pregnant. The father is her boyfriend, a twenty-five-year-old man with brown eyes and dark short hair and prominent black eyebrows. He is a nice guy. He helps in Cindy's mother's store. He watches the other kids. But this is the last thing Cindy needs. Her family has run out of money to pay for her stepfather's lawyer. They eventually lose their car and their business and are so far behind on their mortgage that they will soon lose their house. And Cindy misses making her graduation credits because she is home nursing her morning sickness. A few months later she has her baby and hits the books again. It is daunting. She still has not graduated.

Latino in America airs in October of 2009, shortly after I publish the companion book. The reaction is mostly positive; people want more. A few folks complain that the stories are too grim. They are stunned to hear some of the statistics behind them. More than half of all Latinas are pregnant before they are twenty. Three-quarters of the country's illegal immigrants are from Latin America. The number of hate crime attacks on Latinos rose 35 percent in just three years. I have plenty of rosy stories about our sweet success, the promises of our family's cultural heritage, and the resilience of our faith. I tell people I do no one a favor by ignoring the challenges we face.

One thing is certain: I have given ample voice to the complexity of the immigration debate. We visit a church where I ask parishioners how devout Catholics can feel so distant from new immigrants of faith. I follow a girl who came to the United States as a child, only to be arrested and deported twenty years later, away from her American daughter to a country she doesn't remember. I tell the remarkable story of "Marta," who came to the United States as a kid hoping to reunite with the mother that left her as a child. She crosses the searing desert and floats across the Rio Grande in an inner tube, only to later be captured by Border Patrol. I adore her. She is just a kid. She doesn't know about borders or border issues. She just wants her mom.

Marta's walnut-colored hair often covers her big sad eyes, but she is a go-getter like no one I've met. She lands in immigration detention, a nice version of a jail for kids in Miami. I follow her story as she prepares for detention, only to be rescued by a kind-hearted lawyer Michelle Abarca of Florida Immigration Advocacy

Center. She finds a way for her to get a visa. A judge places her in foster care with an African-American woman. She is the kind of dream chaser that Miami has attracted for generations. As surely as the Cubans before her transformed that sleepy backwater into a cultural center, I'm certain Marta too will make her mark. She texts me sometimes and lets me know her grades. She is a ghost in the immigration debate—a striver, a dreamer, a kid who didn't know better. She is not here to take anyone's job or in defiance of the law. She's just a girl who wanted her mother. And when she couldn't find her, she made a life for herself.

About a month after *Latino in America* airs, Lou Dobbs leaves CNN. He says that being a journalist is no longer enough. He wants a shot at tackling the nation's problems and hints he might run for office. He later even tells a Spanish-language TV station that he supports creating a path to citizenship for illegal immigrants. CNN releases him from his contract so he can carry his "banner of advocacy journalism" elsewhere.

CNN creates a new unit for me after *Latino in America*. They call it In America and they staff it with fourteen people. The idea is to let me grow this concept of allowing voiceless communities a chance to speak. I also want to chart the journeys of marginalized individuals, to show them as people, not as issues or topics of debate. I pack my office and move to another floor where I can sit with my new colleagues. I don't find out until later that I'm actually sitting in Lou Dobbs's old office. I'm glad I never criticized him. Because now the pressure is on me.

· CHAPTER TWELVE ·

MISSION TO HAITI

Ο ne of the things about covering news is that you are constantly losing your footing. One minute nothing is happening; the next minute everything is coming undone. That's the way it felt on January 12, 2010, just a day after most of my staff is hired for the new In America unit. We feel slightly aimless and CNN is still searching for an executive producer to run the unit. The staff is working from desks that are set far away from each other, assembling boxes for our big move. The producers are brimming with ideas. Everyone is anxious about what this new assignment will mean. I have no idea what to tell anyone. I know we have an extraordinary opportunity, and that's good enough for me. I am excited about all the new communities we can explore: gays, conservatives, Muslims, women, and onward. Right now we're doing nothing. Then I walk through the newsroom just before 5 p.m. and everything suddenly changes.

The newsroom in the New York office of CNN on Columbus Circle is set up almost like a theater. There are rows of interconnected desks that all face a small stage area in the front with banks of TV screens. There are managers facing the opposite direction with the screens behind them. It looks a bit like Mission Control running a moon shot from Houston, except that instead of looking out over the launching pad the staff have their backs to the most spectacular view of Central Park you've ever seen. When a major news item rolls in over the wire service, a soft beep emerges from the terminals. Every head tilts down to read the wire, then snaps back up to see how quickly the network gets the latest news onto TV. This time the news is so big the beeps merge into a solid tone that is menacingly insistent. Eyes pop wide open and lips part. Then someone shouts: "We need crews!"

It's quickly clear what's going on. A massive earthquake estimated to be of magnitude 7.0 had struck fifteen miles west of Port-au-Prince, the capital of Haiti. Early reports say the damage is so intense that a plume of dust covers the city for twenty minutes. The size of the quake and its location mean there will be bodies. The poverty of the island means this can only be a major disaster—something along the lines of Hurricane Katrina or the tsunami in Indonesia, maybe even worse. Haiti is one of the poorest countries in the world; its government and infrastructure are already fractured. The country depends heavily on foreign aid, is patrolled by a UN peacekeeping force, and has suffered two major hurricanes in the last six years. The buildings are so poorly designed that a school collapsed all on its own in 2008 and ninety people died. There is no doubt in our newsroom that this will be a major story. CNN, more than any other network in the world, ignites when there is big international news. Everyone is on the phone instantly, trying to get us into Haiti.

The people on my fledgling staff are anxious. Our unit is called In America and the biggest story of the year is unfolding outside the United States. "This is CNN. When something like this happens, you need to be there. It's when people watch us most, when viewers count on CNN. It's why we work here," one of my producers tells me. I am dying to go. The newsroom duties just vanish at moments like this. I'm a journalist. I have a perspective on how to tell the human story that is unique. I won't go and do what everyone else is doing. I will add something more. I need to be there. But how am I going to get in?

At the moment no one is asking me to go. The focus is on getting Anderson Cooper and Dr. Sanjay Gupta into the earthquake zone. That makes total sense. Anderson lives to cover these disasters; his is the voice of immediate distress. Sanjay needs to be there because there is obviously going to be an enormous medical component to this story. They also have shows. I am the anchor of a long-form unit that is only twenty-four hours old. Getting me into Haiti is important but it won't happen instantly and I'm just chomping at the bit.

I grab my producers and we go from office to office. The bosses shake their heads as if to say, "We get it. Just hold on!" My associate producers call anyone they know who has any connection to Haiti. Reports stream in about the extent of the damage. The presidential palace is gone. The UN mission and the main cathedral are gone. The head of the UN mission and archbishop are said to have perished. CNN has this brilliant service called iReport where regular folks can e-mail photos and videos and help us tell a story when we're not there. The iReports from Haiti are stunning, streets full of bodies and rubble and people screaming and running around in fear.

The earthquake hit before most people left work. Children are still in many schools and stores are full. In the first hours of a natural disaster, figures on the number of deaths are wild guesses and are usually inflated. But this time, everyone in my newsroom shares that same sick feeling that the first estimates of a quarter of a million dead might just stick.

I go home that night and want to scream up at the sky. How unimaginably awful it must be in Haiti. I want to be there. I want to help in the way reporters can help. I want to spread the word of what the people need. Instead, I walk down the snowy streets of New York and text my producers about ideas on how to get in. I know the musician and humanitarian Wyclef Jean from my work on *Black in America*. He is probably the best-known Haitian in the United States and a man with a firm commitment to his home country. I reach out, hoping I can travel to Haiti with him. I try everyone I know with a plane or helicopter. At 10:00 p.m., Anderson goes live on CNN from New York with Wyclef Jean as a guest. Wyclef reaches across the anchor desk and offers to go in with Anderson. There goes that idea. I spend most of the evening fuming by BlackBerry to one person or another until exhaustion takes over.

By the next day it's clear CNN has beaten the other American networks into Haiti and commandeered one of the only habitable hotels. They are sending in a "flyaway" satellite dish and supplies. They are already sending back video via technology called a BGAN, a laptop with satellite capacity that allows you to compress video and send it. The live shots are a bit pixilated when reproduced on the air, but the roughness seems appropriate in this case. This is one of those moments when CNN's news-gathering strength on these stories is just remarkable. Anderson Cooper is the first American TV reporter coming live from Haiti. His reports are extremely disturbing. I can see that look in his eyes that I'd seen in the reporting from Indonesia and New Orleans.

There is an emotional line you cross as a reporter from feeling an embarrassing thrill at the magnitude of the story you are telling to experiencing a sinking feeling in the pit of your stomach. There is no thrill in this man's eyes. I know him well enough to see that he is shaken.

My frustration is taking its toll on my family. At some point Sofia says with exasperation, at the dinner table, "Somebody better send Mommy to Haiti." The only thing worse than a last-minute departure is no departure at all. As young as she is, Sofia's been around long enough to know there will be no peace till I go. I put my kids to sleep that night focused on how to get into Haiti.

A few days later, Rose and I visit the offices of our Senior Vice President of Newsgathering, Nancy Lane, a true news junkie who has been with CNN for many years. I make my case again. "Nancy, you know if you send us you're going to get stories no one else will think to do." She nods her head like I'm stating the obvious. Within twenty-four hours, another of our bosses, Senior Vice President of Programming Bart Feder, gives us a green light and urges us to focus hard on something no one else is doing. He wants us to come back with something special so the pressure is on. We are bound for Haiti.

We leave on a chilly New York morning loaded down with survival gear and enough bug spray to kill giant swarms of critters. We have a dozen jars of Vicks VapoRub. If you shove enough of it up your nose it can overwhelm the smell of decaying bodies. It's a trick photographers in Iraq have passed along. Rose and I had been told we'd pick up one of the photojournalists already working in Port-au-Prince. So it is just us and this wild plan to fly into Santo Domingo and drive overnight in a convoy carrying food and water and generators to our colleagues. No one is sure what the security situation will be and our guards look nervous. One guy keeps complaining that he'd been promised a weapon but didn't have one. Neither of us wants to drive so we hit the ground in Santo Domingo trying to find another way in.

The actor Vin Diesel had been on our plane into the Dominican Republic with his sister. They help fund a program for budding filmmakers in the DR and Haiti in coordination with the president of the Dominican Republic. They are going see if their young filmmakers have survived the quake. Vin is a handsome and muscle-bound action movie star. We met ten years ago when I was anchoring *Weekend Today*, and even though his films like *The Fast and the Furious* and *xXx* are meant for teenage boys, I am a huge fan. In those ten years he has grown into a major movie star, but our real connection is the color of our skin—he's a mix of something, too. We never discussed it.

Vin's sister falls into this category of people who use their association with the rich and famous to create and pass forward goodness in the world. She helps her brother establish charities and looks for people to help. She's delightful and gives her brother a bigger sense of purpose beyond making action flicks. The two of them decide they can help me get into Haiti—so they ask the Dominican president if his helicopters flying into Port-au-Prince might have room for two more. The action hero takes action. It's why I love this guy.

A few hours later we are in the air on a military chopper. One thing we learn quickly about Haiti is that it operates more on rumor than hard fact. Whispering erupts in a crowd and a mass of people rush forward even if they don't know what they're rushing toward. There are always reports on fresh incoming dangers, perceived and imagined. In this country it's always been somewhat like this; in the midst of a natural disaster, it is even worse.

We leave Santo Domingo with a flight plan that calls for us to make a stop in the border town of Jimani, where refugees are rumored to have amassed. But when we set down, the biggest commotion is from all the Haitian boys fighting to get Vin Diesel's autograph. There are international aid organizations coming through on their way to Port-au-Prince. A small number of injured Haitians have been taken to a hospital on the Dominican side, but there is not much else. We fly out over the road we were supposed to drive into Haiti on. It had been billed as treacherous, but as far as we can see it's paved and has little traffic. We smile at each other, unable to speak over the roar of the helicopter rotors. Maybe Port-au-Prince will be the same way. Then one of the Dominican pilots writes on a notepad *la zona*, the zone, and points up ahead.

I feel my mouth drop open to suck in air. When something is this shocking you need more oxygen to help you process what you're seeing. Port-au-Prince simply looks flattened. A thick layer of concrete dust hovers above the entire city. The silence coming from down below is disturbing, like the silence at a wake that will eventually be interrupted by a long wail. Nothing seems to be moving. Every now and then a clearing appears and a smattering of makeshift tents dots the landscape. The helicopter flies lower and banks so we can get a better look and take some pictures. The few people walking around don't even look up at the sound. It is like looking down on zombies. Tarps are strewn everywhere, covering mysterious mounds of things we can't see. You can make out people sifting aimlessly through rubble. So many normal things are missing—traffic, commotion, trees, lights, children.

There is so much cream-colored concrete with all its surfaces facing upward that the sun reflects off Port-au-Prince. The glare is blinding and I have to keep blinking my eyes to keep looking. I don't want to look. I have to look. I can't look. I look. I can't believe what I'm seeing. None of us in the helicopter can look at each other. I look down one last time before we land. Then I can't look anymore.

The Dominican embassy in Port-au-Prince has its own landing pad. I don't even want to think about the fact they have needed a private way to escape, given the history between these two countries. We are greeted there by multiple security guards and drivers hired by CNN. CNN doesn't know what to expect and they are ready for riots, looting, and violence of all types. From the moment we move onto the streets of the city, it's clear to me we're unlikely to see any of that. The people look shattered, sad, exhausted, not desperate or angry. There is not enough life left in anyone for violence right now. People are desperately searching for survivors in the rubble, collecting remains, and looking for places to sleep or get a drink of water. The streets that are open have little traffic. The air smells odd, not like human remains but of something unnatural and abnormal, like what you might expect to smell at an animal shelter. I'm wearing construction boots that look barely strong enough to walk these streets and most of the people have on sneakers or sandals.

The scene at the CNN workspace couldn't be more of a contrast. CNN descends on stories like these and erects a mirror of its offices back home. It's quite amazing. I often think all of us should go run an aid organization, provided we had the same resources. They have trucked in the necessary satellite equipment, a network of computers, generators, and gas and water, a mountain of supplies—everything from PowerBars to tampons. There are fifty employees camped out at La Plaza, an old Holiday Inn that faces a huge square where the massive presidential palace has indeed collapsed. There are not many other habitable places to stay and most of the network reporters are stuck in the airline terminals, reportedly upset that we've taken so much space.

Rose and I drop our stuff in a dirty room at La Plaza and right away venture out into the square to do a story on the emerging tent city in the center of town. All of Port-au-Prince seems to be living on the streets. There have been a series of aftershocks and no one wants to go inside, even if they have someplace to go. A big tarp stretches across trees just outside our hotel. Here, three men and a woman dressed in surgical gear are running a walk-up clinic with the barest of medical supplies. The place is packed with people but there is practically no noise. There is a young boy clutching a mangled toy. A woman lies on the ground nursing a horrific gash to her leg. No one seems to be crying. Their eyes express shock. A trash truck moves slowly past them overloaded with bags. Flies swarm around the patients' wounds.

It's hard to know what to even ask people that look so tired and beaten. What story do you tell here? What story can you tell? People look so broken. We are walking around with two body-guards, two translators, two CNN staffers, and a pair of pho-tographers testing a new 360-degree video camera. But we are not attracting any attention because everyone around us is totally and utterly lost in his or her head.

We walk deeper into the swarm of people because we're not sure what else to do. A hose dangling from our hotel offers free water and a long line of mostly women is collecting it in buckets to take into the crowd. Today seems to be the day every woman has decided she needs to clean off her kids. The children stand there naked and silent being doused by soap and water even though they are standing on dirty streets of rubble, trash, and urine. A few people have lit fires but there doesn't seem to be much cooking. Most folks are just sitting around corralling their children, who seem too scared to move. There is a man selling cell phone charges off a car battery. There are a few small groups of people surrounding badly injured relatives lying in the crowd.

We approach a woman tending to her father and suddenly the atmosphere shifts dramatically. The woman jumps up, startling everyone around her. She begins to yell at us in English, tears streaming down her face. "Someone must help us. What are we to do? Help us, anybody help us," she yells. Behind her a boy lying on the ground erupts into a spasm that looks like at epileptic fit. We yell over to one of our guards we think has medical training and he moves in to assist her as the boy calms down. As we walk out of the crowd, he looks half annoyed that we've involved him at all.

CNN reporters and producers are arriving at the most horrible moments and are being pressed to pitch in. Anderson's team has been in particularly difficult situations, arriving at collapsed buildings where people need help digging out, being stopped by people who need a lift to get critically injured victims to make-shift hospitals. Dr. Sanjay Gupta is grabbed by a man needing care for a five-week-old baby. We have arrived before any substantial amount of aid. There are a few instances where you feel like you have to get involved, even though reporters are supposed to remain impartial observers. This is one of those stories, which challenges the usual boundaries more than any I've seen. Everyone needs help. A country has been severely wounded.

I am astounded at how people in such catastrophic circumstances strive to maintain their dignity. On a patch of street, a woman spreads a blue piece of plastic and puts food in one corner, her kids in another, their clothes in a third. Then she sweeps the street around her. She is sweeping garbage in a neat square around her space even as they settle down in the middle of thousands of people, rubble and trash. This is her way of keeping order, sanity, and grace in the face of horror.

The people of Haiti are often described as resilient because they have weathered coups and terrible violence, poverty and miserable injustice. But what I am seeing today is what I saw at the tsunami and Katrina, human dignity on proud display, the gut-wrenching ability of human beings to press on in the face of tragedy. The cultures are different but the fundamental strength comes from the same place. There is no cavalry on the hilltop. Tomorrow may not be a better day; it may be worse. They have only themselves and their fellow survivors. They have the power of one. A home collapses into ten thousand piles of brick and a mother picks them up one by one until she finds her beloved child. A man can't find his wife but searches alone, without sleep or water, because he will be propelled by hope until hope runs out. Children wander the streets at risk because there is no one to care for them, but they wander nonetheless, looking for the next best thing. We can exclaim our anger at governments or curse the sky at our own God, but there are moments when the higher power must come from within.

We make our way to this ugly monument that rises far above the city's tallest building. It was supposedly built to honor the return of President Jean Bertrand Aristide after years in exile following a coup. The concrete has fallen off the metal staircases that criss-cross up into the sky. The entire thing is just one big exposed stairway to nowhere. We decide to walk up to the top because no one has yet gotten a good look at the center of the city from this key vantage point. At the top we all stand there breathless, initially from the climb, then from what we see. As we saw from the ground, the presidential palace has collapsed, and there are great slabs of stone scattered like playing cards. We get a sense of the vast expanse of homeless people surrounding it. A single crane is plowing into the government's tax building, where people, and money, are trapped inside. There are little puffs of smoke from fire and dust clouds of concrete rising into the air.

We pull out equipment to do a live shot from on high. I look out onto Port-au-Prince as the hot sun crashes into a haze of dust. The skyline is this orange yellow, and Haiti delivers perhaps the only ugly sunset I've ever seen. Down below us I see tens of thousands of families out in the unforgiving heat, frightened and helpless and in shock. They have no place to go. I turn the camera toward them and begin to report.

The heat is so intense it hangs in the air like a heavy blanket. I lay faceup, feeling the heat press down on top of me. I am sleeping on a damp bed in La Plaza, on the main square, where the tent city has evolved. I am wearing most of my clothes. My shoes and a flashlight are next to the bed. The place is designed like a motor inn with doors opening onto big open courtyards and parking lots, so it is one of the only reasonably safe places to sleep outside—or so we think.

The night before, Rose and I had filed for CNN.com, sent video, done live shots, driven through horrible wreckage, walked deep inside a sprawling tent city of survivors and filed a story, all on no food. We are wiped. We returned to La Plaza with our cameraman, Orlando, to this intense operation. Anderson, Sanjay, a flotilla of reporters and technicians are scattered around this dismal pool writing into laptops fired by generators. CNN has brought in boxes of PowerBars and water and the hotel is cooking up something that smells great but looks dreadful. The hotel has a small window of generator power and water, but none of us are touching the showers. Anderson and Sanjay look thin, burnt, and anxious. We give each other half hugs and then vent about the stress, which is nothing compared to that of the Haitians who surround us.

Sadness hangs over all of us. The reports have drawn rescue workers, aid, inspired enormous acts of heroism, even some by our own staff. But there is no shaking the feeling of having walked through a city littered with bodies and consumed by unbearable grief. My mind can't register how many schools we went by today, completely crushed, with tiny desks and notebooks sticking out from beneath rubble. Someone's children are in those buildings. Just outside our door families are sleeping on dirty concrete with no food or water or peace of mind. This is a tragedy far beyond anything that any of us has experienced, even with all our grim worldwide treks as reporters for an all-news network. In our courtyard, a man sits with a bleeding child hoping an aid worker will appear. A woman walks about with a wounded leg. The bartender has lost most of her family and asks if we can spare anything that could be used as a tent.

I go to bed trying to shut down my brain, calm my spirit, get a few hours of sleep so I can face another grim day. The hotel is full so we share a room, though neither of is brave enough to sleep alone anyhow. Rose insists on showering in the darkened room, but I can't bring myself to step in the tub, which looks dirty and dank from humidity. I take a bath with baby wipes and brush my teeth with bottled water. We place flashlights and food

in bags we can grab quickly, then we turn off the biggest flashlight and vow to get some sleep.

We are both aware that neither of us is sleeping. A mouse
tangles with a PowerBar and Rose throws something at it. I could
care less. I can barely breathe deeply enough to conjure sleep.
We try texting each other's families. The only way we know it is
the twenty-first century is that in a place where there's no food or
water and a quarter million dead people around us—our Black-
Berrys are working just fine. I go in and out of sleep until my
neck is sore. At 5 a.m. we both finally just get up and start talking
about all the stories that need to be told. I am in midsentence
when Rose interrupts me and says breathlessly: "What's that?"

"Run," I scream.

We race out the door barefoot. I feel like I am running on a
waterbed. I had lived in California so I know the feeling of an
earthquake, but I've felt nothing like this. Rose beats me out the
door and turns her head to me.

"Run! Run!" Rose yells as loud as she can for the benefit of
anyone still asleep. I yell "Run" too. The walls move, trees shake,
and glasses crash from the bar. Doors burst open and half-naked
people emerge. "Run, run, run!" Our hall opens right onto the
open-air courtyard, but you need to go through another hall to
get to the parking lot. Just as we take the turn leading outside,
a man crashes to the ground behind me. He screams in pain. I
hesitate, then turn back to see if I can help. I can barely stand
up. The aftershock isn't stopping. I can hardly reach him. My
mind flashes to a news report. I've died because I went back for
something. I can't believe I'm thinking that way. It feels real, like
it happened. "Run, run!" There is blood spilling from the man's
head. A woman in scrubs falls by his side. She screams to every-

one to keep running. I barely make it into the parking lot when the shaking finally, mercifully, suddenly, stops.

No one says anything. There is wailing in the distance. The Haitians look terrified; the foreigners stunned. No one even notices that CNN's Karl Penhaul is outside pacing around wearing only his briefs. I am amazed at how many photojournalists are carrying their cameras. CNN has a platform with a concrete room on the second floor, where we are doing live shots. There is no way down but a metal spiral staircase. I am minutes away from my first live shot. Anderson Cooper is up there already, as are reporter Jason Carroll and his producer Justin Dial, my producer from Hurricane Katrina. The risk here is unthinkable. My heart beats so quickly it is throbbing. Is it over? I slowly head back with Rose and we hover over the guy who fell.

"He tripped?" someone asks. "He jumped," a woman says. Medics are wrapping his bleeding head. He is moaning. He was so scared he leapt from the second-floor balcony. We walk past him to the CNN space, where they are frantically counting heads. Someone has braved the spiral staircase to confirm that the half dozen journalists up there are frightened but okay. A manager pulls a list of CNN staff and room numbers and all of us begin to go door to door checking everyone out.

I sit around with everyone after it's over, waiting for the next one. Sanjay looks at me over the breakfast table and says: "It's time to go, but not, huh?" I totally agree. I have no guts. I don't want to die here like the people whose bodies are sprawled out in the sun. It's so dehumanizing. I don't want to die like that. I don't want to die at all.

I hop into a minivan with a team of photographers, producers, security people, and drivers. We go nowhere in Haiti without a lot of people. Our van moves slowly through the city of zombies. The destruction is overwhelming; not a city block appears untouched. Piles of rubble cover entire streets. I am on my way to visit Haiti's orphanages. The country is famous for them. They are houses or buildings where people just drop off their kids out of desperation. Their parents just can't afford to raise them. The children are not all technically orphans, although that is what they are called. The country has an estimated 380,000 of these orphans, and no one knows how many more there are following the earthquake. The United States only allowed 330 adoptions of Haitian kids in the prior year. Now American parents seeking to adopt Haitian children are pressing the U.S. government to expedite the adoption process.

The first place I go sits on a steep slope and the houses are built one atop the other. The choice of this site is frightening considering the seismic activity. The children are mostly sitting out in the sunlight, dirty and hungry. A large room inside is lined with playpens. Babies of all ages sleep and cry as flies menace them. A few of the infants look very sick and thin. A woman is jabbing a very thin baby with a needle over and over trying to get an IV going. A nurse ignores the baby's weak scream.

"She won't survive if we don't get her fluids," she says with no panic in her voice. I try to help hold the child. Then our security guard offers to help with the line. He can't do it, either. The baby is barely strong enough to move but we hold her down. The process is excruciating to watch. It seems like an eternity before the nurse finally takes over and gets it on the third try.

I feel as if I am on some kind of misery tour. I visit another place called Maison des Enfants de Dieu—House of the Children of God. The house is still standing, but the children are afraid to go back inside. The toddlers, barefoot and covered with dust, are huddled under a huge tarp. Most sit calmly, but a few come and wrap their arms around our legs and smile. There are bugs everywhere and not much to eat. Armed bandits scaled the walls twice this week and found so little to steal that they left empty-handed. The director, Pierre Alexis, tells me he is afraid children will get sick and die if they don't get help soon. Even as Americans are pressing the State Department to allow adoptions, people are arriving, a dozen or more each day, to drop off more and more children. The building seems sound, and there is a lot of staff. The director has charities in the United States that help him. We play with the kids and shoot some video.

Then we come upon the truck. Twenty-five babies under a year old are in the back, lying on cardboard and paper. The orphanage keeps running out of formula, so they have fed them water and powdered milk. As we talk to one of the caretakers, a girl erupts with diarrhea. The woman wipes the girl off with the dress of another little girl. One baby gags. Others spit up. It's hot. Flies settle on the kids' faces and heads. These babies are very vulnerable. All of us working this particular story have children, so we have a frame of reference. We all murmur that these children will dehydrate quickly. They will become feverish. They will be bitten by mosquitoes. Pierre Alexis has reason to be frightened.

It brings to mind the Superdome in New Orleans during Hurricane Katrina. The desperate people trapped in this watery urban hell on U.S. soil. I expect nothing of Haiti, yet there are aid workers roaring by in rented trucks and water bottles dropping from the sky. A legion of people from around the world— many unconnected to any relief agency—seems to be descending on Haiti. This makes it all the more remarkable that our government allowed its people to languish in New Orleans. I feel as if the Americans here are the same ones who materialized in Louisiana once they realized that the government wasn't up to the task. They are kindhearted missionaries, lefties and righties, union folks and off-duty law enforcement, rich guys in search of meaning, individuals who live for a chance to help out.

It is almost as if the Americans are responding to a disaster in this nearby foreign country as a way of making up for Katrina. The land is peopled by another group of black folks crying out for help. There is something about this that feels a bit redemptive, like folks who just took matters into their own hands and collectively screamed: We care. Help is on the way. If only they know where the help is needed.

That night I go live using the power from a generator in front of the truckload of babies. I spell out how dire the situation is. I have American parents calling my office who have nearly completed adoptions of some of the children. The adoptions are such a fraction of the solution of this problem, but you don't think like that when you are waiting to bring your baby home. I receive word from an adoptive mother in the United States asking me to look in on her son. I find him and he brightens when I tell him I have spoken to her. He asks if I will read him his Bible. I open it to Matthew 27:46 and read to him: "My God, my God, why hast thou forsaken me?" I stop and look to his questioning eyes and I begin to cry. He doesn't understand why. I can't make it past that line. I do some live reporting from the orphanage that night. As the anchors ask me questions about the conditions, I pan our lights toward the babies, who are retching, wheezing, lying listless from lack of formula. The world is watching. I want the world to see.

The next day we cannot bear to see more orphans and I volunteer us to go check out Jacmel, Haiti's cultural capital, on the Caribbean coast. The trip takes a day and requires us to drive through the curving roads that cut through Leogane, the earthquake's epicenter. Our pickup struggles up hills littered with fallen rock and snakes around boulders until the beach appears. I have come to measure the intangible loss of the earthquake, the art and life on the beach that gives Haiti part of its cultural side. The nation's only film school has lost two buildings. The huge, colorful papier-mâché floats for Carnival, just ten days away, are crushed. The mountains of sheet music for the classes at Ecole Musique are scattered in the ruins of a street named La Berenthe, the labyrinth. It's estimated that 10 percent of the town's residents have perished. They have taken with them a country's film festival, its music studios, the paintings and masks that draw tourists and Haitians to this seaside town of forty thousand.

Left behind are crushed limbs and brain injuries, nursed in an open-air hospital that replaced the real one. Cuban doctors had been working with Haitians when the earthquake hit, and they have continued their collaboration outside. "Where there is life, there is hope," says Dr. Silda Del Torro of Cuba while standing over a four-year-old girl who has drifted in and out of consciousness. Del Torro says the head injuries are very hard to treat under these conditions, and she worries they will be left with crippling injuries. The doctors working in the open air also fear they have reached the limits of their abilities. They aren't orthopedists or anesthesiologists, and some patients with crushed limbs are developing gangrene. There are so many surgeries that need to be done.

This seaside town is just over an hour's drive from the epicenter of the earthquake. It has an airport and a port to bring in tourists. But much of the growing international relief effort has been focused on Port-au-Prince until now. The residents dug out trapped neighbors largely on their own for days. But intrepid Jacmel residents got out word they needed help through the Internet, texts, on Facebook and YouTube. The Cine Institute was left homeless, but its young filmmakers pulled their equipment from the rocks and moved into a building next to the airport. They set up generators, powered up laptops, and started moving images across oceans in a cry for help. "We just got the information out. Our filmmakers just went out and started shooting and sent it away even as their own families were being affected, their homes being lost," says David Belle, the institute's director.

Their plea was heard, and Colombian rescue workers arrived just in time to pull a child from the rubble. Chile sent doctors. Sri Lanka sent security. The French assembled a clinic where parents had dug for a trapped child unsuccessfully for days. Canada brought in the big guns—a navy ship and army helicopter with engineers and supplies. "We brought in light engineering equipment, drills, the jaws of life, anything that can be carried portably," said Robert Brown, a naval commander from Halifax, Nova Scotia. The United States joined the effort, announcing they would fly in C130s with supplies to assist the Canadians in making Jacmel's airport the center of the rescue efforts to southern provinces not touched by the aid sent to Port-au-Prince. The world is coming together in the face of this tragedy. America's ability to play a vital role in the relief effort is on keen display. This is possible when nations come together as friends.

But this town needs so much more than just immediate relief. The days without aid wore down their psyche and hampered relief efforts. "We could have saved so many more people with these guys," remarked a film student as he watched the French set up tents and begin treating a growing line of wounded. Yards away, a teenage music student searches for his flute amidst the remains of his flattened house. So many of the colorful buildings are crushed and damaged. So much of the artistry that made Jacmel special is gone.

But the resilience of the people in this town is energizing. There is so much sadness and widespread destruction but every street has people sweeping, clearing, and even building anew. The town is smaller than the big city, so the response by aid workers seems to scale and within reach of addressing the need. The budding filmmakers have lost family members and homes, but they race around town documenting a disaster, preserving images of heartache and hope, spreading information to interested parties abroad. I feel humbled by their work. They offer me tape of critical moments and we exchange reporting tips. I want to linger in their optimism, but we need to take off before the sun falls or spend the night in the car. I think a lot about the kids in this town, and their work lifts me out of bed every day I'm there.

· CHAPTER THIRTEEN ·

THE LIGHTHOUSE

onathan Olinger is so young he is almost like my baby brother. He's post-college, preadult. He is a devout California Christian who was once a skier who almost turned professional until he took up filmmaking. Jonathan's mom, Tawni, had gotten pregnant as a nineteen-year-old. His father left them and his mother raised him alone in Steamboat Springs, Colorado. Jonathan has a rare heart disease called truncus arteriosus that has required eleven surgeries, three to his heart. Yet he left his ski town to visit thirteen nations because he became captivated by the plight of other children. He has never had any money and doesn't expect he ever will. Yet he gives of himself to others.

Jonathan has the visionary attitude that young folks contribute to America's promise. He believes video can change the world for the better. He is unafraid to just up and travel to some desolate, scary, miserable place to spotlight children in need. He is bold. He founded a small nonprofit organization called Discover the Journey with a few friends, including his girlfriend, the photographer Lindsay Branham. They have taken off for the Congo, Uganda, and Iraq and shot videos. I find him and his faith inspiring. I am a true believer that we have much to learn from youth.

I meet Jonathan in Haiti because he has been shooting video of Maison de Lumiere, the Lighthouse, an orphanage run by Christian missionaries. He began documenting their vision in 2004, charting their progress in the years since. He hustled to get himself back into Haiti as soon as he heard about the earthquake. He is a journalist of the future, detached from many of the old rules that don't apply to him. He mixes his journalism with relief work, Christianity, advocacy, and has personal relationships with people who share his quest for social justice. I am searching for a way out of the mind-set that we are covering the unfathomable, the unfixable, a problem with no solution, another Katrina where the people have been abandoned to a harsh sea.

The moment I arrive at the Lighthouse I find the answer to the question that has been nagging me since we arrived—how does any one person make a difference in the face of such an enormous tragedy? Susette and Bill Manassero came to Haiti at the urging of their oldest daughter, Ariana. She was nine and had saved coins to sponsor needy children in Haiti. She wanted to go for a visit. The Manesseros were indulging her when they came to Haiti and were shocked to find the high rates of poverty, sex trafficking, and child abandonment—some of the worst in the world. The children they met were being abused. They were on what they thought was just a casual visit. They made a drastic decision, one that is inconceivable to so many of us. They sold everything and moved their three young children to Haiti.

What the Manasseros have built in Haiti is stunning to say the least. They have a boys' and a girls' orphanage, a feeding program and ministry, a clinic and sports program. The central component to all of it is the guesthouse. Jonathan has spent a lot of time videotaping there. Christian volunteers come and live at the Lighthouse, bringing their skills and enthusiasm and taking home a commitment to spread the word and raise funds. The volunteers are moved by a desire to leave behind their plastic lives, grasp meaning, and pursue God's grace. The last group that came got much more than they bargained for with this devastating earthquake.

Robert Taylor had volunteered to build furniture. Amese Kubicki had brought her stepdaughters there to get them away from the frivolity of Orange County so she could build some character into them. When I arrive, Robert is working in the clinic helping badly wounded people and Amese is caring for traumatized children. The Manasseros are guiding all these untrained people in critical disaster work while running an orphanage. They have just shut down a clinic they opened to the public. For days, wounded, battered, bleeding people of all ages had overwhelmed the volunteers. Aid workers came to assist but there just weren't enough of them. Volunteers like Robert and Amese assist with amputations and splints, things far outside anything they have experienced. The orphanage just couldn't keep up the pace.

Jonathan has been videotaping the precarious situation here. The forty-seven children are sleeping outside in a big concrete play yard they call the "bins." They are afraid to go inside because of the aftershocks. The walls around the girls' orphanage have collapsed, so they are not secure from bandits. Many of the children are uncharacteristically quiet; some are attached to the laps of volunteers and older children. When we arrive, kids swarm around us instantly, checking out our BlackBerrys and cameras and just wanting to play. There is a girl named Cendy, pronounced "Cenzy" in Creole, with assaulting eyes that look at you while she smiles off into the distance. There are babies everywhere whom people pass off to each of us. The boys run up laughing and want us to take their pictures. They may be sleeping outside but every child couldn't be cleaner or better dressed.

Bill and Susette are amazingly calm bearing all this responsibility, considering they are close to running out of food and water. Bill has a very happy daddy personality in the face of the worst situations. He has a graying beard and mustache and is dressed all in khaki. He is constantly in action, working to keep this place running, fueling up generators, moving furniture, making endless drives back and forth between the various facilities. He pats about a hundred heads an hour. Susette is also in constant motion, delivering orders to an army of volunteers, employees, and older children with a calmness and delicacy that sends everyone off feeling they have been given a vote of confidence. This woman has it all together. It is nearly one hundred degrees outside. An earthquake has just flattened half her city. They are short on everything they need to survive and unsure whether help is on the way. And she is wearing perfectly applied eyeliner and completely coordinated jewelry. She is Cuban American and has that Latina sensibility that makes everyone feel as if they are part of one big family on the move. I like them both instantly.

As soon as we arrive, I seem to enter their whirlwind and just follow where it takes me. There is no way to talk with these people without keeping up their pace. We set up cameras in an effort to debrief Ariana on her inspirational story, and even then she and her younger siblings continue running the orphanage as we are putting on their microphones and sitting them down. I barely spit out a few questions before Susette pulls me off on one of her rescue missions. The Manasseros are treating the crisis as their full responsibility. I am awed.

Until this very moment I felt like I had Katrina stuck in my head, the image of a nonresponsive government and a disempowered public. I came to Haiti expecting nothing from their government and next to nothing from my own, even though its shore is just a quick plane jump away. Now, sitting in a Jeep with this Energizer Bunny of a Cuban woman, I am suddenly transported to another mental place. Susette is just pulling up her bootstraps and hitting the streets like Angela back in Pearlington, Mississippi.

I am rattled. Everyone is, actually. There are not just dead people all over this town, but there are aftershocks big and small. You don't know what to expect or when to expect it. There is not enough food or water and no power at all. So driving through Port au Prince is like driving through desperation. I lose track of how many places we visit where the people need help. Susette has so little to give out, but she has boxes of canned goods and bread and water and is doing her part. We go to another orphanage where the kids are all sitting quietly outside. The director says he is desperate. He has no sponsors in the United States anymore and has no one to call for help. They have no food left and the kids are weak. She hands them all bread and they eat, but there is no long-term solution to deliver.

We walk through a ravine where tents are being raised. The people are eating where they sleep and go to the bathroom. This place can't last. I know no Creole but I have no trouble communicating. I barely use our translators. It's amazing how people can make themselves understood in a crisis. Their French meets my few words of French and Spanish and hands move. The next thing you know, we are walking right behind them to see an injured child or a damaged home. Everyone wants to tell us his or her story. They want America to know they need help.

A school next door has pancaked onto tiny desks and word is it was full of children. People walk by carrying bags of recovered supplies. Cars roar by carrying loads of people, injured and hungry, to unknown destinations. Someone occasionally carries a gun, but mostly they are just normal folk on their way toward nothing in particular. We walk down a ravine, dense with tiny structures fractured by the earthquake. People are living in the rubble of their lives. We take Susette and go visit her former wash lady, who breaks down into her arms. She has five children living in a small one-room concrete hut with a tin roof. Her oldest child, Daniel, used to work for Susette and now goes to college. He is the sole provider for his family and he is missing. She shoves his picture in my hand and wails. I need no translation.

This all feels like it happens in an instant, but it takes a full day. I bounce through the cracked streets of Delmas 73 in Port-au-Prince in Susette's Jeep, racing along as if we are headed for an emergency room even when we are going a few blocks. Tall iron gates with no windows swing open to our last stop. We enter the grounds of Quisqueya Church, a vast grassy enclave where several orphanages have set up tents. There are only enough tents for a few staff people and older children. We can see that most of the little ones are out beneath some trees in playpens.

As we hop out of our vehicle, we can hear the children whimpering like little kittens. The sun is so hot and full it's blinding. The smell of hot grass and child vomit fill the air. We run up as if we are about to push a child past an oncoming train. And then we just stop. The caretakers had covered the playpens with mattresses to block the sun. The heat is trapped inside and the children are withering. I've never met such quiet children. There is not enough food or water at this place, either. Susette's face turns completely cold and she stands at a distance as I walk among the playpens. I push the mattresses aside more than once and a flash of hot air moves in. Flies land on one boy's eyelid. He is too weak to wave them away. A girl struggles to roll over. She is maybe five.

I stop at some boys who look to be about two. I know boys this age. I've had boys this age. Their eyes are missing something. There is no white, just red. The lashes droop as if they are a great weight. Their lips are so dry they blend in with the skin around them. There is no moisture in their skin; not enough water inside them to sweat in the ninety-degree heat. I touch their heads, one by one. The tight little Afro on one boy traps dirt like a bird's nest.

One bald kid has tiny blue veins tracing along his skull like a road map. He rises up suddenly to meet me. I kneel down to meet him. He can barely lift the weight of his dirty diaper. He stands like a drunk. I stroke his back a few times and he falls forward against the railing. His head tilts toward me. His mouth is half open. I look into his eyes and see nothing. I stop. I begin to stand up and move away. The boy suddenly cries out. He has just enough tears left to drop some for me. His tiny chest heaves. His head wobbles unsteadily on his neck. I fall back. "Don't cry. Don't cry," I beg him. He has no reaction.

Then suddenly I just can't take it. The heat inside me rises as rapidly as the heat around me beats down on my head. A swell of emotion settles in my head and I just completely lose it. I begin to cry, too. Our foreheads touch. His is dry. Mine is moist. We are both so hot. His little body trembles. My spine collapses so my back is in a hunch. Some of these children will die this week. Some of these little black children in playpens on this terribly beaten island will die. They will die in the heat. They will die alone. They will wither away whether I do a story about them or not. They will be overcome regardless of whether the word gets out that they need help. They were barely better off before the ground shook, before a legion of rescue workers and journalists descended on their homeland for the umpteenth time in history to tell the story of Haiti's woes. His agony overwhelms me. I can do nothing for this boy. Nothing right now. Nothing tomorrow. Nothing at all, nothing but cry.

I finally let go of this child. The eyes of my colleagues are fixed on me. Susette stands a few feet away and waits. "Jesus, there is so much sadness in this country," I tell her. "How do you do this? How do you go on?"

Susette becomes the first of several people in Haiti who tell me the starfish story. The story is adapted from the works of Loren Eiseley, an American philosopher who wrote many books that were contemplative and humane. His essay "The Star Thrower" is treasured by people who do relief work, whose lives are a mission to help the less fortunate. A man is walking on a beach full of starfish perishing in the sun as the tide rolls out. He comes upon a boy who is throwing them back in the ocean one by one. The man asks the boy why he is bothering with the dying starfish when there are so many of them and he could never save them all.

"It doesn't matter," the man tells him. "It matters to the one," replies the boy.

Susette and Bill take enormous comfort from that story, from narrowing their vision to the group of desperate boys and girls they can rescue in the face of this enormous tragedy. We return to the orphanage at dusk, a vast complex of white plaster and concrete lit by the glow of a generator's lamp. The children are clustering even closer to the adults and some of the volunteers are singing and praying with them. As soon as we enter, a group of them surrounds us once again. It is amazing how children can smile even when they are scared.

Susette has a very firm idea of why she is in Haiti. It's to raise these beautiful kids. She doesn't process adoptions, even though she is supportive of the concept and is adopting two kids herself. Hers is a lifetime commitment. She says early on some of the boys told her she would leave the moment things got hard. Her promise that she would never do that has intensified her devotion. Bill and she barely interact since they are so busy, but their movements are coordinated like some kind of machine with lots of moving parts. Bill begins playing music and trying to lift the children's spirits for what will surely be a night of more aftershocks.

I ask a group of the older ones what they think of the rush to get kids to the United States for adoption. Their English is terrific considering they are learning it here. These children love their orphanage and the Manasseros, so the question is awkward. No one wants to say they don't want to be adopted, because they have no idea why this lady with the TV cameras is bothering to ask. But a few talk of rebuilding Haiti, of being here to help each other out. There are some dreams of escaping the poverty and destruction around them. Then they all begin to talk of adoption with a sadness that is heartbreaking.

"Everything here is destroyed. There is nothing for us. I would miss my family, but they would be happy for me," says a boy into the approaching darkness. "But it would make me sad."

As our evening wraps up, Bill comes charging in with a group of newcomers. They are Christian missionaries who flew themselves into the Dominican Republic, rented trucks and bought food and water, and have arrived at the Lighthouse bringing hope. They do not even know the Manasseros. They had no plan, no government behind them, nothing but a desire to go help. Everyone hugs and cheers and Susette turns to me—and if I am not mistaken, she is gloating. "Miracles do happen," she says. "See, they've heard the starfish story, too." They begin to unload the truck of supplies into their basement as the children sing "Hallelujah" into the hot Haitian night.

We wake up to more aftershocks every few hours that night, sending us into the parking lot each time, exhausted and shaken. The food is making us sick so we're relying on the PowerBars now. I have never had so much bottled water to drink. We spent most of last night filing stories and sending pictures. A massive telethon for Haiti is being simulcast and we are contributing footage. Anderson and Sanjay are both prominently featured, and they are fighting to pick up a fourth wind to make it good.

I am sitting with everyone at the hotel bar eating toast when Reverend Jackson appears out of nowhere, flown in by a private plane. He greets everyone, but none of us has the energy to report a story about anything beyond the disaster. Sanjay and I glance at each other with knowing looks. As hard as it was to get into Haiti, there is no easy way out. The airports are closed and the roads require cars and gas and guts. The aftershocks have put us in a constant state of fear. Reverend Jackson has a plane, our eyes say to each other. How tempting to ask for a lift! But we are staying. Sanjay has been up half the night attending to a woman brought injured into the hotel—not his job to do as a journalist but not one he can push away as a doctor. I am focused on the orphans. Anderson has witnessed the latest of several harrowing rescues of people pinned beneath the rubble. We are reporting an extraordinary story of human tragedy. The sadness in this town is overwhelming.

Rose suggests we pack our bags and carry them in the car. We need to leave at some point. But we know from last night that we are not done with Haiti. We need to tell the story of Bill and Susette Manassero. We need to tell America the story of the starfish, in part to help us all get past the devastation of Katrina. No one expected the government to step up to the plate in a country like Haiti. Practically speaking, there is no government. We had low expectations that the U.S. government would rally for this island when they had not rallied for their own. That leaves us with the power of one, the generosity and spunk of individuals who just take it upon themselves to come help the people they can in whatever way they can. This is the story I want to tell.

We revisit the Maison des Enfants orphanage to see how they have fared. I had done live shots from there for several hours showing the ailing babies in the truck. There was an outpouring of sympathy for their plight when the story aired in the United States. When we arrive, they are loading the babies into a van, and the toddlers and older children into a bus. The staff looks desperate. They say they are making a run for the U.S. embassy with over one hundred kids they believe are eligible for adoption. They think the children need to show up in person in order to be processed, and they are desperate to get them out of Haiti. They take a thick black Sharpie and write "FHG" on all the kids' hands—For His Glory adoption services.

We hop aboard along with a volunteer medical team from Denver, carrying the children who are most ill. The staff leads the children in singing "Hallelujah." They urge the kids to clap and pray. The bus hurtles forward into the steaming hot, dusty, broken streets of Haiti. There are no seat belts and nowhere near enough adults to hold all the little children, so a lot of them are getting knocked about. I have three kids on my lap and one is throwing up. The staff keeps calling their colleagues at the embassy, who can't seem to give them a clear idea of whether they should be coming at all. There is all sorts of debris in the road; it's a very bumpy ride, but also really hot. The temperature rises above ninety degrees. The children are wilting; more are throwing up, really just uncomfortable. One of the medics forces a baby to take Tylenol. They keep telling Tanya Constantino, who is leading the operation, that they are worried about the children's health.

"I don't want to jeopardize the children, but I want to do what's right for them," she says.

I'm afraid for the kids who are already in precarious health. A pickup flies by carrying corpses beneath a tarp, and it takes a moment before I fully appreciate what I'm seeing. I avert my eyes. My photographer, Tawanda Scott, and Rose are standing at the front of the bus videotaping and asking questions as the bus moves. Suddenly, the bus jolts sideways on the road and they get thrown forward into a few other folks who are standing along with some small kids. They are sturdy women so it was a strong jolt. The kids scream and begin to cry. The bus charges forward. There has been a very strong aftershock while we are in motion.

"What if I've made a mistake?" Tanya cries out. Then the van ahead of us stops and one of the staff gets out and comes aboard. "We just got a call from the embassy telling us not to bring the children," says the staff member. Tanya argues with him and urges the drivers to press on. We come within two blocks of the embassy when she finally decides to stop. The children pour out of the hot bus onto the sidewalk, shaken and crying. A few dozen begin to pee and others throw up.

"The children do not want to go back to the orphanage. They want to go to America," Tanya says firmly of the assortment of babies, toddlers, and children around her. The medical team is frustrated. They insist that this is not a good plan. Tanya relents and they decide to turn back. We call CNN on our satellite phone and ask them to speak with the embassy. They tell us the embassy staff never asked the children to come and do not believe the trip is necessary. They have a lot of paperwork to do and can't speed it up without risking children being taken from their parents illegally. Haiti has a big problem with child sex trafficking. Tanya is crestfallen.

I grab Rose and Tawanda and get back into our car with the CNN drivers and security team. We decide to head for the airport, where we have been told other orphanages have gotten the green light to leave. The trip begins to feel like that crazy scene in the movie *Hotel Rwanda*, a frantic race to escape. The stream of people making for the airport seems endless. When we arrive there are twenty-one children whose adoption agencies have completed their paperwork. A team of relief workers from Utah has rented a chopper. They airlift the orphans from their crèche and drop them at the airport into the hands of U.S. soldiers. Tall, broad-shouldered, American servicemen are walking around with tiny Haitian kids, and they are feeding them cold clean water.

A group of wealthy Americans, employees of a tech firm with no connection to the orphanage, have bought and stocked a private plane and come to help. They have volunteered to take these children to Fort Lauderdale. The children cling to whichever adult will pick them up. We make a quick decision to board the plane, get home so we can tell their story. We are carting small kids on our laps, have shown our passports to no one. There is no order at this moment in Haiti, no rules. As we are beginning to move, there is a knock at the airplane door. A man outside begins to beg the pilots to take an American woman and her adoptive son. They begin to cry. The pilots look at each other and relent. We take off with twenty-two kids aboard.

Sometimes, you just do what you can. The adoption issue is so very complicated. It is a fact that it is not a solution to the misery of so many of Haiti's children. There are just not enough adoptive parents to go around, not even considering what it does to a nation of parents for people to take their kids. But for these kids, at this moment, they have embarked on a new life. These absolute strangers just up and got a plane and came to their rescue. The reality of what's happening doesn't hit everyone until we're high in the sky. Then a lot of the guys just stroll down the aisle looking as if their lives have embraced new meaning. Their act of generosity has enhanced them as much as these children. They are high in the sky in more ways than one.

CNN has sent a live truck to the Fort Lauderdale airport, and when we land an incredible human moment unfolds on TV. "We have just landed at Fort Lauderdale International Airport," I say on live national television. "And we're actually very close to where these adoptive parents, we're told, are waiting in a hangar."

What's happening, though, is the children have to be processed through first, so they're going through immigration, they're going through customs, and they will load them back on the plane and roll that plane to the hangar, where they get to meet their American parents.

"But what a day it has been," I say to one of our anchors, feeling like I have landed in some alternate universe. As I'm speaking, the plane finally gets a chance to unload and the adoptive parents rush up the runway screaming with arms outstretched. A little boy smiles and screams "Mommy." His moment of recognition speaks volumes about the relationship he has built with his adoptive mom. A few other children look bewildered, even frightened. The parents are universally in tears. I look at the faces of these Haitian kids in the Fort Lauderdale airport bound for far-off states in the middle of America with their mostly white parents. Each of these little faces has a remarkable story behind it and quite an adventure ahead. I am not done with my work in Haiti. I am just home for now.

My new unit is called In America but I am producing a documentary on Haiti. That makes no sense, but I am so breathless with excitement about this story that all the bosses sign off on it. I enlist Jonathan Olinger, the young man who introduced me to the Manasseros. Jonathan has great footage of the Lighthouse prior to the earthquake. He doesn't really have a focus to what he is shooting, but at the center is the story of the Manasseros' Christian mission to save Haitian kids. Jonathan has a terrific sensibility for people. He is also a genuinely humble guy, which you need to be to have your life's work disassembled by total strangers.

I love the story he is trying to tell, but it isn't ours. We look through his footage to find connections between his work and ours. We keep returning to two compelling images. One is the story of Cendy, the six-year-old girl, who had been at the orphanage since she was a toddler, the niece of the wash lady who had begged us to help find her missing son. Jonathan has recorded the traumatic events of her abandonment. He also has this hard-to-watch footage of the day her parents return to come take her back. The incident spells out the emotional anguish of the orphan story. She is better off with the Christian missionaries who came from California, but these are her parents. He also has footage of Mark Kenson Olibris, who was rescued by the Manasseros from begging on the streets. Jonathan recorded his journey to Cap Haitian to see the parents who abandoned him. There is a remarkable moment when he puts his arm around the father who abandoned him and begins to pray before his entire village.

Both children have survived the earthquake and are living with the Manasseros now. We decide to return to Haiti to shoot a documentary we will call *Rescued*. I want to tell the story of these two real-life orphans behind those worldwide appeals for charity and how their lives were transformed by the kindness of Bill and Susette Manassero.

There is just one catch in this story line. The night after we leave Haiti, bandits assault the Lighthouse. Jonathan captures the terrifying aftermath as Susette and Bill completely lose their composure. Robert Taylor, who came to build things and ended up a medic, now runs security. They gather in the darkness in a panic. By the time the sun rises, these Christian missionaries are calling the Haitian police, an intimidating force, and arming their increasing number of guards to the teeth. The walls cannot be rebuilt so they gather the children to tell them they are moving back inside. A girl who had been crushed and trapped in rubble gets hysterical. She is afraid of the aftershocks. Susette and Bill force the kids inside, dragging mattresses and clothes into the basement of their homes. "Somehow I missed this part in the Christian missionary manual," Bill says, trying to joke away the stress.

Robert is making calls and sending e-mails trying to find everyone a way out. Volunteers are leaving any way they can. He finds benefactors willing to bring in helicopters, maybe even charter a plane. They can't take the kids, but maybe they have to just go. People repeatedly tell Susette she needs to think of her family. She is frightened and under enormous stress but doesn't know what to do. They talk about heading for the hills with all the children, just hopping on a bus and ditching their life's work at the orphanage. At one point, Robert finds a ranch in the state where they can go. He asks Susette if she can leave it all behind. She cannot take the Haitian orphans with her. "I don't know, maybe, yes. I don't know," she says. She may be about to throw the parable of the starfish out to sea.

CHAPTER FOURTEEN

Rescued

Our second trip to Haiti is less dramatic than the first. It's now mid-February and the airport is open and CNN has plenty of supplies. That doesn't make up for the continuing aftershocks and the fact that the city appears to be in even worse shape. People are still sleeping outdoors and they are worn down by life on the streets. The infrastructure remains the same—there isn't one. The orphanages are still being flooded with children. We've hired Jonathan Olinger to videotape and he has disturbing footage of a mother begging Susette to take in her baby, even though the orphanage is at full capacity. Susette relents, but vows that she will not make the mistake of getting in over her head. There is so much need outside her door.

I arrive in Haiti with Rose and Tawanda, again, and am greeted by my new, temporary team of young Christian filmmakers. Jonathan is invisible when he shoots footage, which makes him a great addition to our team. His partner, Lindsay Branham, shoots stills and also has a way of disappearing into the background.

They connect with a photographer named Josh Newton who shoots affecting stills. He is this tall, fair, muscular guy with full red lips. Suddenly, I am surrounded by all these attractive young Christian journalists on a mission. Their dedication and faith is inspiring. Back home, we have decided our first In America feature will be the story of two gay men having a baby with a surrogate. From Christian missionaries to gay parents, that's the range of my new unit!

I arrive at the Lighthouse not exactly sure what I'm going to find. Bill and Susette haven't left, and the kids are still here, as are the guards. Jonathan reports that all the girls are sleeping in the basement of the Manasseros' home, with two floors of concrete house above them. They are scared every time there is an aftershock, as there was this morning. Cendy, who we are going to profile, has always been shy. She was two when her aunt, Matile, the wash lady, brought her to Bill and Susette because her parents had abandoned her. She was running around a ghetto on her own. She was the youngest girl here for a long time, and Bill Manassero worked to break through her tough exterior. She would run and cry and hide. He cries when he recounts the day she finally extended her hand. "I wondered what happened to this little girl. Who could give up this precious little beauty?" he says.

Then, two years later, when Cendy was four, Jonathan recorded the drama of her life. Her parents showed up at the orphanage unannounced to pick up their daughter. Jonathan's footage of that afternoon is disturbing. Cendy clung to Susette, terrified and stressed, jerking back each time her mother reached out to touch her. She had known only the Manasseros. Susette looked equally traumatized. She and Bill are legal guardians of all the children but their parents can take them back. "If they had wanted to take her we would have given her up. We have barbed wire and walls to keep bad people out, not to keep anyone in," she said. "The parents are entitled to take their own children." But it would have been heartbreaking all around.

Cendy's parents left, secure in the knowledge that their daughter was doing fine. The father occasionally returns to ask after her, but the mother never came back. The girl I meet barely talks at all. Her hair has been shaved down, which makes her haunting eyes all the more piercing. Cendy dislikes the cameras from the beginning. She plays constant hide-and-seek with us, even when I give her a flip cam so she can take pictures on her own. She is lanky, with very dark skin, almost like dark chocolate, shiny and lovely, offsetting those big eyes. She walks out hand in hand with Ariana Manassero, whose dreams of helping Haiti began all of this. Ariana has walnut skin and long curly hair. She is like the Oracle to this family and her insights on Cendy are illuminating.

Ariana is just a teenager, not a therapist. But she is extraordinarily insightful and pragmatic. Cendy is lonely in life, brokenhearted, gaining distance from people in response to their distance from her. She has no single adult in the world who is responsible for her, no one she can fully count on, no plan B. The orphanage is giving her an education, food, shelter from a cruel world outside. Ariana believes in the power of overwhelming love as a great healer of the spirit. It's not exactly a prescription from a doctor, but her plan for Cendy is just to shower her with love every day so she recognizes what it feels like, so that it grows inside her soul. The entire staff and many of the older kids have adopted that plan.

Cendy sits by herself lost in sadness several times a day. Someone always interrupts her. A lot of our footage of this little girl ends up reflecting those moments, when the warmth of a stranger intervenes on a cloudy day. I watch this process a few dozen times over the course of our trip and marvel at what I'm watching. The power of one person is exhilarating to me, the notion that this vast expanse of disaster does not have to bring you down, that it can inspire you to rise up and own a piece of the solution. The idea of Susette and Bill leaving Haiti and shutting down the orphanage is inconceivable. It would be devastating for kids like Cendy, who are unaware that such a conversation has even been contemplated, let alone taken place, which it has.

Mark Kenson Olibris also has a lot to lose if the Manasseros leave Haiti. He came to the Lighthouse at age fourteen. He is now the caretaker for the guesthouse. He has received food and an education. He walks around fueling the generator and purifying water, helping move all the children's things inside because of the fear of more thieves. He lives in a private room that he shows off proudly. He has come a long way from a life on the streets. He has built a life for himself.

Mark Kenson takes us on a walk to the girls' orphanage, where a crew of volunteers is making repairs. I am struck by how calm he is even under enormous stress. Mark Kenson has one of those faces that looks happy even when he is sad. He has large, bright eyes and a wide smile. He looks like he takes a bath twice a day and irons his clothes. He is handsome and gentle, polite and sweet. He is clearly someone driven by his faith. This was a young man whose conversion to devout Christianity was the glue that held together his life.

We talk about his wretched childhood in Cap Haitian, where his parents struggled to provide for him. He lowers his voice whenever he talks about how tough it was for his family. Then he delivers the defining information of his life. His parents sold him as a child slave. "You were a *restavec*?" I ask him, the Creole word for "stay with," which is the name given to children sold in Haiti's legal child slave trade. He mumbles, "Yes," and looks down. I ask him again about his sister. "Her too," he mumbles again and looks down. It is hard to tell if he is shamed by that fact or just sad that it was true. He was sold to a lady who made him and his sister call her "auntie."

"How much money did the woman pay for you?"

"One hundred and twenty Haitian dollars."

"Which is how much? Ten to twelve dollars U.S.? Someone bought you for twelve dollars. Do you ever think about that?"

"No. I'm just happy."

"Doesn't it make you mad?"

"No."

"Angry?"

"No," he says; his parents were poor. His humility and calm are unnerving. How could he not be angry? Then he says something that leaves me with deep admiration for this young man. He has a very limited education and so many reasons to feel angry and lash out at the cruelties of the world around him. Yet, he says matter-of-factly, "I'm just happy it all turned out." Haiti, he explained, is a place where many people have nothing, where even the hardest-working young man can never seem to find a job. This is a place where so many people beg or sell trinkets on the street. How could he be angry with his parents if they had nothing to give him and no way to feed him? Selling him and his sister meant they would get to Port-au-Prince and maybe find their fortune, perhaps get adopted away to the United States and a better life. Selling their own children to a stranger was a way of giving them hope. He has a profound understanding of the circumstances faced by his parents.

I ask Mark Kenson to jump atop a Jeep with me and go visit the place where he had lived as a child slave. I want to understand how fifty thousand children lived legally as slaves in this country and how a young man who had suffered as he had suffered could be so resilient, so understanding, so strong in the face of this latest indignity—an earthquake hitting an island already hit hard by poverty. We drive to La Saline, a ghetto by the edge of the sea that was already in such miserable condition it's hard to tell if the earthquake did any damage. A flotilla of garbage floats atop the sewage that runs in canals along the homes. Large black sows poke through the trash for food in constant competition with the children, who are naked and bone thin. La Saline is assembled from refuse, discarded tin and cardboard, wood boards and boxes. There is nothing to lose here when a natural disaster hits, yet there is everything to lose.

Mark Kenson leads me through the narrow alleys that divide the structures as Tawanda records our journey. We walk past unattended children who have barely learned to walk. Many are naked, crying, and clearly ill. Those children used to be him, running out daily into the streets to beg, then beaten if they came back with nothing. Jonathan and Josh Newton both lean over the edge of our pickup with their cameras, tall white guys in fading T-shirts hovering over a sea of screaming children. "Photo! Photo!" the children yell, and Josh captures images of big eyes looking up at him. The people who lived around and knew Mark Kenson cannot believe their eyes when they see him, surrounded by photographers, arriving in a car, well fed, well groomed, a warm smile across his face. Children crowd around him in awe. Jonathan snakes into the slum ahead of us. He may have grown up as a competitive snowboarder but his energy blends in comfortably in the third world these days. Jonathan's only distraction is he keeps stopping to interact with the kids. I really admire this about him. I am like so many Americans with my single focus on work. Life is not work. Life is life. A stop to admire a child's smile and a smile back enriches us both, even in all this sadness. He will take away from this a mental album to go with his footage, memories that will drive his quest for social justice. I watch him and realize I can walk away from this with so much more than a story. Josh with his full blue eyes has captured the attention of half the girls in the slum and giggles break out. There is something oddly happy about this scene.

We come upon a woman who rented space to the lady who enslaved Mark Kenson and his sister. The lady who enslaved him is gone, but this woman lets us see the hut where he used to live, hot but neat, with buckets of food packets from the World Food Program. Josh walks in and snaps photos. Mark puts his arms around the woman and her husband, as if they are all at a family reunion. I am overcome by the smell, the heat, and the terrible conditions. Mark is sweating profusely but smiling a wide smile. I can't believe how neat and tidy this dump is. It reminds me of the people sweeping their little square in the street; it's about dignity. "What do you think when you come here?" I ask him.

"I thank God," says this grateful young man. "I thank him."

And then he does something surprising. He thanks me for taking him to see where he'd come from. "I could have never come here on my own," he says.

"Why not?" I ask him. He smiles at me and looks around him. It is obvious. To come back with a film crew and a story worth telling is a triumph. Instead of feeling sad when he revisits his past, he is coming back to celebrate his good fortune.

Mark Kenson tells me that he has been through so much in life that he does not see the earthquake as daunting. It is a reason to work harder. He believes he can help build a better Haiti for the future. His experience being schooled and raised by the Manasseros makes him believe that he can someday open an orphanage for his own people. That plan was supposed to include his sister, Mona, who was also taken off the streets by an orphanage that was not far away from the Lighthouse, and Mark Kenson had been able to visit her often. He obviously loves his sister dearly. She is his only real family, the only relative who has been around all his life and accompanied him through his journey.

We offer to take Mark Kenson to Mona's orphanage to see what had become of her. That is the first time I see that smile drop from Mark Kenson's face. Since we are profiling him for our documentary, Bill and Susette Manassero have called the directors at her orphanage to find out what had become of her. A family in Texas has adopted her. The paperwork was expedited because of the earthquake, so he never had a chance to say goodbye. Mark Kenson has lost his only close relative to adoption. He has been working so hard at the Lighthouse after the earthquake that he hadn't been by to see her in time. But knowing she is gone doesn't soften the blow of walking through the iron gates of her orphanage and seeing the emptiness she'd left behind.

Hal Nungester, the director, lets us all look around and shows us pictures of Mona on the computer. Mark Kenson's eyes scan the premises, as if she will pop up at any moment. Her bottom bunk bed is made and an old suitcase is jammed beneath. Several stuffed animals sit lonely atop her bed. It is obvious he misses her. Hal's whole mission is to support adoptions, and Mark Kenson is torn about the idea—it has cost him his sister—so a small amount of tension hangs in the air. "It was her choice and I'm happy for her," Mark Kenson says of his sister. But he also laments that she will be one less young person around to build a future Haiti. I ask him if he is sure he will stick around. He nods affirmatively. "Even if I left for a while I would return," he says. "My country needs me."

Hal listens in and grows redder as my questions to Mark Kenson continue. "I'm angry that there are factions that are saying we should turn these kids back in to their families, when Mark Kenson obviously can't even take care of himself, let alone his little sister. He's living in an orphanage so he can't provide for himself. We got her from a police station," Hal says.

"How did Mona come to you?" I ask.

"She had been arrested. She was on the street, about twelve years old, little teeny tiny thing. She had scars all over her body where she'd been beat. It's just starting to come out now about some of the abuse that she suffered while she was here in Haiti. Because while she was in Haiti she was afraid to talk about it, but she's talking with her family about it now in the States."

Hal says he sees no future in Haiti for kids like Mark Kenson and Mona because the unemployment rate hovers at 80 percent. "The people who are hungry now were hungry before the earthquake. They're getting fed somehow because the Internet and international community has stepped in, and we do appreciate that. But what's going to happen when they step out? We're going to go right back to what we had before," he says. Hal says Mona dreamed of going to the United States to live with a new family and get an education. His orphanage taught her English to prepare her for adoption. Hal commends Mark Kenson for staying behind to help rebuild his country. "I don't think he's naive. I think he's the hope of Haiti. I really believe that if we had more young men like him, we could do something, rather than just wallowing in hopelessness," he says.

Touring this orphanage leaves me feeling confounded. It is

very hard to tell at some of these orphanages where the effects of poverty end and the dislocation of the earthquake begins. All the children are sleeping outside, their belongings strewn about as if they are at a weekend sleepaway camp. The building is unaffected by the earthquake, but it feels dingy and upended inside. The furniture is pushed against the walls and belongings are scattered aimlessly around the floor. Hal's wife is traveling. There are as many as 125 children in this place at any one time. The Nungesters also take children who are considered unadoptable. So in a large living room in the front, ill and listless children lay in oversized playpens. One boy's head is so inflated by fluid that it fills the entire width of a pack-and-play, monstrous and bloated. Hal says it is too late for surgery. He is being medicated heavily until death can bring him relief.

The orphanage system has been laid bare to the eyes of the world since the earthquake and it is heart-wrenching. Children's faces cry out on TV appeals for aid. People want to help. But it is not clear exactly how they can. The word "orphan" means a lot of things in Haiti, and everyone is quick to tell you that it doesn't just mean children whose parents are deceased. Some orphans live at orphanages with their parents. Others are left at orphanages by a parent who has every intention of reclaiming them someday. Others are handed over by parents for reasons of poverty, not because they want to lose their children. The country has a hundred licensed orphanages that care for dozens of children and another sixty-seven adoption crèches. But every community has several more unlicensed homes for children, many run by American missionaries, according to local authorities.

We take Mark Kenson back to his own orphanage, where he resumes his role as a force in this operation, living proof that the

Manasseros' contribution goes far beyond giving day-to-day help to needy children. He is a young man whose life is now devoted to building a country he adores. That is the power of one person's kindness to another. That philosophy is on full display when we arrive. Loud teenage music, in both Creole and English, booms from inside the bins, overcome at times by the laughter of children's voices. The place is still recovering from an earthquake, the directors are considering shutting down, but there is a party going on?

We enter to find Susette in a basketball jersey and tennis shoes playing a full game of basketball with the teenage boys. Bill is helping a DJ connect more music. Cendy offers up her first genuine smile as volunteers race behind her and a group of girls in a game of duck duck goose. Mark Kenson joins a soccer game in another area of the concrete bin. A group of laughing boys launches a kite and Jonathan hops on the roof to help them navigate. They are used to his visits and barely notice his camera. One thing is clear. Susette and Bill are going nowhere.

"What would have happened to Cendy and Mark Kenson if you had left?" I ask her.

"They would have been left behind. I don't know. That's why we couldn't leave," she says.

"What would you hope for her to be? What would you want for Cendy at her best?"

"A self-assured child who loves herself, loves others, loves God, has peace with who she is. And does whatever God's given her to do well. Whatever that is. Whatever she wants to aspire to be. We just want to be able to help her heal. Bad things happen, earthquakes happen, orphans happen. Poverty is here. I wish we didn't have to live here. We're here because we feel we're supposed to be here and Cendy is here with us. So we're trying to do the best we can with her. There is no absolute. There is no perfect."

The next day Susette and Bill do the opposite of give up and leave—they open a school! Just half of Haiti's children ever see the inside of a classroom. The earthquake destroyed three-quarters of the schools that exist. The Manasseros decide they will open their own. Ariana takes Cendy to class the first morning, where a very serious Haitian gentleman who calls himself "Mr. Lavinsky" begins teaching her to read. Mr. Lavinsky says flat out that Haiti will never recover from this earthquake. Navi, Cendy's nanny, agrees. She lost ten family members in the disaster. Navi and Mr. Lavinsky show up each day in any case, pushing everything forward. Susette and Bill and the volunteers are single focus. They do not believe they can save all of Haiti, but they do believe they can save their fifty kids. They truly are the starfish people, running something that best approximates Disaster Camp.

The sounds of children learning bounce off the walls of the new building as Susette brings in jugs of water, toilet paper, and snacks. A team of carpenters who showed up to volunteer has built these terrific desks and chairs that look like pews. The place smells strongly of fresh-cut wood and new paint. A generator almost overwhelms the voices of the teachers, but it allows lights and fans. Susette runs off to figure out how to feed a tent city they've erected across the street. She tells us for maybe the tenth time she has been warned to not lose focus, not get spread too thin. So every move is calculated against how many supplies they have. Her priority has to be security and food. Bill shows up and we walk around the new place. I ask him to look back on Cendy's life at the orphanage, all the twists and turns that came before her sitting in the classroom reciting letters in the middle of a disaster zone. "I love her," he blurts out, and suddenly begins to cry.

That evening the sunset crashes down on the concrete yard, painting it with a patina of orange. Bill and Ariana play guitar and feed children from the neighborhood. The children get caught in the spirit, heads tipping back to sing to God. Mark Kenson looks mesmerized; Cendy is at peace. Susette stands off to the side, her perfect eyeliner unaffected by the heat.

Weeks later, Wyclef Jean, Haiti's most famous musician, writes me a song called "Rescued" for our documentary. The meaning plays out in this big concrete bin. "Anger got the best of me. So if you're listening we need better policies," he sings to his guitar. "They will rescue us. Who will rescue them?"

Rescue is not as simple as the government rushing in like cavalry when the storm hits. I learned that they don't even do that sometimes while covering Hurricane Katrina. Haiti teaches that rescue is about what you as an individual do for others; it's what you do for yourself when you seize the opportunity to help. Rescue is about the guy who jumps in his own boat to yank you off the roof when the floodwaters rise. Rescue is your soul and your spirit rising above your feelings of frustration and entitlement, about the moment you decide this big unsolvable problem belongs to you, too. It's about the moment you choose to pick up the phone and demand action on behalf of someone who can't. It's when you scream aloud at the authorities that something has to get done. It's about the choice you make to take responsibility for a problem you didn't create and just go out and assist a total stranger. That's the moment of rescue, when you rescue yourself from frustration or indifference or lack of power, and step up to offer help.

I don't return to Haiti until mid-June. The documentary has aired in May and I am onto other things. I just want to go back. I decide to take my oldest daughter, Sofia, who is nine. She looks totally thrilled we are going together. So am I. I see this as an opportunity to share with her a major lesson I have learned from my time in Haiti. That one person can change the world, if only by changing a piece of it. She takes a breath when we land, not from the jolt of the plane but out of pure excitement. I am so happy to be taking this trip with her. The people in the plane clap and so does she.

I love the sight of her rolling her luggage through the airport behind me. I love that she is seeing what I do. I delight in explaining to her that a plane to a place devastated by an earthquake is jammed because there are so many people who want to help. Half of all Americans say they plan to give money to help Haiti, and over a billion dollars have already poured in. Sofia has brought pencils and art supplies, cards and Reece's Pieces for Bill. She is jazzed to be able to come help at the orphanage. Her hair is gathered in a low ponytail. She's wearing a T-shirt with "I am happy!" written on it. The place sparkles from the hot sun. The windows that were shattered post-quake have been repaired. The chaos I remember from our last trip here has faded. The two of us probably look odd walking out to an airport full of military helicopters with tents set up on the grass next to the runway.

One of the CNN security people who worked with us on our last trip picks us up at the airport. He looks like a secret agent and acts like one. He blinks at immigration and we walk through. We stand in one long line where it's baking hot, but everyone is calm. The baggage claim, inoperable the last time we were here, is churning along. We are thirty minutes early so there's a calm that's unusual at the airport. Outside we make a brisk pace out the airport gates. Sofia scoots along like a pro, energized by the coolness of being in this new country with this secret agent guy and all the hubbub. We arrive at the tent city, which is even bigger this time and feels more permanent. There are "snaker" stores, lean-tos with gleaming white American brands. Tons of rubble have been swept into piles. They look like they are there for good. The place looks cleaner. Or at least more organized.

We drive by Robert Duvall's soccer camp. He is a Haitian man designated a hero by a special program of CNN. I met him when he came to an event for my documentary. He has a large football-field-sized space with cows grazing on the sidelines. He used to run a soccer camp to mentor kids. Now he has installed tents donated by Italian volunteers. They stand in tiny rows in one corner. Duvall had worried about the tent cities encroaching on his soccer camp, but he's managed to have it both ways, creating housing and keeping his beloved camp. The tents feel like they're not going anywhere soon. There are very few places to escape the sun.

We drive on through Cite Soleil. "Goats! Goats!" says Sofia. "Pigs." She sees them running through metal shacks where hundreds of thousands of people live. She is such a city girl that she drives through Haiti's biggest slum and notices a pig. There are bullet holes in some of the walls. There are some markets, but garbage and plastic water bottles choke the canal. There is no clean water here but plenty of empty plastic. I know there are many people who would think this is an odd place to take a little girl. But I feel as if I am opening a door for her, and also, quite frankly, for me. I am not here to report, on a crazy mission scraping at the edges of danger. I am here to teach my daughter that we must never get far from the grief and joys of the people around us. That we share a place on this chaotic earth with people of varied means. That we live in a land of possibilities, those we seize for ourselves and those we create for others.

We drive over mountains of dirt, literally piles of garbage. But the streets are full of workers. Markets with fruits and candies and ginger root. At one end, there's a port. The water is so blue, we are tempted to jump in. Baby pigs wander the streets. "What's that?" I ask when I see a bright blue-and-white building that looks newly built. A new police station right in the middle of Cite Soleil. I guess something is being built. We zip past barbershops, women cooking in these massive metal tubs. On the main road, it's stunning how little has changed structurally. I look into Sofia's eyes. It's all so new to her.

We arrive at the Lighthouse. Children surround Sofia. Cendy appears and suddenly begins hiding in case I have any more cameras. Sofia intrigues her. She is fascinated by my relationship to Sofia. Sofia plays all the hand games I played with Cendy on my visits. Sofia is fair like her father and is already getting red from the sun. She crouches down and extends her palms in a game of nerves—will the other person slap your palms before you retreat? Cendy remembers when I did this with her. She looks at me and immediately connects with my daughter. It is a fascinating dance. Sofia has seen the documentary where Cendy's story of abandonment is told. I wonder what is going on in the heads of these two little girls. The boys get in line to play, too. "Me next. Me next!" they shout. Sofia's connected and she's beaming. She's figured out how to break through as a stranger and she's proud of herself.

Susette's warm hug is my first real greeting in Haiti. Now I feel as if I have really arrived. She gives me a look that makes up for the two months since we've seen each other. We don't even have to talk about how important the documentary was for her and her work. The report was a nonjudgmental human look at the kind work of Christian missionaries and the lives of two orphans. It wasn't a debate or an issues piece about Christianity, adoption, race, or politics. There was no back-and-forth. It is a new voice for me, a style of reporting that does great service to the human story. You just tell people about one person's life and chart their journey. Then leave the judgments and takeaways to the viewers.

Susette is still on her personal mission. The subject of her work today is a baby they are trying to evacuate. She pulls me into her rush. I glance over at Sofia, who looks at me like she wants to stay. The hot sun splashes sparkly bits of light on the vast concrete bin. The laughter bounces against the walls and mixes into a cheery symphony of children's sounds. Mark Kenson is here, too, smiling and excited to see someone who has met Wyclef Jean, Haiti's big star. The playground is full of optimism and life. Sofia heads down the street to the girls' dorm to work on crafts with the older girls. Cendy races after her, so they can stick together. How crazy is that! So I leave my nine-year-old playing in an orphanage in Haiti, which somehow at that particular moment seems like the safest place in the world.

We head out to look for a doctor who can do tests on the baby Susette and Bill are trying to evacuate. We take a treacherous road through collapsed buildings. The city looks exactly the same as it did days after the quake in many places. A building that was leveled just sits there pancaked flat. Susette tells me the women who were sitting on the sidewalk under the building selling fruits and vegetables were all crushed to death in the quake. But now I'm worried that we're going to impale our car, or even ourselves, on the metal bars sticking out from the house. Our driver slowly rolls by the debris. All the drivers in Haiti seem to be pros at dodging metal and stone.

We meet Vanessa, who runs Angel Mission Haiti. She shows me a picture of her seventeen kids—two biological and more than a dozen others. She explains what documents are needed to get the baby evacuated to get his medical care in Pennsylvania. They need legal documents that are notarized, promise letters from the hospital and the cardiac surgeon who will do the work. Vanessa is a stout woman with short hair and a suntan. She wears shorts and a bright short-sleeved shirt, almost what someone would wear on a Caribbean vacation. She is covered with beads. She's moved her desk outdoors because her Internet has failed today and she's borrowing from a neighbor. The downside of this arrangement is she's hot, so she's arranged bedsheets around her to try to block the sun out.

A hospital in Philadelphia has promised surgery for free, but the sticking point seems to be that humanitarian parole has ended. Humanitarian parole is what the U.S. government gives someone who is brought into the country without a visa. The baby has big eyes and surgical tape holds a feeding tube in place. He is six months old and weighs seven pounds. His twin, a girl, is doing better. Their mother has been feeding her but had been ignoring him a bit, afraid to bond because she sensed he might not survive. Now they realize he has an operable heart problem, the same heart problem that Jon Olinger has. The surgery is straightforward, but impossible in Haiti. His name is Adriano.

I go back to the Lighthouse to find Sofia having a tougher afternoon. She is having trouble communicating. A lot of the kids have not mastered English and she knows no Creole. She accompanies the Manesseros to the feeding program where hungry neighborhood kids come eat. She looks very sad. It makes me sad.

She tells me she doesn't know how to help people who are living in tents. I tell her she is doing what she can do by being here. She gets back to taking care of little girls, applying stickers and playing games. The boys find her fascinating. They all like her. A little boy named Richard says: "You are so pretty." I say "Thanks." He says, "No. No. Sofia! Sofia. Sofia is so pretty." They're sort of awkward around her. But her heart is breaking. I think it will make her grow up a bit, see that there is a larger world around her and she can make it better, if even in a small way. I hand her my camera. I tell her it will help her communicate with the kids. She takes their pictures and they take hers.

A group of seven kids, three girls, four boys, organize a performance. The clouds roll in just in time to provide some cover from the blazing sun. All the children begin to giggle as the cables are rolled out into the bins. A computer reboots and goes "dun dun dun dah!" They all laugh at the universal sign for it's on. They are so cute. A hip-hop tune comes on and they do their dance: "Uh uh uh uh. I'm free from sin." It's Christian rap. When the music ends there are big cheers.

The next group is the smaller kids. The cheers are deafening. Cendy is in a summer dress, lacy and gauzy and lavender. She's got new braids. She ignores me but loves Sofia. I could have used Sofia on the last trip when we ran around trying to get her picture. Cendy, quiet, shut down, camera shy, retreating little Cendy is going to dance with nine other kids! Katie, a volunteer from California who's been reaching out to Sofia, leads them in a song. "There are seven. There are seven.

"Con-tin-ents. Con-tin-ents."

Cendy stomps her foot to the song. She is so cute.

People are yelling out names: Keso, Markendy. I give my BlackBerry to Eli, the Manesseros' son, to e-mail my own son,

Charlie. "I hope to meet you one day." I've sent a picture to Celia and Charlie, who are e-mailing sorrowful notes about missing Sofia and me. Jackson has gone to watch the World Cup with Brad. We wind up inside the house, where the flies are ignoring the merciful cross-breeze. A screen door would cost $1,000, so Eli is sent to get a fly swatter. He is ten and strong and the flies have no chance. The Manasseros are living in a new house that is big and airy, much bigger than their last one, which was tagged with a yellow mark that means the cracks make the house unsafe. Get them fixed or move out. So they moved out. There is a big living room with a TV on the first floor. We are in the guest room downstairs. Upstairs there are three more bedrooms, with bunk beds for the kids. And there is the most amazing view from the upstairs veranda—stunning, and over the rooftops. It's lovely.

The next morning Sofia wakes up before me and I'm told she's upstairs having a tea party. By breakfast every child in the house has Silly Bandz, the latest kid craze back home. A boy named Fanfan is wearing seven on his right arm—all the way from the wrist to under his armpit. He's getting ready to go off to school. Sofia has given him every dinosaur-shaped Silly she has. Kenny has three on his left arm, and one on his right wrist. He wanted lobsters and alligators. And the N.Y. for the New York Yankees. They are a hit. I watch Sofia watch the small children, who switch effortlessly between English, French, and Creole. I feel like all my lectures on teaching her to speak other languages have just been outdone by this moment.

It's the last day of school so there are ice cream treats. Whitney, a tall auburn-haired girl from California, came to teach. She was promoted to principal after her first day. She's leaving, and so is Ashley, who works in the clinic. Susette says they've had such great volunteers. Some have come from their church, some from the Web site, some drawn by our documentary. The heat is getting to Sofia. It must be ninety-five degrees today and there are no clouds. She's flushed and has finally agreed to knot her hair up on her head. She spent part of the morning giving out treats to neighborhood boys, who asked me first for water (I had none) and then to take their photo. She is still so quiet, nodding her head yes and no.

Adriano is ailing and the orphanage is still working on his case. Meanwhile, I get to hold him on my lap. He isn't squirmy like most babies his age, which reflects his ill health. But he has that warm baby summer smell and hope in his eyes. I feel a peace come over me like I have not felt in ages, not through the rush of work or even the incredible moments of joy I experience each day with Brad and the kids. I am sitting in Haiti, where a quarter million people died in an excruciating catastrophe. Their government is fractured; their history promises little revival. American generosity is far-reaching but fleeting. These kids will likely never know the advantages and possibilities handed to people like me just a boat ride away. I have a sick child on my lap. But I can help. I can be here. I can hold Adriano on my lap while they successfully negotiate his rescue. I can tell his story. I can teach my daughter that she may just bring these kids stickers and smiles today but the growth in her heart can help her reach far beyond this sunny afternoon in Haiti.

CHAPTER FIFTEEN

GOING HOME

I don't often go to Smithtown, even though my parents' home is still out near the beach. But today I cruise along the Long Island Expressway, the unwelcoming flat-line highway that cuts across the island of my birth. I am off to visit the home where six black kids grew up surrounded by white kids feeling utterly American, yet somehow outside the main.

An exit away from Smithtown, in Patchogue, a white boy who dated black and Latino girls has been accused of killing a guy from Ecuador because he hates "illegal aliens." I feel like my next assignment needs to be to find out why. But I know I will never have a full answer. Jeffrey Conroy is nineteen. I met his parents weeks ago when the trial first began. Now he has been convicted and sentenced to twenty-five years in prison despite a tearful apology to the judge. He is one of seven teenagers who described going out "beaner hopping" and stabbing to death a man named Marcelo Lucero. The U.S. Justice Department is now probing bias attacks against Latinos on Long Island. This is my hometown. Conroy's parents are incensed over the sentence. But that day his mother approached Lucero's brother in the hallway at the courthouse. She cried and told him she was so sorry about what had happened. Her son has a swastika tattoo and a lightning bolt tattoo, which together symbolize white power. Jeffrey told the courtroom he was there when Lucero was killed but that a friend had been the one to plunge the knife into him. Again, I just don't get the anger.

Today, I blow through many towns like Patchogue now ripped with tension over immigration. I can't understand at what moment Long Island became a flash point in debating the status of these latest immigrant newcomers. There are towns with enormous wealth out here that seem troubled by the presence of people seeking low-paying jobs as contractors. There are blue-collar mini-cities where people gripe about lost jobs. It's a complex debate, but one I'd like to someday get at the heart of. I am certain this will be my next big story.

But today I am on a quest to recapture my youth, to see where things stand back home. When you touch base with your childhood memories there is always a risk. I swing by the home of Angela Cinqmani, the girl who I believed to be the only other Latina at my school. A hilarious scene unfolds. Her tiny white cottage is overgrown with vines and is now collapsing on the far side of an enormous lot. A big McMansion is being built on the rest of it, tall and brick with Sopranos detail. It looks about 90 percent done but is obviously empty. I yell and knock because there is light on in the little house.

It takes a long while and then out comes Angela all grown up. She immediately recognizes me. I tell her I am writing my own story and have mixed memories of Smithtown. She begins immediately to tell her tale without me asking. She was miserable in school, chesty and bigmouthed, by her own account, and, she admits with enormous pride, secretly very rich. "I had a hundred and eight absences in English because I wasn't a morning person," she says in a very thick Long Island accent. We never had a conversation this long in high school, so I feel as if I'm getting to know her for the first time. It begins to rain. She clearly wants to talk but doesn't want to let me inside either of her houses.

At this point her mother approaches the front window in a see-through white nightie and begins banging her cane against the glass. "AAAAAANNNGELA. Shud up! Just shud up and get your ass back in here," she says, as if she is the very originator of the heavy Long Island accent.

"Coming, Ma," Angela replies and continues. "I had big boobs." She confirms that she was a C cup in third grade. "The vice principal told me I was a hazard. I lived in detention. I was best friends with a big albino girl. I had maybe one or two others, but they stole my boyfriend so I skipped graduation and prom."

"Get inside. Shud up. Come inside now," her mother yells. She bangs the cane on the window again. I begin to back up.

"Coming, Ma," Angela yells back. Her eyes throw me a conversation-closer look.

I blurt out the reason I'm here. I need perspective. I ask her about being Latino in Smithtown. We weren't friendly, but we were the only ones, I tell her. "Latino?" she says, laughing gently. "I'm freaking Italian." She stalks back into her house and I begin to laugh, mostly at my memory of myself.

I instinctively know how to find Shevoy Onley's little one-story house. I sit out front for a while and just stare at the lot where it used to be. There is now this beautiful suburban two-story house presenting itself as Smithtown's suburban best. I go up to knock and see if they know what has happened to the Onleys. And it is Shevoy herself who answers the door—all grown-up! We stare at each other, give the predictable screech and hug. I walk into this beautiful brand-new house. She has built her own fabulous house atop the tiny old one where she lived with her parents. The front bedroom where we used to have sleepovers is now a playroom for her eighteen-month-old son and five-year-old daughter. Shevoy's husband stares at me like I'm some ghost from her past. I guess I am.

Shevoy has returned to this community to raise her own kids. It's a statement on how far both she and Smithtown have come. Shevoy looks exactly the same, and we fall right back into the banter of our youth. I tell her I'm writing about Smithtown, and she laughs aloud. I ask if she remembers how people treated us. "I didn't worry about how other people treated us because we had each other," she says. "I knew we were different but Mom would say, 'You worry about the person you are inside.'" Shevoy recalls so many of the best memories of my youth: the giggling sleepovers and the games out on the lawn. Yet the best recollections of all are the looks we gave each other in the halls, our shared strength. It is remarkable how one person's friendship can turn bad to good. "Kids would say things, and I knew my feelings were hurt but I didn't know why," remembers Shevoy. She ended up working in Child Protective Services, where she met her husband, who is half white and half Ecuadorean.

Shevoy's parents were also immigrants. They came from Bermuda searching for new opportunities. Her aunt had married an American and moved to Smithtown. She sold him on the square lawns and safe streets. Shevoy was thrilled when she found Orestes and me in school. "It was at least three of us then. And we were like interchangeable to folks. We all knew the rules. We were not going to fight anyone about anything. We knew we were different but no one was going to risk his or her life over that. We knew we wouldn't date and you just didn't get upset about that."

Her recollections reaffirm the reality of my youth. Yet it doesn't upset me in the least. Here we are, all grown-up, having seized the opportunity our parents won for us. That she built this big house atop her parents' old house is all you need to know about what happened to Shevoy. "For my parents, I've gone beyond expectations," she says as she begins to give us a tour of her ample closets and wide-open living room. Her lawn seems endless. Her children go to school with the children of the same folks who ignored her back in school. The kids are mostly white, but there are also kids who are Indian, Spanish, and black. Occasionally someone will assume she is mother to one of the others. A few folks will tell her that her fairer daughter must look like her father. But she proudly tells the census her children are black, Latino, and white. In the end, she won.

I can't go visit Corinne Vargas in Smithtown, the woman who was denied a federally subsidized cash voucher so she could move to my hometown. She never got the opportunity to live there. Smithtown settled the lawsuit but the town never admitted to discriminating against anyone ever. Corinne and the other plaintiffs were finally given Section 8 vouchers in 2009. Her daughter was five when she applied for the voucher in a moment of distress. She is now eleven. She went looking for housing but, after years of only seeing white applicants, the home owners with eligible rentals turned her down. "I got sixty days to look for a shit hole in the middle of a palace and people wouldn't even rent me the shit hole," she says, laughing.

The years that went by cost her dearly. She was in a homeless shelter for ten months one year. The housing she finally found was in an environment totally foreign to her solid, working-class family roots. She was an only child to hardworking American parents, family-loving Puerto Ricans who stuck together and swept their little patch of Oakdale, Long Island, no matter what was going on outside. She lived in three different apartment complexes that were overrun by drug dealers.

"I was in a ghetto, surrounded by danger and noise. You can have the poorest people on earth but they can have self-respect," she said. "These were not those people. I was scared. My daughter can only walk five to eight steps and all I wanted was to be able to take her out the door to do that. And I couldn't even take her out to play catch." There was a fire once. She was moved in and out; a single mother with a completely disabled child had to pack and move a household of furniture.

She remembers the day she got the letter from Smithtown so vividly, like reading the numbers on a lotto ticket and thinking you've got the winning number. She had walked into the town office that day wondering about the possibilities for her child in Smithtown, about the great pool at the Y and the proximity of the beach. The day they wrote "INELIGIBLE" and circled that word, she felt herself deflate.

There is something about places like Smithtown that is more than just about good schools and low crime. There is a psychic peace that grows in a child's mind when they can walk out the back door and just stare up at the treetops to watch the sunshine sparkle through the leaves. The emotional anguish of being a shut-in, of fearing the world outside your door, of not even knowing that help is on the way, is immeasurable. For Corinne and her little girl, there was no Bill Huntington, the man who sold my parents the land to build their house. She didn't even have the chance to find her way in a place where she wasn't wanted. She might have been a great addition to Smithtown, someone whose talents and good spirit enriched the community around her. We will never know. Her American story is of a person whose opportunity was denied, a lesson in why that is not what this country should be about.

"I am very proud to be Corinne Vargas versus Smithtown," Corinne says of her case. "If I can change one person's life then this was a victory. This was never about money. This was about saying you cannot do this for another decade—you cannot do this to another mother. I am just one person, but one person can open a door. The town had all these opportunities, all these possibilities, but there were no possibilities for me."

Corinne eventually did find a home in Bohemia, a nice area not far away that is slightly more diverse. Her daughter can spend the entire day outside in the sunshine now. Corinne put up a mini six-hole golf course and a plastic pool. "I know that my kids won't go through what they would have gone through in Smithtown, so it's okay," she says. "Sometimes what looks like perfection on the outside is not the same inside." She has few neighbors because she lives along a commercial strip. But at night it's very quiet. She loves the silence. She has a two-year-old child now, too. She has her justice and she has her own Smithtown. She has a shot at seeing her new baby grow up and get what she couldn't have.

I was given all the opportunities Corinne never got. I pledge to live my life aware of that truth, to refuse to rush by trouble, to stop and at least bear witness to what is happening to people like Corinne. I was fortunate enough to enjoy a childhood in Smithtown that gave me every resource possible to succeed in life. That means I have a responsibility to give back. That sounds obvious and simple, but not everyone does it. I can't change the entire world, but I can work on my little piece of it. I can at least give voice to people whose plight goes unnoticed, to make sure they are heard in the middle of the shouting matches that sometimes pass as debate. I can scrape below the surface of a pretty town and unearth what's going on inside. I can help in my own small way. That is the least any of us can do.

I don't have to go far to see how lucky I was. My old house in Smithtown looks exactly as it did the last time I lived there when I went off to college. None of us has thought about moving back there, but my parents never get it together to sell. The land is so vast and green and the trees shelter the property from the world around it. The smell of wild grasses blows through the air. The Quaker meetinghouse and the horse stalls remain close by and the connecting streets are quiet enough for a bike ride. The beach at the inlet beckons the horseshoe crabs, and I make a mental note to bring the kids. I have come a distance since my little tribe came here to seize the promise of America. Life is sometimes about what's possible.

· ACKNOWLEDGMENTS ·

T his book captures a lifetime of memories, lessons learned and experiences beyond my wildest imagination. I am thankful for the people who've helped me recall them accurately and given me my own world of opportunities.

It is hard to write about yourself without the advice and guidance of friends and mentors. I would like to thank Kim Bondy, Jeanne Blake, and Bob Bazell for being brilliant mentors and even more valuable friends.

I thank my wonderful agent, Lisa Queen, my insightful editor, Ian Jackman, and publisher Ray Garcia for believing in this project and working around my frenetic reporting schedule. There aren't enough thanks to give to my coauthor, Rose Arce, who's not only become a wonderful writing partner, but who also vowed to wake me up during the aftershock of an earthquake in Haiti, should I sleep through it. Her partner, Mafe, and daughter, Luna, deserve my gratitude for giving up their time with her.

I thank Jon Klein and Bart Feder for understanding the importance of this project. They are the reason for my success at CNN. They've given me a great opportunity to report on stories that often go uncovered. My new boss, Geraldine Moriba, is also my new friend. I see a long future ahead of us making documentaries that tell the stories of Americans whose voices need to be heard. Marianna Spicer Joslyn, Barbara Levin, David Bohrman, and Justin Dial were immensely helpful to me in making this book good. My reporting would never come to fruition without the efforts of CNN's photojournalists, especially those that accompanied me to hot spots like Haiti, Thailand, Chile, and through the storms of New Orleans. My stories come to life because of editors like Carl Graf and Al DiSanti and the production staff of my In America team, particularly my invaluable assistant Robert Farfan, senior producer Michelle Rozsa, and producer Kimberly Arp Babbit, who were invaluable to *Black* and *Latino in America*. I thank my young interns Sara Mahmood and Anddy Matos for their help on this book. I also owe plenty to my CNN colleagues from the national and international desks who take our reporting teams effortlessly and safely through terrible storms and scary earthquakes. I thank my reporting colleagues Anderson Cooper, Sanjay Gupta, Thelma Gutierrez, Roland Martin, Susan Candiotti, Miles O'Brien, Katie Couric, and so many others who see the challenges of good and honest reporting as our collective effort.

I am thankful also to Shevoy Onley for the memories restored and for being there from the beginning. Corinne Vargas shared a painful story that is a life lesson to all of us. So did the people in Shenandoah, Pennsylvania, Cindy Garcia of East LA, "Marta" of Miami, Michael Eric Dyson, Tina Smith and her family, Kenneth Talley, Susette and Bill Manassero, Cendy Jeune, Mark Kenson Olibris and so many others who open up their lives to me. I am a better reporter and a better person because I had a chance to listen in.

The most important contribution to this book was made by my parents. By recalling the stories of my childhood, they made me want to explore the history of Long Island and civil rights. It is a privilege to be able to finally tell the story of their journey as well and credit them with all the possibilities they gave me in life. I thank my siblings, who share my history and always have my back: Maria, Cecilia, Tony, Estela and Orestes. I am also grateful to my in-laws, nieces and nephews, for their support.

My deepest thanks to my husband, Brad, and my children: Sofia, Cecilia, Jackson and Charlie. They make great sacrifices so I can do my work. I do this for them and their future.